assessing
YOUTH behavior

Using the Child Behavior Checklist in Family and Children's Services

Edited by

Nicole S. Le Prohn

Kathleen M. Wetherbee

Elena R. Lamont

Thomas M. Achenbach

Peter J. Pecora

CWLA Press
Washington, DC

Proceedings from the Child Behavior Checklist Roundtable, sponsored by Casey Family Programs, Seattle, Washington

CWLA Press is an imprint of the Child Welfare League of America. The Child Welfare League of America is the nation's oldest and largest membership-based child welfare organization. We are committed to engaging people everywhere in promoting the well-being of children, youth, and their families, and protecting every child from harm.

CHILD WELFARE LEAGUE OF AMERICA, INC.
HEADQUARTERS
440 First Street, NW, Third Floor, Washington, DC 20001-2085
E-mail: books@cwla.org

CURRENT PRINTING (last digit)
10 9 8 7 6 5 4 3 2 1

Cover design by James D. Melvin
Text design by Meredith Simpson

Printed in the United States of America

ISBN # 0-87868-777-7

Library of Congress Cataloging-in-Publication Data
Assessing youth behavior using the child behavior checklist in family and
 children's services/ edited by Nicole S. Le Prohn...[et al.]
        p. cm.
    Includes bibliographical references and index.
    ISBN 0-87868-777-7
        1. Child Behavior Checklist. 2. Behavioral assessment of children. I. Le Prohn, Nicole Suzanne.

RJ503.5 .A845 2001
618.92'89075—dc21

2001035373

Contents

Tables

Figures

Acknowledgments

This book was made possible through the efforts of many individuals, in addition to the editors and chapter authors. The participants at the CBCL Roundtable in Seattle, Washington, asked thought-provoking questions, and the discussions that resulted provided additional material for the presenters to incorporate into their chapters.

Casey Family Programs (Casey) provided the funding necessary to bring the participants together. Ruth Massinga, President and Chief Executive Officer of Casey, Jean McIntosh, Executive Vice President—Strategy and Program Development, and James Marquart, Executive Vice President—Operations, all supported this work and encouraged the effort. Research Services staff, especially Kelly Sim and Vince Payne, assisted with the Roundtable and subsequent follow-up work.

We appreciate the support of the Child Welfare League of America as this book was brought to completion. Their patience and interest in the project were instrumental in this effort.

Finally, we are indebted to the caregivers—parents, foster parents, and child care workers—who complete the assessments for the children and youth. This book would not have been possible without them.

1

Introduction

Nicole S. Le Prohn, Elena R. Lamont, Peter J. Pecora, and Kathleen M. Wetherbee

Although child and family services in the United States constitute, in many ways, a large and troubled enterprise, there are pockets of excellence. It has become increasingly important to identify and replicate these quality child welfare practices. Rates of child abuse have escalated, leading many to describe the current state of child protection as a national emergency and crisis (American Humane Association et al. 1998). In 1995, more than one million children were confirmed as victims of maltreatment (U.S. Department of Health and Human Services 1997), a 271% increase since 1977. At the same time, the population of children in foster care has grown dramatically. As of September 1998, there were 560,000 children in foster care (U.S. Department of Health and Human Services 2000), compared to a foster care population of 275,000 in 1984 (U.S. House of Representatives 1996).

The costs associated with child protection and foster care likewise have grown. In 1997, public child welfare agencies spent almost $12 billion on child welfare services (U.S. House of Representatives 1996; Lipner & Goertz 1996). The increasing budget outlays for child welfare services have attracted heightened scrutiny from funders and politicians. At the same time, there has been a greater emphasis on quality of services and accountability. Quality refers to the achievement of success on a range of attributes, including access, consistency of service, and capacity to effectively address the needs of children and families. Accountability refers to the achievement of results at a reasonable cost.

Program quality and accountability can be maximized through the linkage of reliable and timely data in order to answer five questions:

- What are the needs and strengths of children and families?

- Which worker actions and services are provided to whom?

- What short-term, intermediate, and long-term outcomes are achieved?

- Which services are most beneficial to whom?

- What does it cost to provide the services and achieve the desired outcomes?

Unfortunately, most child and family service agencies are able to answer only the first two questions. Although they are able to identify the needs and strengths of clients and the services that are provided, they are not able to track outcomes, differential effectiveness, or costs. They have few tools to assist them in assessing the outcomes for individual clients or in documenting broader program outcomes. Many agencies struggle to find tools that can reliably assess how children are doing, and even when such clinical tools are identified, agency administrators often are uncertain whether these tools reliably document program success.

A key tool that is available to child welfare agencies is the Child Behavior Checklist (CBCL). This reliable and valid instrument has been used for several years in mental health settings. More recently, child welfare agencies and researchers in child welfare settings have discovered the value of the CBCL in meeting clinical and research needs. Many practitioners and researchers who have been using the CBCL, however, work in isolation and have not had opportunities to share the knowledge they have gained. Casey Family Programs (Casey) recognized the need to bring together agency and university-based researchers who have used the CBCL to present information on their studies and discuss how the CBCL and its companion instruments—the Teacher's Report Form (TRF) and the Youth Self-Report (YSR)—can best be used in child welfare settings.

The 1997 CBCL Roundtable

In 1997, Casey invited 30 researchers to a two-day roundtable in Seattle so that they could share their knowledge and experiences in using the CBCL. Some researchers were affiliated with universities, some with large public agencies, and others with small private, not-for-profit agencies. All were currently using or had used the CBCL as a research instrument, an assessment tool, or both. Appendix A lists the participants and their affiliations.

Each participant was invited to present a paper on his or her work with the CBCL, the TRF, and the YSR. Several participants agreed to present papers to facilitate knowledge sharing and discussion. The presentations served as the basis for a rich discussion of the benefits and challenges of using the assessment tools with children in foster care. Participants learned from one another how the instruments were being used with this group of children; the problems encountered and the successes realized; and the special issues that arose as they applied to new population instruments originally designed for use with children living with their birth parents.

One recommendation that emerged from the Roundtable was that the proceedings be compiled so those child welfare professionals interested in using the CBCL could benefit from the discussions that had taken place. This book is designed to provide the field of child welfare with a summary of the knowledge that was developed through Roundtable discussions.

An Overview

This book provides many examples of how the CBCL may be used in practice and research, including chapters that highlight different statistical techniques for analyzing data and presenting results. The various chapters discuss the implications of research using the CBCL for practice, policy, and administration of child welfare programs.

The research studies reported in this book are unique in several ways. First, some of the studies have small samples. Such studies are rarely published because they generally are viewed as lacking the rigor of studies with larger samples. Many public and private agencies, however, are able to conduct only small-sample studies because they have little or no funding for research and few research staff. Although small samples limit statistical power to detect differences and replicability, such studies make important contributions to a better understanding of outcomes in foster care. Second, all the studies in the book have a single instrument in common, the CBCL (although several studies used additional instruments). This focus provides practitioners and researchers with multiple examples in which the CBCL was used, examples that can facilitate the use of this instrument in other program settings.

Finally, the studies illustrate the range of methodological issues that can arise when the CBCL is used for assessment or research purposes, including issues related to the passage of time between assessments and the impact of using multiple informants.

In Chapter 2, Thomas Achenbach (the primary developer of the CBCL), Peter Pecora, and Gay Armsden provide an overview of the CBCL, describing how the tool is completed and scored. The authors offer suggestions for using CBCL results in child welfare settings. Chapters 3 through 9 present the results of a number of research studies that used the CBCL in a variety of settings. Each of these chapters is authored by a researcher who presented at the Roundtable. In Chapter 3, Craig Anne Heflinger and Celest Simpkins present their research on young people in state custody in Tennessee. Using the CBCL and the Child and Adolescent Functional Assessment Scale (CAFAS) (Hodges 1990), they found that most youth had high levels of mental health problems and that juxtaposing CBCL and CAFAS scores produces intriguing results. In Chapter 4, William Shennum, Debra Moreno, and JoAnna Caywood (all associated with Five Acres—The Boys' and Girls' Aid Society of Los Angeles County) describe the routine use of the CBCL as part of quarterly evaluations of youth in residential treatment. The researchers examine the relationship between demographic variables of youth and behavioral improvement, and they conclude that the CBCL provides a useful method for tracking youths' achievement over time.

Mark Courtney and Andrew Zinn of the University of Wisconsin-Madison report in Chapter 5 on the early results of a longitudinal investigation of treatment foster care services. Their study of children served by the Professional Association of Treatment Homes (PATH), a private not-for-profit agency that operates foster homes in several Midwestern states, examines the use of CBCL and the association between CBCL scores as reported by foster parents and youths' discharge outcomes. The researchers also explore the relationships between CBCL scores and YSR scores for a subset of youth. In Chapter 6, David Hickel, another agency-based researcher, reports on the use of the CBCL at intake, discharge, and 3-months post-discharge for 10 youth in residential care. Using a within subjects, repeated measure design to evaluate treatment effectiveness, he finds that youths' reported problems at intake improved during treatment and did not change significantly after they were discharged to their home. Sydney Hans and her colleagues at the University of Chicago report in Chapter 7 on behavior problems of children born prenatally exposed to drugs. Their longitudinal study follows 10-year old youth, collecting data from teachers on the TRF, and compares outcomes for children living with their biological mothers and children living with other caregivers. Their findings suggest that policies that support the separation of substance abusing mothers from their children may not be in children's best interests.

In Chapter 8, Roger Phillips of Pinebrook Services for Children and Youth discusses the use of the CBCL in a variety of foster care programs. He presents data on the behavioral difficulties of youth served by the agency in the past and currently. He examines the relationship between CBCL ratings and social workers' clinical judgments and discusses at length the usefulness of the CBCL as a practice tool. Researchers from the Casey Family Program—Gay Armsden, Peter Pecora, Vincent Payne, and Charles Joyce—present data in Chapter 9 from the agency's use of the CBCL in 1991 and 1992. They profile youth at time of entry into Casey programs and compare CBCL and TRF data. The researchers pose questions about the use of the instruments in clinical practice and with youth in foster care in particular.

Chapters 10 and 11 present a variety of issues regarding the use of the CBCL in practice and research. In Chapter 10, Kathleen Lenerz of Casey Family Services discusses the agency's implementation of the CBCL as a routine part of agency practice. She identifies a number of implementation hurdles, including difficulties ensuring consistent administration of the CBCL. She offers suggestions for implementation efforts in other agencies. In Chapter 11, Kathleen Wetherbee and Thomas Achenbach discuss methodological and statistical considerations when the CBCL is used in research investigations. They discuss issues related to design and analysis when using multiconstruct measures such as the CBCL. They address which scores to use under which circumstances in order to maximize information, and they identify the issues that typically arise when planning analytic strategies. The researchers discuss issues such as statistical power and validity and review recommendations from the American Psychological Association's Task Force on Statistical Inference.

Finally, in Chapter 12, Pecora, Armsden, Le Prohn, and Achenbach pull together the themes that emerge from the chapters and review the challenges that researchers and practitioners face when using the CBCL, TRF, and YSR.

Conclusion

The CBCL Roundtable generated a number of recommendations to advance the use of the CBCL for research and practice purposes. One recommendation, a CBCL user's guide for staff who provide child and family services, has been implemented (Achenbach, Pecora & Wetherbee 1998). This book is designed to provide further information to professionals in the field of child welfare. It is hoped that practitioners, administrators, and researchers will find answers to the questions with which the field struggles, particularly the short, intermediate, and long term outcomes that are achieved for children served through child welfare services.

References

Achenback, T. M., Pecora, P. J. & Wetherbee, K. M. (1998). *Child and Family Service Workers' Guide for the Child Behavior Checklist and Related Forms.* Burlington: University of Vermont Department of Psychiatry.

American Humane Association, Children's Division; American Bar Association, Center on Children and the Law; Annie E. Casey Foundation, Casey Family Services; The Institute for Human Services Management; & The Casey Family Program. (1998). *Assessing outcomes in child welfare services: Principles, concepts, and a framework of core indicators.* Englewood, CO: American Humane Association.

Hodges, K. (1990). *Child and adolescent function assessment scale and global level of functioning.* Unpublished scale. Ypsilanti: Eastern Michigan University.

Lipner, R. & Goertz, B. (1996). *Child welfare priorities and expenditures.* W-Memo, 2(8). Washington, DC: American Public Welfare Association.

U.S. Department of Health and Human Services. (1997). *Child Maltreatment 1995: Reports from the States to the National Child Abuse and Neglect Data System.* Washington, DC: U.S. Government Printing Office.

U.S. Department of Health and Human Services, Administration for Children and Families, Administration on Children, Youth and Families, Children's Bureau. (2000, April*). The AFCARS Report.* [On-line]. Available: http://www.acf.dhhs.gov/programs/cb/stats/afcars

U.S. House of Representatives, Committee on Ways and Means. (1996). *1996 Green Book.* Washington, DC: U.S. Government Printing Office.

2

Using the Child Behavior Checklist 4-18, Teacher's Report Form, Youth Self-Report, and Related Measures in Child and Family Services

Thomas M. Achenbach, Peter J. Pecora, and Gay Armsden

The Child Behavior Checklist (CBCL), Young Adult Behavior Checklist (YABCL), Teacher's Report Form (TRF), Youth Self-Report (YSR), and related measures can provide some of the assessment data that is essential for sound clinical practice, program evaluation, and more formal research studies. This chapter discusses the utility of standardized assessment of behavioral and emotional problems and competencies. It also summarizes the three measures, with an emphasis on the items, structure, reliability, and validity of the CBCL and TRF. Finally, the chapter offers a few practical suggestions for using these measures in child and family services.

Standardized Assessment of Behavioral and Emotional Problems and Competencies

The Nature of Standardized Assessment Procedures

Standardized assessment can contribute to the evaluation of the strengths and needs of children served by professional staff in child welfare, education, mental health settings, and other fields. The measures described in this chapter are compatible with other assessment procedures that professionals may use, but they can add valuable information that may not be easily obtained by other procedures. Standardized assessment procedures involve the use of forms that allow for reports and ratings of children's problems and competencies by a variety of individuals who work with children and youth. Parents and parent surrogates, such as foster parents, complete some forms. Other forms are completed by daycare providers and preschool teachers of 2- to 5-year-olds; schoolteachers of 5- to 18-year-olds; clinical interviewers; and observers of children's behavior in classrooms and other group settings. Finally, some forms are designed to obtain self-reports from youths and adults up to age 30.

Responses obtained from the involved informants are scored in standardized ways to enable a comparison of responses from the various informants who may have different perspectives on the child and to compare a child's scores with the norms for the child's age and sex. Responses may be both close-ended, with a range of responses provided, or may be open-ended, encouraging respondents to describe the child's strengths and concerns in their own words. Clerical staff may score close-ended responses, but professionals should examine the responses to open-ended items. The scores obtained from informants are displayed on profiles to facilitate the comparison of different informants' reports and comparison of the child's scores with norms. The norms enable ready identification of both strengths and concerns, as is discussed more fully later.

Why Use Standardized Assessment?

Much of the information that child and family workers obtain about children comes from interviews and narrative reports, which necessarily must be tailored to the individual case. Tailoring assessment procedures to each case requires a considerable investment of time and contacts with multiple individuals. Standardized assessment differs from this process in several ways.

Standardized assessment is efficient and economical.

Standardized assessment makes it possible to obtain, quickly and economically, a detailed picture of a child's functioning as viewed by different informants. Information from parents, foster parents, caregivers, teachers, and adolescents early in the evaluation process can save time that would otherwise be spent interviewing individuals on aspects of the child's functioning readily tapped by assessment forms. Armed with information from the standardized assessment regarding the child's specific problems, competencies, and areas of concern, professionals can focus their efforts on issues that cannot be assessed with standardized procedures.

Standardized assessment provides documentation for decisions.

Standardized assessment via the CBCL, TRF, YSR, and related instruments provides documentation regarding placement and service decisions. Because the profiles clearly display specific problems, competencies, and areas of concern, they can guide the selection of the appropriate placement for the child and the services needed by the child. Increasingly, funders are requiring explicit documentation for placement and service decisions.

Standardized assessment supports outcome evaluation.

Standardized assessment provides outcome evaluations for individual children and for programs. Outcome evaluations require that standardized assessment data be collected at the beginning of services and again at a subsequent point in order to determine whether there has been improvement in the problem and competence scores. In the case of formal evaluations of program effectiveness, statistical analyses are required to compare changes among children who receive specified services with changes among children who receive different services or no services. In the case of less formal evaluations of outcomes for individual children, children's initial profiles may be visually compared with their profiles following services or placement.

The Child Behavior Checklist (CBCL) and the Young Adult Behavior Checklist (YABCL)

Child Behavior Checklist for Ages 2–3 (CBCL/2-3)

The CBCL/2-3, which is completed by parents and parent surrogates, lists 99 problems to be rated by the informant, and requests the informant to describe any additional problems, illnesses, and disabilities of the child; identify the most pressing concerns about the child; and list the "best things" about the child. (See Figure 2-1: The CBCL/2-3 for 3-year-old Benny Brown). With regard to each of the 99 listed problems, the informant rates each problem as "0" if it is not true of the child; "1" if it is somewhat or sometimes true; and "2" if it is very true or often true. The ratings are based on the child's functioning over the preceding two months. The CBCL/2-3 can generally be completed in about 10 minutes.

Child Behavior Checklist for Ages 4–18 (CBCL/4-18)

The CBCL/4-18 includes a variety of competence and open-ended descriptive items and problem items that are scored 0, 1, or 2 like the items in the CBCL/2-3 (Achenbach 1991a). Parents and parent surrogates are asked to base ratings on the preceding 6 months, although the time period can be shortened if the informant, such as a foster parent, has not known the child for a 6-month period. The first page of the CBCL/4-18 requests information about competencies, such as the child's involvement in sports, nonsports activities, groups, and work. The second page of the CBCL/4-18 requests information about the child's friendships, relationships with significant others, school functioning, illnesses and disabilities, greatest concerns about the child, and "best things" about the child. (See Figure 2-2: The CBCL/4-18 for 12-year-old Gloria Chavez). The competence portion of the CBCL/4-18 takes 5 to 10 minutes to complete, and the portion related to problems and other issues takes about 10 minutes.

CBCL Sections and Items

The two major sections of the CBCL are the Competence Section and the Problem Section. The items in both sections were selected from a pool of childhood competencies and behavioral and emotional problems suggested by literature reviews and interviews with parents and mental health professionals. Problem behavior scales were developed using principal component analyses, with separate analyses for boys and girls and for three age groups defined by important developmental transitions.

Competence Section

The 20 competence items are grouped according to content into three scales: Activities, Social, and School. Items include the child's involvement in play activities (such as sports, organizations, and hobbies); involvement in work activities (such as chores); friendships; and functioning at school. On the Activities scale, both the number of activities and how the child compares to peers are scored. Scores on the three scales are summed to yield a Total Competence score.

Figure 2-1. Page 1 of the CBCL/2-3 Completed for 3-year-old Benny Brown.

CHILD BEHAVIOR CHECKLIST FOR AGES 2-3

For office use only
ID # 731223

CHILD'S FULL NAME — First: BENNY   Middle: SHAWN   Last: BROWN

GENDER: ☑ Boy ☐ Girl   **AGE**: 3   **ETHNIC GROUP OR RACE**: WHITE

TODAY'S DATE: Mo. APR. Date 4 Yr. 1998

CHILD'S BIRTHDATE: Mo. MAR. Date 3 Yr. 1995

PARENTS' USUAL TYPE OF WORK, even if not working now (Please be specific—for example, auto mechanic, high school teacher, homemaker, laborer, lathe operator, shoe salesman, army sergeant.)

FATHER'S TYPE OF WORK: unKnown

MOTHER'S TYPE OF WORK: Nurse's Aide

THIS FORM FILLED OUT BY:

☑ Mother (full name): ANGELINA BROWN

☐ Father (full name): _____

☐ Other—Specify full name & relationship to child: _____

Please fill out this form to reflect *your* view of the child's behavior even if other people might not agree. Feel free to print additional comments beside each item and in the space provided on page 2.

Below is a list of items that describe children. For each item that describes the child *now or within the past 2 months*, please circle the *2* if the item is *very true* or *often true* of the child. Circle the *1* if the item is *somewhat or sometimes true* of the child. If the item is *not true* of the child, circle the *0*. Please answer all items as well as you can, even if some do not seem to apply to the child.

0 = Not True (as far as you know)   1 = Somewhat or Sometimes True   2 = Very True or Often True

0 1 ②	1. Aches or pains (without medical cause)
0 ① 2	2. Acts too young for age
0 ① 2	3. Afraid to try new things
0 ① 2	4. Avoids looking others in the eye
0 1 ②	5. Can't concentrate, can't pay attention for long
0 ① 2	6. Can't sit still or restless
⓪ 1 2	7. Can't stand having things out of place
0 ① 2	8. Can't stand waiting; wants everything now
0 1 ②	9. Chews on things that aren't edible
0 1 ②	10. Clings to adults or too dependent
0 ① 2	11. Constantly seeks help
0 ① 2	12. Constipated, doesn't move bowels
0 1 ②	13. Cries a lot
0 ① 2	14. Cruel to animals
0 1 ②	15. Defiant
0 1 ②	16. Demands must be met immediately
0 1 ②	17. Destroys his/her own things
0 ① 2	18. Destroys things belonging to his/her family or other children
0 ① 2	19. Diarrhea or loose bowels when not sick
⓪ 1 2	20. Disobedient
0 ① 2	21. Disturbed by any change in routine
0 1 ②	22. Doesn't want to sleep alone
⓪ 1 2	23. Doesn't answer when people talk to him/her
0 ① 2	24. Doesn't eat well (describe): won't eat fruits, veggies
⓪ 1 2	25. Doesn't get along with other children
⓪ 1 2	26. Doesn't know how to have fun, acts like a little adult
⓪ 1 2	27. Doesn't seem to feel guilty after misbehaving
⓪ 1 2	28. Doesn't want to go out of home
0 1 ②	29. Easily frustrated
0 ① 2	30. Easily jealous
0 ① 2	31. Eats or drinks things that are not food—don't include sweets (describe): Sometimes dirt
0 ① 2	32. Fears certain animals, situations, or places (describe): Dogs

0 ① 2	33. Feelings are easily hurt
⓪ 1 2	34. Gets hurt a lot, accident-prone
⓪ 1 2	35. Gets in many fights
0 ① 2	36. Gets into everything
0 ① 2	37. Gets too upset when separated from parents
0 ① 2	38. Has trouble getting to sleep
0 ① 2	39. Headaches (without medical cause)
⓪ 1 2	40. Hits others
0 ① 2	41. Holds his/her breath
⓪ 1 2	42. Hurts animals or people without meaning to
0 ① 2	43. Looks unhappy without good reason
0 1 ②	44. Angry moods
0 1 ②	45. Nausea, feels sick (without medical cause)
⓪ 1 2	46. Nervous movements or twitching (describe): _____
⓪ 1 2	47. Nervous, highstrung, or tense
0 1 ②	48. Nightmares
⓪ 1 2	49. Overeating
⓪ 1 2	50. Overtired
⓪ 1 2	51. Overweight
⓪ 1 2	52. Painful bowel movements
⓪ 1 2	53. Physically attacks people
⓪ 1 2	54. Picks nose, skin, or other parts of body (describe): _____
0 ① 2	55. Plays with own sex parts too much
0 ① 2	56. Poorly coordinated or clumsy
⓪ 1 2	57. Problems with eyes (without medical cause) (describe): _____
⓪ 1 2	58. Punishment doesn't change his/her behavior
0 ① 2	59. Quickly shifts from one activity to another
0 ① 2	60. Rashes or other skin problems (without medical cause)
0 ① 2	61. Refuses to eat
⓪ 1 2	62. Refuses to play active games
⓪ 1 2	63. Repeatedly rocks head or body
0 ① 2	64. Resists going to bed at night

Please see other side
7-96 Edition

Page 1 of the CBCL/2-3 completed for 3-year-old Benny Brown.

Figure 2-1 continued. Page 2 of the CBCL/2-3 completed for 3-year-old Benny Brown.

0 = Not True (as far as you know)	1 = Somewhat or Sometimes True	2 = Very True or Often True

0 (1) 2   65. Resists toilet training (describe): *Doesn't want to use toilet*

(0)(1) 2   66. Screams a lot

(0) 1 2   67. Seems unresponsive to affection

0 (1) 2   68. Self-conscious or easily embarrassed

0 (1) 2   69. Selfish or won't share

(0) 1 2   70. Shows little affection toward people

(0) 1 2   71. Shows little interest in things around him/her

(0) 1 2   72. Shows too little fear of getting hurt

(0) 1 2   73. Too shy or timid

0 (1) 2   74. Sleeps less than most children during day and/or night (describe): *No naps, goes to sleep late*

0 (1) 2   75. Smears or plays with bowel movements

(0) 1 2   76. Speech problem (describe): _____

0 (1) 2   77. Stares into space or seems preoccupied

0 1 (2)   78. Stomachaches or cramps (without medical cause)

(0) 1 2   79. Stores up many things he/she doesn't need (describe): _____

(0) 1 2   80. Strange behavior (describe): _____

(0) 1 2   81. Stubborn, sullen, or irritable

0 (1) 2   82. Sudden changes in mood or feelings

0 1 (2)   83. Sulks a lot

0 1 (2)   84. Talks or cries out in sleep

0 (1) 2   85. Temper tantrums or hot temper

(0) 1 2   86. Too concerned with neatness or cleanliness

0 1 (2)   87. Too fearful or anxious

(0) 1 2   88. Uncooperative

(0) 1 2   89. Underactive, slow moving, or lacks energy

0 1 (2)   90. Unhappy, sad, or depressed

(0) 1 2   91. Unusually loud

0 (1) 2   92. Upset by new people or situations (describe): *Visitors who he doesn't know*

0 (1) 2   93. Vomiting, throwing up (without medical cause)

0 (1) 2   94. Wakes up often at night

(0) 1 2   95. Wanders away from home

0 1 (2)   96. Wants a lot of attention

0 1 (2)   97. Whining

(0) 1 2   98. Withdrawn, doesn't get involved with others

0 (1) 2   99. Worries

100. Please write in any problems your child has that were not listed above. *Keeps asking where Daddy is*

0 (1) 2

0 1 2

PLEASE BE SURE YOU HAVE ANSWERED ALL ITEMS.   UNDERLINE ANY YOU ARE CONCERNED ABOUT.

Does the child have any illness or disability (either physical or mental)?   ☒ No   ☐ Yes—Please describe:

What concerns you most about the child?

*Seems very unhappy.
Kind of immature.*

Please describe the best things about the child:

Very loving and cute.

Page 2 of the CBCL/2-3 completed for 3-year-old Benny Brown.

Figure 2-2. Page 1 of the CBCL/4-18 competence items scored for 12-year-old Gloria Chavez.

CHILD BEHAVIOR CHECKLIST FOR AGES 4–18

Please Print

For office use only
ID # 163121

CHILD'S FULL NAME — FIRST: *Gloria*   MIDDLE: *Rosa*   LAST: *Chavez*

SEX: ☐ Boy ☑ Girl   **AGE:** 12   **ETHNIC GROUP OR RACE:** *Latina*

TODAY'S DATE: Mo. *May* Date *5* Yr. *97*

CHILD'S BIRTHDATE: Mo. *Feb* Date *1* Yr. *85*

GRADE IN SCHOOL: *6*

NOT ATTENDING SCHOOL: ☐

Please fill out this form to reflect *your* view of the child's behavior even if other people might not agree. Feel free to print additional comments beside each item and in the spaces provided on page 2.

PARENTS' USUAL TYPE OF WORK, even if not working now. *(Please be specific—for example, auto mechanic, high school teacher, homemaker, laborer, lathe operator, shoe salesman, army sergeant.)*

FATHER'S TYPE OF WORK: *Mechanic*

MOTHER'S TYPE OF WORK: *Food Service Worker*

THIS FORM FILLED OUT BY:
☐ Mother (full name) _____
☐ Father (full name) _____
☑ Other—name & relationship to child: *Maria Garcia-Foster* MOM

I. Please list the sports your child most likes to take part in. For example: swimming, baseball, skating, skate boarding, bike riding, fishing, etc.

☑ None

	Compared to others of the same age, about how much time does he/she spend in each?				Compared to others of the same age, how well does he/she do each one?			
	Don't Know	Less Than Average	Average	More Than Average	Don't Know	Below Average	Average	Above Average
a. _____	☐	☐	☐	☐	☐	☐	☐	☐
b. _____	☐	☐	☐	☐	☐	☐	☐	☐
c. _____	☐	☐	☐	☐	☐	☐	☐	☐

II. Please list your child's favorite hobbies, activities, and games, other than sports. For example: stamps, dolls, books, piano, crafts, cars, singing, etc. (Do *not* include listening to radio or TV.)

☐ None

	Compared to others of the same age, about how much time does he/she spend in each?				Compared to others of the same age, how well does he/she do each one?			
	Don't Know	Less Than Average	Average	More Than Average	Don't Know	Below Average	Average	Above Average
a. *reading books*	☐	☐	☑	☐	☐	☐	☐	☑
b. _____	☐	☐	☐	☐	☐	☐	☐	☐
c. _____	☐	☐	☐	☐	☐	☐	☐	☐

III. Please list any organizations, clubs, teams, or groups your child belongs to.

☐ None

	Compared to others of the same age, how active is he/she in each?			
	Don't Know	Less Active	Average	More Active
a. *Church Group*	☐	☐	☑	☐
b. _____	☐	☐	☐	☐
c. _____	☐	☐	☐	☐

IV. Please list any jobs or chores your child has. For example: paper route, babysitting, making bed, working in store, etc. (Include *both* paid and unpaid jobs and chores.)

☑ None

	Compared to others of the same age, how well does he/she carry them out?			
	Don't Know	Below Average	Average	Above Average
a. _____	☐	☐	☐	☐
b. _____	☐	☐	☐	☐
c. _____	☐	☐	☐	☐

Page 1 of the CBCL/4-18 competence items scored for 12-year-old Gloria Chavez.

Figure 2-2 continued. Page 2 of the CBCL/4-18 competence items scored for 12-year-old Gloria Chavez.

Please Print

V. 1. About how many close friends does your child have? ☐ None ☐ 1 ☑ 2 or 3 ☐ 4 or more
(Do *not* include brothers & sisters)

2. About how many times a week does your child do things with any friends outside of regular school hours?
(Do *not* include brothers & sisters) ☐ Less than 1 ☑ 1 or 2 ☐ 3 or more

VI. Compared to others of his/her age, how well does your child:

		Worse	About Average	Better	
a.	Get along with his/her brothers & sisters?	☐	☐	☐	☑ Has no brothers or sisters
b.	Get along with other kids?	☐	☑	☐	
c.	Behave with his/her parents?	☑	☐	☐	
d.	Play and work alone?	☑	☐	☐	

VII. 1. For ages 6 and older—performance in academic subjects. ☐ Does not attend school because _____

Check a box for each subject that child takes	Failing	Below Average	Average	Above Average
a. Reading, English, or Language Arts	☐	☐	☐	☑
b. History or Social Studies	☐	☐	☐	☑
c. Arithmetic or Math	☐	☐	☑	☐
d. Science	☐	☐	☑	☐

Other academic subjects—for example: computer courses, foreign language, business. Do *not* include gym, shop, driver's ed., etc.

	Failing	Below Average	Average	Above Average
e. _____	☐	☐	☐	☐
f. _____	☐	☐	☐	☐
g. _____	☐	☐	☐	☐

2. Does your child receive special remedial services or attend a special class or special school? ☑ No   ☐ Yes—kind of services, class, or school:

3. Has your child repeated any grades? ☑ No   ☐ Yes—grades and reasons:

4. Has your child had any academic or other problems in school? ☐ No ☑ Yes—please describe:

Conflicts with teachers

When did these problems start? *4th grade*

Have these problems ended? ☑ No ☐ Yes—when?

Does your child have any illness or disability (either physical or mental)? ☑ No   ☐ Yes—please describe:

What concerns you most about your child?

Low self-esteem. Doesn't try to develop new skills. Gets very angry.

Please describe the best things about your child:

Likes books. Wants to do well in school. Helpful at home.

PAGE 2

Page 2 of the CBCL/4-18 competence items scored for 12-year-old Gloria Chavez.

Problem Behaviors Section

This section is composed of 118 specific problem items and 2 open-ended problem items that ask parents to describe the child's current emotional and behavioral problems. (See Appendix A for a list of CBCL problem scales and items.)

Eight problem scales have been empirically derived for children ages 4 to 18:

- Withdrawn

- Thought Problems

- Somatic Complaints

- Attention Problems

- Anxious/Depressed

- Delinquent Behavior

- Social Problems

- Aggressive Behavior

One scale, Sex Problems, also was derived for children under 12 years of age. In addition, scales are summed to provide scores for Internalizing Problems (e.g., sadness and worrying) and Externalizing Problems (e.g., arguing and fighting). The sum of scores for all problem items yields a Total Problems score.

Use of the CBCL

The CBCL is intended to provide standardized descriptions of behavior rather than diagnostic inferences. The instrument's authors advocate a multiaxial assessment model, in which CBCL reports are integrated with information from other sources such as teacher reports, cognitive assessments (such as language and perceptual-motor tests), physical assessment, and direct assessment of the child through interviews, observation or youth self-reports for children aged 11 and older (Achenbach 1991b). (See Reference Notes 1 and 2 for information on the validity and reliability of the CBCL). The use of multiple approaches facilitates a comprehensive evaluation of the child. Consistent with this multi-axial approach, the instrument's authors have developed the Teacher's Report Form (Achenbach 1991c) and the Youth Self-Report (Achenbach 1991d), both of which have counterpart scales to the CBCL. These instruments are described later.

The Young Adult Behavior Checklist for Ages 18-30 (YABCL)

The YABCL obtains standardized descriptions of young adults from individuals who know them well, such as parents, parent surrogates, and spouses. Ratings are based on the preceding 6 months, but the time period may be shortened if necessary. The YABCL can be used to assess the functioning of young adults who were placed in foster care or received services when they were younger; young adults who are being considered for foster care placement or services; and young adult parents of children who receive services. The YABCL can provide comparative data, for example, for an individual who was assessed with the CBCL/4-18 when placed in foster care at age 16 in order to evaluate changes in problems and competencies and identify service needs. The CBCL/4-18 and the YABCL both have norms for individuals at age 18 and, as a result, either may be used for 18 year olds. Typically, the CBCL/4-18 is more appropriate for 18-year-olds who live with parents and attend high school, where as the YABCL is more appropriate for 18-year-olds who are more independent. The YABCL takes about 10 to 15 minutes to complete.

Maximizing Information from Parents and Parent Surrogates on the CBCL and YABCL

The CBCL and YABCL may be completed by an adult who lives with or knows the child or youth, including birth, adoptive, step, and foster parents; relatives such as grandparents, adult siblings, aunts, and uncles; and staff who work with children and youth in institutional and group home settings. Both instruments are accessible to parents and parent surrogates as they require only fifth grade reading skills. If an informant cannot read English but can read another language, translations are available in 61 languages. If there are questions about an informant's ability to complete the form, the interviewer may hand the informant the form, retain a second copy, and offer to read the questions aloud and write down the informant's answers. Informants who can read will usually begin answering the questions without waiting for them to be read, but this procedure can avoid embarrassment and errors that may arise if an informant is unable to easily read the form. Even when informants cannot read well, having the form before them allows them to see the format of the questions. Although the form may be administered as a telephone interview, it is advisable to send informants the form and ask them to look at the form while the telephone interviewer asks the questions. Informants will differ in the knowledge they have of a child's competence and behaviors and may judge the child in different ways. As a result, it is important to compare reports from multiple informants who know the child.

Forms Completed by Teachers and Daycare Providers

Other than parents, teachers are often the most important adults in children's lives. Because they see children in contexts quite different than the home and have different perspectives than parents, teachers can often contribute crucial information. For young children, daycare providers may similarly contribute crucial information about children's functioning outside the home. Forms, therefore, have been developed to compare reports by teachers and daycare providers with reports by parents and parent surrogates. These forms request that ratings of problems be based on the preceding two months.

Caregiver-Teacher Report Form for Ages 2–5 (C-TRF)

The C-TRF is similar to the CBCL/2-3 and contains most of the same items. It replaces problems that are apt to be observed only at home with problems that are more apt to be observed in daycare and preschool settings. The C-TRF takes about 10 minutes to complete.

Teacher's Report Form for Ages 5–18 (TRF)

The TRF provides standardized descriptions of problem behaviors, adaptive behaviors, and academic functioning in children 5 through 18 years of age (Achenbach 1991c). The TRF has many of the same problem items as the CBCL/4-18 but substitutes school-specific items for home-specific items. (See Reference Notes 3 and 4 for information regarding the validity and reliability of the TRF).

Problem behaviors

The TRF has 118 specific problem items and two open-ended problem items. Teachers rate the specific problem items for the child as "Not True," "Somewhat or Sometimes True," or "Very True or Often True." Based on 2 broadband factors, scale scores are summed to provide Internalizing and Externalizing scores. The syndrome scales included on the broadband scales are the same as on the CBCL. Summing all problem items yields a Total Problem score.

Eight scales from the 118 specific problem items have been empirically derived for the TRF. These scales have the same labels as CBCL scales, but the item content differs somewhat from the CBCL. These problem-behavior scales were developed using principal component analyses of scores for children referred to mental health or special education services. Analyses were conducted separately by gender and age (5–11 and 12–18 years). (See Appendix B for a list of TRF problem behavior scales and items.)

Consistent with the multiaxial approach discussed earlier, TRF problem-behavior scales have counterpart scales on the Child Behavior Checklist (Achenbach, 1991c).

Adaptive behaviors and academic functioning

In place of the activities and social competence items of the CBCL/4-18, the TRF requests teacher ratings on four adaptive characteristics: how hard the child works in school; how appropriately the child behaves in school; how much the child is learning; and how happy the child is. The four items are added to create a summary score called "Adaptive Functioning." Respondents also report school performance relative to grade level (Academic Performance Score). Information is requested about special school services that the child received and the child's ability and achievement test scores, if available. The TRF takes about 15 to 20 minutes to complete.

Self-Report and Observation Forms

Youth Self-Report for Ages 11–18 (YSR)

The YSR has many of the same competence and problem items as the CBCL/4-18. Like the CBCL, the YSR problem items are rated 0, 1, or 2, based on the preceding 6 months. The YSR, however, omits CBCL items that are not appropriate for ages 11 to 18 and items that youth are unlikely to report about themselves. The YSR takes about 15 to 20 minutes to complete. If a youth's ability to complete the YSR independently is questionable, an interviewer may administer it according to the procedure outlined earlier for the parent forms.

Young Adult Self-Report for Ages 18–30 (YASR)

The YASR has many of the same problem items as the YABCL but also has substance use items and adaptive functioning items that are scored on separate scales. The adaptive functioning items tap relations with friends and family, functioning in educational and job situations, and relations with spouse or partner, if the respondent has had such a relationship in the preceding 6 months.

Semistructured Clinical Interview for Children and Adolescents Ages 6–18 (SCICA)

The SCICA is designed for use by professionals with experience in conducting clinical interviews with children of the ages to be assessed. Because it covers the topics typically included in initial clinical interviews, it can be used in the initial evaluation. The SCICA protocol form provides instructions, topic questions, and activities, such as a kinetic family drawing and tasks for screening fine motor and gross motor functioning.

The protocol form also provides columns in which the interviewer separately notes observations regarding the child's behavior and self-reports by the child.

Following the interview, the interviewer scores one set of items to describe the child's behavior and a second set to describe the child's self-reports. The items can then be entered on a profile of syndrome scales by clerical staff, using either the SCICA hand-scored profile or a computer-scoring program. The information from the SCICA includes both the standardized item and scale scores displayed on the profile and the interviewer's notes, impressions, and inferences as would be obtained from traditional clinical interviews. The SCICA takes from 60 to 90 minutes to administer, depending on whether achievement subtests are included to assess the child's academic functioning.

Direct Observation Form For Ages 5–14 (DOF)

The DOF is used to record a 10-minute sample of a child's behavior in the classroom and other group setting. During a 10-minute period, the observer writes a narrative description of the child's behavior and checks boxes on the DOF to indicate whether the child is on-task at the end of each 1-minute interval. After the 10-minute observation period, the observer scores items that are then displayed on a profile. Because children's behavior may vary considerably from one occasion to another, it is desirable to obtain 10-minute samples of behavior on different days. The DOF computer program can average all item and scale scores for up to six observation sessions and print a profile based on these averaged scores. To indicate how a child's observed problems differ from those of other children observed in the same setting, the program can provide a comparison profile based on the averages of scores from two other children observed on up to six occasions.

DOF observations may be done by paraprofessionals, including teacher aides and childcare workers. The DOF is especially useful for documenting specific behaviors while the child is in the classroom or in group activities, where direct observations may detect behaviors that may not be readily assessed by other means.

Table 2-1 summarizes the forms that may be used by child and family social workers.

Profiles for Scoring the Forms

Each of the forms can be scored on a profile that displays the ratings of each competence, adaptive functioning, and problem item. The profile also provides a graphic display that depicts the child's standing on syndrome scales of behavioral and emotional problems. Each syndrome consists of behavioral and emotional problems that were found to co-occur in statistical analyses of large samples of children. Descriptive names for the syndromes summarize the kinds of problems comprising each syndrome scale.

Hand-Scored Profiles

Hand-scored versions of the profiles are available so that users who lack computer facilities can transfer data from the rating forms to profile forms. Instructions are provided that enable clerical staff to score the CBCL/2-3 profile in about 5 minutes. The hand-scored profile for the C-TRF and the problem portion of the CBCL/4-18, YSR, and TRF also take about 5 minutes to score. Figure 2-3 shows a profile scored from Benny Brown's CBCL/2-3 with six syndromes displayed: Anxious/Depressed, Withdrawn, Sleep Problems, Somatic Problems, Aggressive Behavior, and Destructive Behavior.

The information in Figure 2-3 is based on Ms. Brown's rating (0, 1, or 2) of each problem for Benny and a determination of a total score for each syndrome based on adding the 1 and 2 ratings of the problems comprising the syndrome. The syndrome score is then marked in the column of numbers in the graphic display above the syndrome. After the scores for all 6 syndromes have been marked in the graphic display, a line can be drawn from one score to the next to show the child's profile pattern, as Figure 2-3 illustrates for Benny.

On the left side of the profile is the percentile for each of Benny's syndrome scores. The percentiles, which are based on a large normative sample of children, indicate how a particular child scores in relation to other children of the same age. Benny's score on the Anxious/ Depressed syndrome, for example, is at the 98th percentile for the normative sample of 2- and 3-year-olds. Based on Ms. Brown's ratings, Benny's score on the Anxious/Depressed syndrome was in the top 2% of scores obtained by the normative sample of children – that is, 98% of children in the normative sample obtained scores lower than Benny's score.

The broken lines on the profile in Figure 2-3 demarcate a borderline clinical range from the 95th to the 98th percentile of the normative sample. On the Anxious/Depressed syndrome, Benny's score was at the top broken line (the upper limit of the borderline clinical range) and, therefore, of concern. Benny's score on the Anxious/Depressed syndrome, however, was not quite high enough to be in the clinical range, which is above the top broken line. In contrast to his scores on the Anxious/Depressed syndrome, Benny's score on the

Table 2-1. Forms that May be Helpful to Child and Family Workers

Name of Form	*Filled Out By*
Semistructured Clinical Interview for Children and Adolescents for Ages 6-18 (SCICA)	Interviewers
Direct Observation Form (DOF) for Ages 5-14	Observers
Child Behavior Checklist for Ages 2-3 (CBCL/2-3)	Parents & surrogates
Child Behavior Checklist for Ages 4-18 (CBCL/4-18)	Parents & surrogates
Young Adult Behavior Checklist for Ages 18-30 (YABCL)	Parents & surrogates
Caregiver-Teacher Report Form for Ages 2-5 (C-TRF)	Daycare providers & preschool teachers
Teacher's Report Form for Ages 5-18 (TRF)	Teachers
Youth Self-Report for Ages 11-18(YSR)	Youths
Young Adult Self-Report for Ages 18-30 (YASR)	Young adults

Withdrawn syndrome, was much lower, falling at the 50th percentile. This score indicates that Ms. Brown reported only as many problems of this syndrome as were reported for the lowest 50% of the normative sample of 2- and 3-year-olds.

Computer-Scored Profiles

For all the forms, computer-scoring programs are available and are easily utilized by any individual who is familiar with desktop or notebook computers. These programs make it possible to enter the data from any form in about two minutes. The program then prints a profile like the one shown for Benny Brown in Figure 2-4. The layout of the computer-scored profile is similar to that of the hand-scored profile shown in Figure 2-3.

T Scores (Standard Scores)

For each syndrome, the program prints out T scores as well as raw scale scores. T scores are standard scores that indicate how a child's score compares with the scores of a normative sample of peers. For example, a T score of 67 indicates that a child's scale score is at about the 95th percentile of the scores obtained by a normative sample of peers. In other words, a T score of 67 indicates that the child scored higher than about 95% of her peers. A T score of 70 is at about the 98th percentile of the normative sample, and therefore, is higher than the scores of about 98% of a child's peers. Even though the number of items and the possible range of raw scores differ from one scale to another, a particular T score, such as 67, indicates approximately the same degree of elevation on all scales.

As an example, the Withdrawn scale has 14 items. The sum of the scores on 14 items can range from 0 to 28, because each item can be scored 0, 1, or 2. The Sleep Problems scale has only 7 items, whose sum can range from 0 to 14. Conversion of the Withdrawn and Sleep Problems raw scores to T scores provides common sets of numbers that indicate the same degree of elevation on both scales. Even though the raw scale scores have different meanings on the Withdrawn and Sleep Problems scales, a T score of 67 on either scale indicates that

Figure 2-3. Hand-scored CBCL/2-3 profile for Benny Brown.

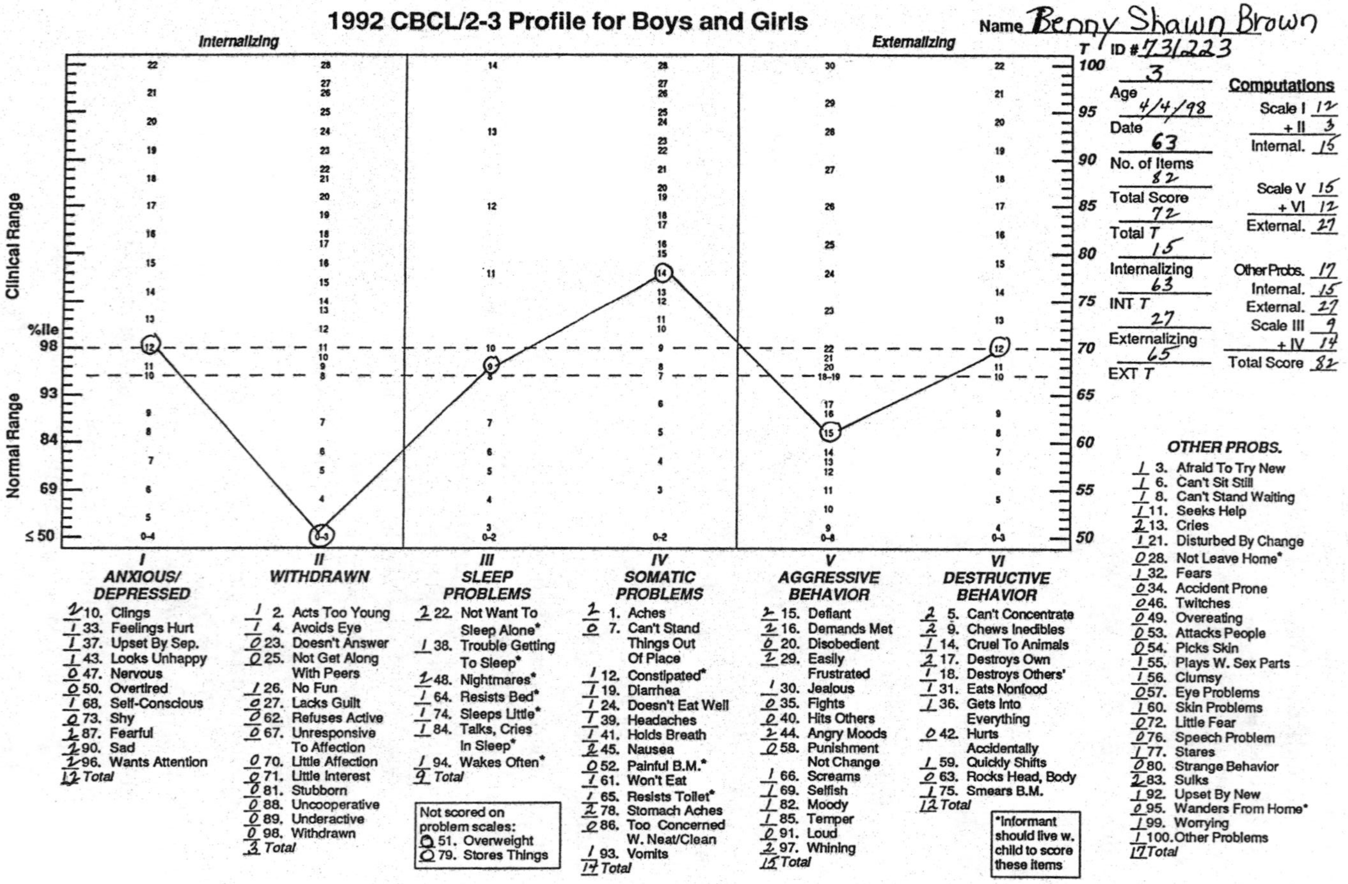

Hand-scored CBCL/2-3 profile for Benny Brown.

Figure 2-4. Computer-scored CBCL/2-3 profile for Benny Brown.

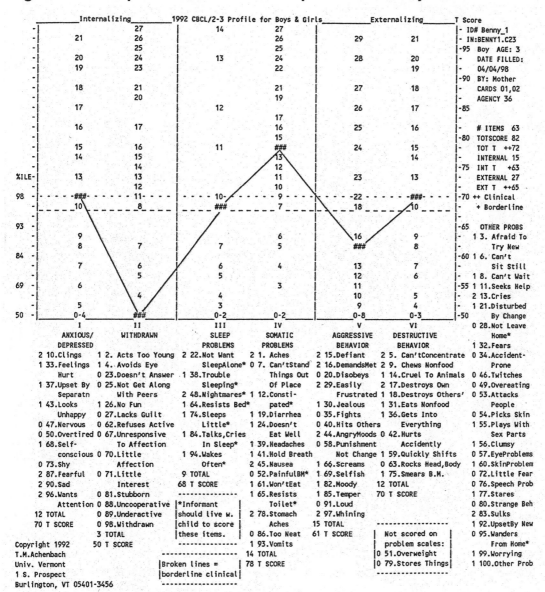

Computer-scored CBCL/2-3 profile for Benny Brown.

a child is at the 95th percentile on that scale – that is, the child's score is higher than the scores obtained by 95% of peers.

Cross-Informant Comparisons

Another feature of computer-scoring programs is their ability to provide comparisons of up to 5 forms (or, with the new Windows program, up to 8 forms) that have been completed by different individuals for the same child. Because each parent, surrogate, caregiver, and teacher may see different aspects of a child's functioning and may have different standards for reporting what they see, there is seldom perfect agreement among them. If a child's problems appear significant enough to warrant a comprehensive evaluation, it is helpful to have forms completed by several relevant adults. For adolescents, it is helpful to obtain their views of their problems and competencies by having them complete the YSR. If the child's functioning in school is relevant for an evaluation, the C-TRF or TRF can be completed by one or more teachers.

When 2 or more individuals have completed forms for a child, the computer program can print the profiles from each informant, which can then be visually compared to identify similarities and differences in the elevations and patterns of syndrome scores. Alternatively, the program can print side-by-side comparisons of scores obtained from each informant on each problem item. Figure 2-5, for example, shows side-by-side comparisons of the problem items scored by Benny Brown's mother, aunt, and grandmother. These 3 relatives agreed in a rating of 2 ("Very true or often true") to the first item of the Anxious/Depressed syndrome (upper left corner of Figure 2-5). That item, abbreviated as "10, Clings," refers to the item on the CBCL/2-3 listed as "10, Clings to adults or too dependent". By contrast, Figure 2-5 shows that the second item of the Anxious/Depressed syndrome, abbreviated as "33, Feelings Hurt" for the CBCL2-2 item, "33, Feelings are easily hurt," was scored 1 by Benny's mother but 0 by his aunt and grandmother. The differences in ratings on this item indicates that it is a less consistent problem than "10, Clings to adults or too dependent." A review of side-by-side comparisons of scores obtained from different informants facilitates the quick identification of problems that are absent according to all informants, problems that are present according to all informants, and problems that may be more variable because they are reported by some informants but not others.

The computer program also provides a side-by-side comparison of the T scores obtained from each informant on each syndrome scale. Figure 2-6 displays the side-by-side T scores obtained from Benny's mother, aunt, and grandmother. Additionally, the program provides T scores for Internalizing and Externalizing groupings of syndromes and total problems, also illustrated in Figure 2-6. A comparison of T scores from each informant on each syndrome allows a quick determination of which syndromes are scored in the normal range by all informants (T scores below 67) and which syndromes are scored in the borderline range (T scores 67 to 70) or clinical range (T scores over 70) by any informant. The program prints a cross (+) beside scores that are in the borderline range and two crosses (+ +) beside scores that are in the clinical range.

As an example, Figure 2-6 shows that Benny's mother scored him in the borderline clinical range (T score = 70) and Benny's aunt and grandmother scored him in the clinical

Figure 2-5. Side-by-side comparisons of item scores from CBCL/2-3s completed by Benny's mother, aunt, and grandmother.

I ANXIOUS/DEPRESSED

Item	Mo C23 1	Aunt C23 2	Grandma C23 3	4	5
10. Clings	2	2	2	-	-
33. FeelingsHurt	1	0	0	-	-
37. UpsetBySep	1	2	2	-	-
43. LooksUnhappy	1	2	1	-	-
47. Nervous	0	1	2	-	-
50. Overtired	0	0	1	-	-
68. SelfCon	1	1	2	-	-
73. Shy	0	0	0	-	-
87. FearFul	2	2	1	-	-
90. Sad	2	2	2	-	-
96. WantsAttn	2	2	2	-	-

II WITHDRAWN

Item	Mo	Aunt	Grandma	4	5
2. ActsYoung	1	2	1	-	-
4. AvoidsEye	1	0	1	-	-
23. Doesn'tAns	0	1	1	-	-
25. NotGetAlong	0	0	0	-	-
26. NoFun	1	1	2	-	-
27. LacksGuilt	0	0	0	-	-
62. Refuses	0	0	0	-	-
67. UnrespAffct	0	0	0	-	-
70. LittleAffct	0	0	0	-	-
71. LittleInt	0	0	0	-	-
81. Stubborn	0	0	1	-	-
88. Uncooprtive	0	0	0	-	-
89. Underactive	0	0	1	-	-
98. Withdrawn	0	0	0	-	-

III SLEEP PROBLEMS

Item	Mo	Aunt	Grandma	4	5
*22. NoSleepAlone	2	1	2	-	-
*38. TroubleSleep	1	1	2	-	-
*48. Nightmares	2	2	1	-	-
*64. ResistsBed	1	2	2	-	-
*74. SleepsLittle	1	2	1	-	-
*84. Talks,Cries	1	1	0	-	-
*94. WakesOften	1	1	1	-	-

IV SOMATIC PROBLEMS

Item	Mo C23 1	Aunt C23 2	Grandma C23 3	4	5
1. Aches	2	1	1	-	-
7. Can'tStand	0	0	1	-	-
*12. Constipated	1	0	1	-	-
19. Diarrhea	1	1	2	-	-
24. NotEatWell	1	2	2	-	-
39. Headaches	1	1	0	-	-
41. HoldBreath	1	2	1	-	-
45. Nausea	2	2	1	-	-
*52. Painful BM	0	0	0	-	-
61. Won'tEat	1	1	1	-	-
*65. ResistToilet	1	1	1	-	-
78. Stomachaches	2	1	1	-	-
86. TooNeat	0	1	0	-	-
93. Vomits	1	1	2	-	-

V AGGRESSIVE BEHAVIOR

Item	Mo	Aunt	Grandma	4	5
15. Defiant	2	1	1	-	-
16. DemandsMet	2	2	2	-	-
20. Disobeys	0	0	0	-	-
29. Frustrated	2	1	2	-	-
30. Jealous	1	1	0	-	-
35. Fights	0	0	0	-	-
40. HitsOthers	0	0	0	-	-
44. AngryMoods	2	1	2	-	-
58. PunishNoChng	0	0	0	-	-
66. Screams	1	1	2	-	-
69. Selfish	1	1	1	-	-
82. Moody	1	2	1	-	-
85. Temper	1	1	1	-	-
91. Loud	0	0	0	-	-
97. Whining	2	1	0	-	-

VI DESTRUCTIVE BEHAVIOR

Item	Mo C23 1	Aunt C23 2	Grandma C23 3	4	5
5. Can'tConcen	2	1	2	-	-
9. ChewsNonFood	2	1	1	-	-
14. CruelAnimals	1	2	1	-	-
17. DestroysOwn	2	2	2	-	-
18. DestroysOthr	1	2	1	-	-
31. EatsNonFood	1	0	0	-	-
36. GetsInto	1	2	1	-	-
42. HurtsAccidnt	0	0	0	-	-
59. QuickShifts	1	2	1	-	-
63. RocksBody	0	0	0	-	-
75. SmearsBM	1	1	1	-	-

VII OTHER PROBLEMS

Item	Mo	Aunt	Grandma	4	5
3. AfraidNew	1	1	1	-	-
6. NotStill	1	2	2	-	-
8. Can'tWait	1	1	1	-	-
11. SeeksHelp	1	2	1	-	-
13. Cries	2	1	2	-	-
21. DisturbChng	1	1	1	-	-
*28. NotLeave	0	0	0	-	-
32. Fears	1	1	1	-	-
34. AccidntProne	0	0	0	-	-
46. Twitches	0	0	0	-	-
49. Overeating	0	0	0	-	-
53. AttackPeople	0	0	0	-	-
54. PicksSkin	0	0	0	-	-
55. PlaySexParts	1	2	1	-	-
56. Clumsy	1	1	1	-	-
57. EyeProblems	0	0	0	-	-
60. SkinProblem	1	1	1	-	-
72. LittleFear	0	0	0	-	-
76. SpeechProb	0	0	0	-	-
77. Stares	1	0	0	-	-
80. StrangeBehv	0	0	0	-	-
83. Sulks	2	1	1	-	-
92. UpsetNew	1	0	1	-	-
*95. Wanders	0	0	0	-	-
99. Worries	1	1	0	-	-
100. OtherProb	1	1	2	-	-

"Mo.C23.1" is ID# Benny_1: Boy age 3. Filled out on 04/04/98 by Mother. Cards 01 02; Agency 36.
"Au.C23.2" is ID# Benny_2: Boy age 3. Filled out on 04/04/98 by Aunt. Cards 01 02; Agency 36.
"Gm.C23.3" is ID# Benny_3: Boy age 3. Filled out on 04/04/98 by Grandma. Cards 01 02; Agency 36.
- -
* Informant should live with child to score these items. ?? or M means missing data.

Side-by-side comparisons of item scores from CBCL/2-3s completed by Benny's mother, aunt, and grandmother.

Figure 2-6. Side-by-side comparisons of scale scores from CBCL/2-3s completed by Benny's mother, aunt, and grandmother.

```
                              For Reference Samples
        For this Subject      25th %ile Mean 75th %ile   Agreement between:
  Mo.C23.1 x Au.C23.2 =  .68     .41    .51    .63        Mother and Aunt is above average.
  Mo.C23.1 x Gm.C23.3 =  .64     .41    .51    .63        Mother and Grandma is above average.
  Au.C23.2 x Gm.C23.3 =  .65     .41    .51    .63        Aunt and Grandma is above average.
- - - - - - - - - - - - - - - - - - - - - - - - - - - - - - - - - - - - - - - - - - - - - - -

     T Scores for 6 Syndrome Scales on the CBCL/2-3

     Scale                    Mo.C23.1  Au.C23.2  Gm.C23.3
  1. Anxious/Depressed          70+       76++      79++      -          -
  2. Withdrawn                  50        54        62        -          -
  3. Sleep Problems             68+       70+       68+       -          -
  4. Somatic Problems           78++      78++      78++      -          -
  5. Aggressive Behavior        61        57        57        -          -
  6. Destructive Behavior       70+       73++      67+       -          -

     Internalizing             63+       66++      71++      -          -
     Externalizing             65++      63+       61+       -          -
     Total Problems            72++      72++      72++      -          -

          +Borderline Clinical Range   ++Clinical Range     M = Missing Data
- - - - - - - - - - - - - - - - - - - - - - - - - - - - - - - - - - - - - - - - - - - - - - -
```

© Copyright 1999 by T.M. Achenbach. Reproduced with permission.

range (above $T = 70$) on the Anxious/Depressed syndrome. All 3 informants reported problems of the Anxious/Depressed syndrome above the 95th percentile for children in the normative sample. By contrast, all 3 informants scored Benny in the normal range on the Withdrawn syndrome.

Profiles on Competence and Adaptive Functioning Scales

The CBCL/4-18 and YSR contain items that tap involvement in activities, social relationships, and school performance. These items are scored on competence scales, as illustrated for Gloria's hand-scored profile on the CBCL/4-18 provided in Figure 2-7. On the CBCL/4-18, the 3 competence scales are entitled Activities, Social, and School. Unlike the problem scales, low scores on the competence scales (which indicate a lack of competence) are clinically important. Gloria's score on the Activities scale in Figure 2-7 is in the clinical range because it is below the bottom broken line; her score on the Social scale is in the borderline clinical range because it is between the two broken lines; and her score on the School scale is in the normal range because it is above both broken lines. High scores on the competence and adaptive scales (as is the case for Gloria's School scale) identify areas where the child is doing well, and, thus, provide documentation of children's strengths. As discussed earlier, the profile for the TRF has scales for academic performance and adaptive behaviors. As with the CBCL/4-18 and YSR, low scores in these areas indicate poor functioning, whereas high scores indicate strengths.

Data-Processing Options

Table 2-2 presents several options for obtaining and scoring data. When the behavioral and emotional problems of only a few children are being assessed, it may be most practical to use

Figure 2-7. Hand-scored CBCL/4-18 competence profile for 12-year-old Gloria.

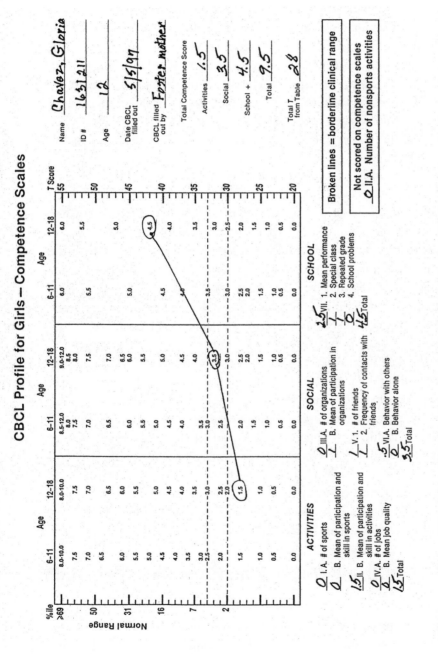

Hand-scored CBCL/4-18 competence profile for 12-year-old Gloria.

the classic forms like the one that was shown in Figure 2-1 for Benny Brown. These forms may be scored either on hand-scored profiles like the one shown in Figure 2-3 or on computer-scored profiles like the one shown in Figure 2-4. Even for small numbers of children, however, computer scoring is quicker and more accurate than hand scoring. Computer scoring also offers two additional advantages: the capacity to compare ratings by multiple informants (as shown in Figures 2-5 and 2-6) and the storage of data for later tabulations and analyses.

To avoid the labor of hand scoring and key entry into a computer program, two options are worth considering. One option is the use of machine-readable versions of the forms on which informants fill in "bubbles" to indicate their answers. The filled-in bubble forms are fed through a scanning machine that uses a special CBCL Scanning Software Package to transmit the data to a desktop computer. The computer then prints out a scored profile. The second option is the use of the CBCL Client-Entry Program. This program enables parents, parent surrogates, adolescents, and teachers to use a desktop or notebook computer to key enter their own CBCL/4-18, YSR, or TRF answers in response to user-friendly instructions on the computer screen.

Summary

The Child Behavior Checklist for Ages 2-3 (CBCL/2-3), Child Behavior Checklist for Ages 4-18 (CBCL/4-18), and Young Adult Behavior Checklist (YABCL) are completed by parents and parent surrogates to report behavioral and emotional problems. The Youth Self-Report (YSR), Young Adult Self-Report (YASR), Caregiver-Teacher Report Form for Ages 2-5 (C-TRF), and Teacher's Report Form for Ages 5-18 (TRF) obtain data from others. The Semistructured Clinical Interview for Children and Adolescents (SCICA) is used to record and rate children's behavior and self-reports during an interview. The Direct Observation Form (DOF) is used to record and rate behavior in-group settings.

Each form can be scored either by hand or by computer to produce profiles that display the scores for each problem item and each syndrome scale. Open-ended items encourage respondents to describe strengths and concerns in their own words. The computer-scoring programs for the parent, teacher, and self-report forms can compare scores from multiple informants for each child or young adult. The profiles show the child's pattern of syndrome scores in comparison to normative samples of peers. Broken lines on the profiles indicate a borderline range and a clinical range for syndrome scores that are high enough to be of concern. Strengths are indicated by high scores on the competence profiles of the CBCL/4-18 and YSR and on the academic and adaptive functioning profiles of the YASR and TRF. Figure 2-8 presents a flow chart of the typical use of the forms.

Use of the CBCL and Related Instruments in Research and Practice

Use of the CBCL and related instruments varies from one child welfare agency to another. The CBCL and TRF, for example, may be administered at different points in time, including at

Table 2-2. Obtaining and Scoring CBCL/4-18, TRF, and YSR Data

Obtaining Data	*Scoring Data*
1. Informant fills out classic forms using pencil or pen.	(a) Key enter data via scoring program.
	(b) Hand score profile forms.
2. Informant fills out machine-readable "bubble" forms.	Scanning software package transmits data froma fax or scanner to a profile-scoring program.
3. Informant enters data into computer.	Client-entry program transmits data to profile scoring program.

intake to support the initial assessment and decision making process; at regular intervals or at a midpoint in the child's program; and at case closure or at a key age for the child such as when he or she reaches 18 years. The CBCL, TRF and YSR may be used in connection with a range of interventions, including Wilderness Work Programs, intensive group work, intensive employment or mentor programs, and use of psychotropic medications. These instruments also may be utilized in connection with special case reviews or the placement of a child in more intensive treatment or as a tool to track a child's progress over time.

The CBCL, YSR, YASR, and YABCL

Use of the CBCL and related instruments provides important benefits for child welfare professionals. Applications of the standardized forms can be tailored to particular situations. The instruments completed by parents and parent surrogates can be routinely used for most children and young adults served by child and family social workers. Even when birth parents are unavailable or are poor informants, other relatives, foster parents, and child care workers may know the child, adolescent, or young adult well enough to complete the CBCL/2-3, CBCL/4-18, or YABCL. In most cases, adolescents and young adults can provide self-reports on the YSR and YASR. In other cases, the forms can be administered as interviews. In those situations, it is helpful to provide the informant a copy of the form to look at while the interviewer asks about each item.

Use of the forms requires little time from child welfare professionals because they are completed by others or in brief interviews. The forms are compatible with other procedures such as casework interviews. When completed before such interviews, the forms can save interview time. The professional can ask the informant whether he or she has any questions about the form or would like to say more about any items, and the responses can be used to guide interviewing.

The forms also provide information that can strengthen interviews. Especially with adolescents who are reluctant to discuss problems, the YSR frequently serves as an "ice breaker" that facilitates subsequent interviews. Adolescents often report problems such as suicidal ideation and feelings of rejection that they are more willing to discuss than would be the case if initially confronted with these issues in a face-to-face interview. When an

Figure 2-8. Flowchart of typical use of the forms

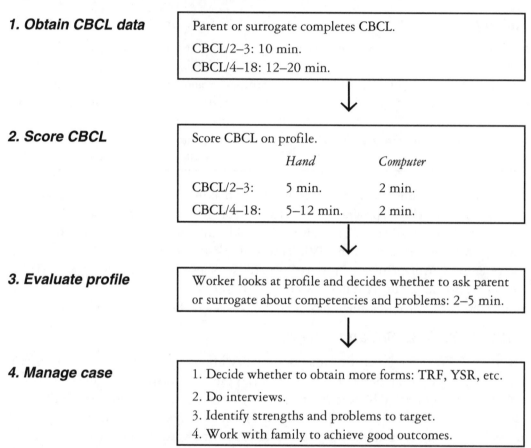

1. Obtain CBCL data
> Parent or surrogate completes CBCL.
>
> CBCL/2–3: 10 min.
> CBCL/4–18: 12–20 min.

2. Score CBCL
> Score CBCL on profile.
>
> | | *Hand* | *Computer* |
> |-----------|-----------|-----------|
> | CBCL/2–3: | 5 min. | 2 min. |
> | CBCL/4–18: | 5–12 min. | 2 min. |

3. Evaluate profile
> Worker looks at profile and decides whether to ask parent or surrogate about competencies and problems: 2–5 min.

4. Manage case
> 1. Decide whether to obtain more forms: TRF, YSR, etc.
> 2. Do interviews.
> 3. Identify strengths and problems to target.
> 4. Work with family to achieve good outcomes.

© Copyright 1999 by T.M. Achenbach. Reproduced with permission.

adolescent indicates such problems on the YSR but does not mention them in an interview, the responses can be highlighted and the adolescent asked to talk more about them.

Completed forms and their scored profiles provide standardized documentation of the child's or young person's strengths and problems. The inclusion of completed forms and profiles in the case record allows comparisons with data from other sources and provides baselines against which to measure changes and outcomes over the course of interventions or placements. Re-administration of the forms on later occasions allows comparisons with previous profiles. The forms also provide information that can be provided to other professionals who are working with the child or young person.

The C-TRF, TRF, and DOF

For children who attend school or day care, information from teachers and caregivers is often essential. Teachers and caregivers work with children in important life contexts that differ from the home, and their perspectives are apt to differ from those of parents and parent surrogates. Problems and adaptive strengths that are evident in educational and day care settings can be important in understanding children's overall development.

The C-TRF or TRF can be administered by mail. The form should be accompanied by a release from the parent or parent surrogates, an explanatory letter, and a return envelope. Alternatively, the forms can be administered as telephone interviews, but, as discussed earlier, a copy of the form should be provided to the informant before the interview.

In residential and day treatment settings that provide schooling, routine use of the TRF as part of each child's ongoing assessment can be quite helpful. The TRF can be scheduled at regular intervals, such as every 3 or 4 months, starting at 2 months after the child enters the school. This practice generally is not a burden to teachers because classrooms in treatment settings usually have few students, and students enter class and are assessed at different points in time. The DOF can also be used periodically to document specific behaviors observed over 10-minute intervals by a paraprofessional such as a teacher aide.

Like the parent and self-report forms, the C-TRF, TRF, and DOF and resulting profiles can be placed in case records to document a child's functioning; can be provided to other professionals who need information about the child; and can be re-administered to measure changes in response to interventions and placements. In addition, the information can be used to document needs for special education services.

Use of the SCICA

Evaluations of children usually include face-to-face interviews. Interviews may be conducted in children's homes, temporary placements, foster homes, or in social workers' offices. Children's behavior in interviews may be affected by stressful experiences, the conditions of the interview, and the characteristics of the interviewer. Interviewers' styles and what interviewers say to children and infer from children's behavior may also affect their evaluations. Consequently, conclusions about a child may differ from one interviewer to another and between an interviewer and other informants such as parents or teachers.

The SCICA provides a semi-structured protocol that is adaptable to a wide range of situations and interviewer styles. Unlike highly structured diagnostic interviews, it does not consist of yes-or-no questions about symptoms, but instead provides leading questions that encourage children to talk about important feelings, experiences, and areas of their lives. The interviewer is free to pursue issues that arise and to formulate questions as needed. Because the interviewer notes and scores observations of the child's behavior and what the child says, a rich clinical record can be obtained even for children who say little.

If the SCICA is used early in the evaluation process, the social worker can compare the profile scored from the SCICA with profiles scored from the other forms such as the CBCL and TRF and can identify similarities and differences in how the child appears in the interview versus and the child appears to others. Major differences should be explored to determine whether they reflect important contrasts in the way the child behaves in the interview situation, with parent figures, and in school. On the other hand, when a profile scored from ratings by one informant disagrees markedly from profiles scored from all other informants, attention should be given to the informant's credibility.

Working with Mental Health, School, and Medical Personnel

Mental health, school, and medical personnel may need information about a child from child and family social workers, and conversely, social workers may need case information from mental health, school, and medical personnel. The profiles scored from the CBCL family of forms are familiar to many mental health and school professionals and are becoming increasingly familiar to pediatricians. As a consequence, these profiles provide a way to easily and efficiently communicate information about children's competencies, adaptive functioning, and problems. With appropriate permission, social workers can provide copies of the completed forms and profiles to other professionals and can likewise request copies of the CBCL family of forms and profiles from other service providers. The standardized forms, because they are used by different disciplines for many purposes, can support evaluations and service plans by a range of service providers. Ongoing assessment is also made possible by the re-administration of the forms by other professionals involved in serving the child.

Summary

There are multiple applications of the CBCL and other standardized forms: routinely obtaining the CBCL from parents or parent surrogates; obtaining the YSR from adolescents; obtaining the C-TRF for children who attend day care or preschool and the TRF for older children; and re-administering the forms periodically to monitor changes in children's functioning over the course of placement or services. Social workers can use the SCICA in evaluation interviews, adapting it as needed. The completed forms and profiles can be used to communicate, efficiently and concisely, information about a child among the many professionals who may be involved.

The Strengths and Limitations of the CBCL and TRF

Strengths of the CBCL and TRF

The CBCL and TRF are two of the most widely used child assessment measures in the world and have norms by different gender and age groups. These forms require little time to complete and provide a high level of information regarding children's difficulties and strengths. In less than 30 minutes, a professional can gather assessment information that ordinarily requires a 2- or 3-hour interview.

Child welfare staff report that the CBCL helps them determine the issues that require further exploration and, importantly, the child's behaviors that may be dangerous to the child himself or others. Many agencies routinely distribute children's scored CBCL profiles during child intake conferences and other case staffings. At the same time, because the CBCL has been shown to be sensitive to changes in behavior over time, it can be used to evaluate social service programs and specific treatment interventions. However, as subsequent chapters will indicate, these results may vary and certain statistical properties of the instruments need to be carefully considered and used for data analyses.

Limitations of the CBCL and TRF

Although the CBCL and TRF are among the most comprehensive assessment measures available, no measure is perfect. Researchers, agency staff members, and others have identified the following limitations of one or both measures:

- Unfamiliar raters. The CBCL (and to a much lesser extent the TRF) format and set of questions do not allow an assessment of the familiarity of the informant with the child whom he or she is rating. As a result, care must be exercised when selecting individuals to complete the measures.

- Respondent bias. CBCL scores can be skewed if the caregiver who completes the form does not accurately report competencies or problems. As an example, a child's current foster parent may not be confident that the program serves children who have serious behavior problems and may minimize the child's poor behavior in one or more areas.

- Limited data for various ethnic groups. It should be noted that the CBCL problem syndromes were delivered on a sample of 4,455 children who were referred for mental health services (Achenbach 1993), and the scale norms were based on a national sample of 2,368 youth between the ages of 4-18 years old, with 27% of the sample children of color (Achenbach 1991a). Many international studies have been conducted using the CBCL, and some 100 publications report data for various American ethnic groups. The instrument manuals for the CBCL and TRF also report the associations of the scales with ethnicity, with socioeconomic status controlled. For most of the items and scales, ethnicity did not have a significant effect on the item's scores. Users, however, can use these manual sections to determine whether ethnicity is significantly associated with scale scores. Agencies may find it helpful to develop specific profiles for the major ethnic groups that they serve in order to determine whether their client population may vary or be similar to other groups or programs.

- Agency misuse of the forms for ADHD classification. Some child welfare agencies have been using the CBCL problem behavior scales to diagnose children as attention deficit and hyperactivity disordered (ADHD). Several studies have shown strong associations between ADHD diagnoses and CBCL scores. Although the CBCL is helpful for indicating whether further testing for ADHD should be conducted (Edelbrock, Costello & Kessler 1984), the scale scores alone should not be the sole basis for making diagnoses.

- Under-reporting of child strengths on parent-reported competence scales. Some practitioners have noted that the scale and item analyses for the parent-reported competence section of the CBCL (Activities, Social, and School functioning) allow a child to score only up to the 69th percentile and at first glance, having a highest possible score of 69% would tend to show youth in a more negative light than what their activities, participation in social events, and school achievement would indicate. The 69th percentile, however, indicates that the child's functioning is higher than 69% of the non-referred normative sample. Because of this pattern, it is important to carefully review the open-ended questions of the competence section of the CBCL and use a "multi-axial" approach to assessment (Achenbach 1991a).

Conclusion

This chapter has provided an overview of the CBCL, TRF, YSR and related forms. It is intended to offer a foundation for the following chapters which report the results of various studies using these instruments in child and family social services.

Authors' Note

This material has been extracted and adapted with permission from the following: Achenbach, T. M., Pecora, P. J. & Wetherbee, K.M. (1998). *Child and family service workers' guide for the Child Behavior Checklist and related forms.* Burlington, VT: University of Vermont, Department of Psychiatry. All rights reserved. Special thanks to Kathleen Wetherbee and Kelly Sim for their contributions to both these papers.

Reference Notes

1.   Reliability of the CBCL.   One-week test-rest reliability scores, which assess the stability of scale scores over time, were generally high for reports by mothers of nonclinically referred children 4-16 years-old (N = 80). The mean correlation coefficient (r) for competence scales was .87 and for problem scales was .89. Lowest reliability scores were obtained for the Activities Scale (mean r = .70) (Achenbach 1991b). CBCL scores also proved stable over a 1- to 2-year period in a study of children 6 to 8 years old (Achenbach et al. 1991b). When both parents completed the CBCL for a child, inter-parent agreement correlation coefficients for clinical and non-clinical samples of children were relatively good (average r = .65 to r = .75). Lowest inter-parent agreement scores were found for Thought Problems (.48), Somatic Complaints (.52) and Sex Problems (.52). Differences in mean scores between mothers and fathers did not exceed chance level. Averaged across referred and non-referred samples, internal consistencies of the problem section scales were generally well above .70 (using Cronbach's alpha as the statistic), which indicates that the items on the scales belong together. Alpha's for the competence scales were lower, ranging from .54 to .62 (Achenbach 1991b).

2.   Validity of the CBCL. CBCL items show a significant association with referral status of children, with clinically referred children scoring in the direction of lower adjustment. CBCL scales were moderately to highly correlated with analogous scales on two widely accepted instruments: the Conners (1973) Parent Questionnaire and the Quay and Peterson (1983) Revised Behavior Problem Checklist (Achenbach 1991b; Achenbach & Edelbrock 1978; Weissman, Orvaschel & Padian 1980). Several studies have demonstrated a relationship between psychiatric diagnosis (using DSM typology) and scores on the pre-1991 CBCL (Edelbrock & Costello 1988; Weinstein et al. 1990) and post-1990 CBCL scales (Chen et al. 1994). CBCL scale scores significantly discriminated between referred and non-referred children, controlling for demographic effects. In addition, classifications of scale scores as normal-range versus clinical-range discriminated significantly between demographically matched referred and non-referred children (Achenbach 1991b). The CBCL has also proven sensitive to differences between treated and untreated children in intervention studies

(Kazdin et al. 1987; Webster-Stratton 1984). This ability indicates that the scale can be used to help compare the effectiveness of different interventions.

3. Reliability of the TRF. Test-rest reliabilities obtained over one to four-week intervals for ratings of 8-9 year-olds were uniformly high, averaging r = .90 for the adaptive functioning scales and r = .92 for the problem scales. Inter-teacher agreement for a referred sample of children averaged r = .54, with a range of r = -.00 (Withdrawn scale, younger girls) to r = .87 (How Happy, older girls). Overall, the least inter-teacher agreement was found for older boys. Internal consistencies (Cronbach's alpha) of the problem syndrome scales, averaged across referred and non-referred samples, ranged from .70 to .96 (Achenbach 1991c).

4. Validity of the TRF. Most TRF items differentiate children referred to mental health services from demographically matched non-referred children, with referred children scoring in the direction of lower adjustment. TRF scales also show substantial correlations with analogous scales on the well-known Conners Revised Teacher Rating Scale (Goyette, Conners & Ulrich 1978). TRF scale scores, as well as the clinical-cut points on the scale scores, significantly discriminate between referred and non-referred children in the expected directions, controlling for demographic effects. In addition, classifications of scale scores as normal versus clinical-range discriminate significantly between demographically matched referred and non-referred children (Achenbach 1991c). A number of studies have demonstrated relationships between diagnostic status (such as Attention Deficit Disorder, Hyperactivity, and emotional disorders), academic achievement and classroom adjustment, and pertinent TRF problem scores (Edelbrock, Costello & Keesler 1984; Harris et al. 1984; Hoge & McKay 1986). Referral status, compared with demographic variables, consistently accounted for the largest proportion of the variance in TRF scores in a series of multiple regression analyses by the instrument developers. Modest associations between socioeconomic status and TRF scores were found (Achenbach 1991c).

References

Achenbach, T.M. (1991a). *Integrative Guide for the 1991 CBCL/4-18, YSR, and TRF Profiles.* Burlington: University of Vermont Department of Psychiatry.

Achenbach, T.M. (1991b). *Manual for the Child Behavior Checklist/4-18 and 1991 Profile.* Burlington: University of Vermont Department of Psychiatry.

Achenbach, T.M. (1991c). *Manual for the Teacher's Report form and 1991 Profile.* Burlington: University of Vermont Department of Psychiatry.

Achenbach, T.M. (1991d). *Manual for the Youth Self Report and 1991 Profile.* Burlington: University of Vermont Department of Psychiatry.

Achenbach, T.M. (1993). *Empirically based taxonomy: How to use syndromes and profile types derived from the CBCL 4-18, TRF, and YSR.* Burlington: University of Vermont Department of Psychiatry.

Achenbach, T.M. (1997a). *Guide for the Caregiver-Teacher Report Form for Ages 2-5.* Burlington: University of Vermont Department of Psychiatry.

Achenbach, T.M. (1997b). *Manual for the Young Adult Self-Report and Young Adult Behavior Checklist.* Burlington: University of Vermont Department of Psychiatry.

Achenbach, T.M. & Edelbrock, C. (1978). The classification of child psychopathology: A review and analysis of empirical efforts. *Psychological Bulletin, 85*(6), 1275–1301.

Achenbach, T.M., Phares, V., Howell, C.T., Rauh, V.A. & Nurcombe, B. (1990). Seven-year outcome of the Vermont intervention program for low-birthweight infants. *Child Development, 61,* 1672–1681.

American Humane Association, Children's Division, American Bar Association, Center on Children and the Law, Annie E. Casey Foundation, Casey Family Services, the Institute for Human Services Management, and The Casey Family Program. (1998). *Assessing outcomes in child welfare services: Principles, concepts, and a framework of core indicators.* Englewood, CO: American Humane Association

Chen, W.T., Faraone, S.V., Biederman, J., & Tsuang, M.T. (1994). Diagnostic Accuracy of the Child Behavior Checklist Scales for Attention-Deficit Hyperactivity Disorder: A Receiver-Operating Characteristic Analysis. *Journal of Consulting and Clinical Psychology, 62*(5), 1017–1025.

Conners, C.K. (1973). Ratings scales for use in drug studies with children. *Psychopharmacology Bulletin: Pharmacotherapy with children.* Washington, DC: U.S. Government Printing Office.

Dubowitz, H., Feigelman, S., Harrington, D., Starr, Jr., R., Zuravin, S., & Sayer, R. (1994). Children in kinship care: How do they fare? *Children and Youth Services Review, 16,* 85–106.

Dubowitz, H., Zuravin, S., Starr, Jr., R., Feigelman, S., & Harrington, D. (1993). Behavior problems of children in kinship care. *Developmental and Behavioral Pediatrics, 14,* 386–395.

Edelbrock, C., & Costello, J. (1988). Convergence between statistically derived behavior problem syndromes and child psychiatric diagnoses. *Journal of Abnormal Child Psychology, 16*(2), 219–231.

Edelbrock, C., Costello, J. & Kessler, M.D. (1984). Empirical corroboration of attention deficit disorder. *Journal of the American Academy of Child Psychiatry, 23*(2), 285–290.

Evans, M.E., Armstrong, M.I., Dollard, N., Kuppinger, A.D., Huz, S., & Wood, V.M. (1994). Development and evaluation of treatment foster care and family-centered intensive case management in New York. *Journal of Emotional and Behavioral Disorders, 2*(4), 228–239.

Fanshel, D. & Shinn, E. (1978). *Children in foster care: A longitudinal investigation.* New York: Columbia University Press.

Friman, P., Evans, J., Larzelere, R., Williams, G., & Daly, D. (1993). Correspondence between child dysfunction and program intrusion: Evidence of a continuum of care across five child mental health programs. *Journal of Community Psychology, 21,* 227–233.

Glisson, C. (1994). The effect of services coordination teams on outcomes for children in state custody. *Administration in Social Work, 18*(4), 1–23.

Goyette, C.H., Conners, C.K., & Ulrich, R.F. (1978). Normative data on revised Conners Parent and Teacher Rating scales. *Journal of Abnormal Child Psychology, 6*(2), 221–236.

Harris, J.C., King, S.L., Reifler, J.P., & Rosenberg, L.A. (1984). Emotional and learning disorders in 6-12-year-old-boys attending special schools. *Journal of the American Academy of Child Psychiatry, 23*(4), 431–437.

Hoffart, I., & Grinnell, R.M. (1994). Behavioral differences of children in institutional and group home care. *International Journal of Family Care, 6*(1), 33–47.

Hoge, R.D., & McKay, V. (1986). Criterion-related validity data for the Child Behavior Checklist—Teacher's Report Form. *Journal of School Psychology, 24*(4), 387–393.

Hornick, J., Phillips, D., & Kerr, N. (1989). Gender differences in behavioral problems of foster children: Implications for special foster care. *Community Alternatives, 1*, 35–52.

Hulsey, T.C., & White, R. (1989). Family characteristics and measures of behavior in foster and nonfoster children. *American Journal of Orthopsychiatry, 59*(4), 502–509.

Kazdin, A.E., Esveldt-Dawson, K., French, N.H., & Unis, A.S. (1987). Problem-solving skills training and relationship therapy in the treatment of antisocial child behavior. *Journal of Consulting and Clinical Psychology, 55*(1),76-85.

Landsverk, J., Clausen, J. M., Ganger, W., Chadwick, D., & Litrownik, A. (Under Review). Mental health problems of foster children in three California counties. *Child Abuse and Neglect.*

Lenerz, K., Cannon, B., Johnson-Meester, N., & Peterson, J. (1995). *Intensive family preservation services: An examination of program-specific outcomes.* Boys Town Research Report.

McConaughy, S.H., & Achenbach, T.M. (1994). *Manual for the semistructured clinical interview for children & adolescents.* Burlington: University of Vermont Department of Psychiatry.

McIntyre, A., & Keesler, T. (1986). Psychological disorders among foster children. *Journal of Clinical Psychology, 14*, 297–303.

Quay, H.C., & Peterson, D.R. (1983). *Interim manual for the Revised Behavior Problem Checklist.* Coral Gables, FL: University of Miami, Applied Social Sciences.

Runyan, D. & Gould, C. (1985). Foster care for child maltreatment. II. Impact on school performance. *Pediatrics, 76*, 841–847.

Swire, M.R. & Kavaler, F. (1978). The health status of foster children. In S. Chess & A. Thomas (Eds.), *Annual progress in child psychiatry and child development* (pp. 626–642). New York: Brunner/Mazel.

Webster-Stratton, C. (1984). Randomized trial of two-parent training programs for families with conduct-disordered children. *Journal of Consulting and Clinical Psychology, 52*(4), 666–678.

Weinstein, S.R., Noam, G.G., Grimes, K., Stone, K. & Schwab-Stone, M. (1990). Convergence of DSM-III diagnoses and self-reported symptoms in child and adolescent inpatients. *Journal of the American Academy of Child and Adolescent Psychiatry, 29*, 627–634.

Weissman, M.M., Orvaschel, H. & Padian, N. (1980). Children's symptoms and social functioning self-report scales. Comparison of mothers' and children's reports. *Journal of Nervous and Mental Disease, 168,* 736–740.

Appendix 2A

CBCL Problem Behavior Scales and Items

Internalizing

Withdrawn

42. Would rather be alone
65. Refuses to talk
69. Secretive, keeps things to self
75. Shy or timid
80. Stares blankly
88. Sulks a lot
102. Underactive, slow moving, or lacks energy
103. Unhappy, sad, or depressed
111. Withdrawn, doesn't get involved with others

Somatic Complaints

51. Feels dizzy
54. Overtired
56. Physical problems without known medical cause:
    a. Aches or pains
    b. Headaches
    c. Nausea, feels sick
    d. Problems with eyes
    e. Rashes or other skin problems
    f. Stomachaches or cramps
    g. Vomiting, throwing up

Anxious/Depressed

12. Complains of loneliness
14. Cries a lot
31. Fears he/she might think or do something bad
32. Feels he/she has to be perfect
33. Feels or complains that no one loves him/her
34. Feels others are out to get him/her
35. Feels worthless or inferior
45. Nervous, high strung, or tense
50. Too fearful or anxious
52. Feels too guilty

71. Self-conscious or easily embarrassed
89. Suspicious
103. Unhappy, sad, or depressed
112. Worrying

Social/Thought/Attention Scales

Social Problems

1. Acts too young for his/her age
11. Clings to adults or too dependent
25. Doesn't get along with other children
38. Gets teased a lot
48. Not liked by other children
55. Overweight
62. Poorly coordinated or clumsy
64. Prefers playing with younger children

Thought Problems

9. Can't get his/her mind off certain thoughts; obsessions
40. Hears sounds or voices that aren't there
66. Repeats certain acts over and over; compulsions
70. Sees things that aren't there
80. Stares blankly
84. Strange behavior
85. Strange ideas

Attention Problems

1. Acts too young for his/her age
8. Can't concentrate, can't pay attention for long
10. Can't sit still, restless, or hyperactive
13. Confused or seems to be in a fog
17. Day-dreams or gets lost in his/her thoughts
41. Impulsive or acts without thinking
45. Nervous, high strung, or tense
46. Nervous movements or twitching
61. Poor school work
62. Poorly coordinated or clumsy
80. Stares blankly

Externalizing

Delinquent Behavior

26. Doesn't seem to feel guilty after misbehaving
39. Hangs around with children who get in trouble
43. Lying or cheating

63.   Prefers playing with older children
67.   Runs away from home
72.   Sets fires
81.   Steals at home
82.   Steals outside the home
90.   Swearing or obscene language
96.   Thinks about sex too much*
101.   Truancy, skips school
105.   Uses alcohol or drugs for non-medical purposes
106.   Vandalism

Aggressive Behavior

3.   Argues a lot
7.   Bragging, boasting
16.   Cruelty, bullying, or meanness to others
19.   Demands a lot of attention
20.   Destroys his/her own things
21.   Destroys things belonging to his/her family or other children
22.   Disobedient at home
23.   Disobedient at school
27.   Easily jealous
37.   Gets in many fights
57.   Physically attacks people
68.   Screams a lot
74.   Showing off or clowning
86.   Stubborn, sullen, or irritable
87.   Sudden changes in mood or feelings
93.   Talks too much
94.   Teases a lot
95.   Temper tantrums or hot temper
97.   Threatens people
104.   Unusually loud

Other Problems Not in the Main Scale Groupings

5.   Behaves like opposite sex*
6.   Bowel movements outside toilet
15.   Cruel to animals
18.   Deliberately harms self or attempts suicide
24.   Doesn't eat well
28.   Eats or drinks things that are not food—don't include sweets
29.   Fears certain animals, situations, or places, other than school
30.   Fears going to school

36. Gets hurt a lot, accident-prone
44. Bites fingernails
47. Nightmares
49. Constipated, doesn't move bowels
53. Overeating
56. Physical problems without known medical cause
58. Picks nose, skin, or other parts of body
59. Plays with own sex parts in public*
60. Plays with own sex parts too much*
73. Sexual problems*
76. Sleeps less than most children
77. Sleeps more than most children during day and/or night
78. Smears or plays with bowel movements
79. Speech problem
83. Stores up things he/she doesn't need
91. Talks about killing self
92. Talks or walks in sleep
98. Thumb-sucking
99. Too concerned with neatness or cleanliness
100. Trouble sleeping
107. Wets self during the day
108. Wets the bed
109. Whining
110. Wishes to be of opposite sex*

113. Please write in any problems your child has that were not listed above

* These items are for the "Sex Problems" scale, which is intended for girls and boys ages 4-11 years old only.

Appendix 2B

TRF Problem Behavior Scales and Items

Internalizing

Withdrawn

42. Would rather be alone than with others
65. Refuses to talk
69. Secretive, keeps things to self
75. Shy or timid
80. Stares blankly
88. Sulks a lot
102. Underactive, slow moving, or lacks energy
103. Unhappy, sad, or depressed
111. Withdrawn, doesn't get involved with others

Somatic Complaints

51. Feels dizzy
54. Overtired
56. Physical problems without known medical cause:
    a. Aches or pains (not headaches)
    b. Headaches
    c. Nausea, feels sick
    d. Problems with eyes
    e. Rashes or other skin problems
    f. Stomachaches or cramps
    g. Vomiting, throwing up

Anxious/Depressed

12. Complains of loneliness
14. Cries a lot
31. Fears he/she might think or do something bad
32. Feels he/she has to be perfect
33. Feels or complains that no one loves him/her
34. Feels others are out to get him/her
35. Feels worthless or inferior
45. Nervous, high-strung, or tense

47. Overconforms to rules
50. Too fearful or anxious
52. Feels too guilty
71. Self-conscious or easily embarrassed
81. Feels hurt when criticized
89. Suspicious
103. Unhappy, sad, or depressed
106. Overly anxious to please
108. Is afraid of making mistakes
112. Worrying

Social/Thought/Attention Scales

Social Problems

1. Acts too young for his/her age
11. Clings to adults or too dependent
12. Complains of loneliness
14. Cries a lot
25. Doesn't get along with other pupils
33. Feels or complains that no one loves him/her
34. Feels others are out to get him/her
35. Feels worthless or inferior
36. Gets hurt a lot, accident-prone
38. Gets teased a lot
48. Not liked by other pupils
62. Poorly coordinated or clumsy
64. Prefers being with younger children

Thought Problems

9. Can't get his/her mind off certain thoughts; obsessions
18. Deliberately harms self or attempts suicide
29. Fears certain animals, situations, or places other than school
40. Hears sounds or voices that aren't there
66. Repeats certain acts over and over; compulsions
70. Sees things that aren't there
84. Strange behavior
85. Strange ideas

Attention Problems

1. Acts too young for his/her age
2. Hums or makes other odd noises in class
4. Fails to finish things he/she starts
8. Can't concentrate, can't pay attention for long

10.   Can't sit still, restless, or hyperactive
13.   Confused or seems to be in a fog
15.   Fidgets
17.   Day-dreams or gets lost in his/her thoughts
22.   Difficulty following directions
41.   Impulsive or acts without thinking
45.   Nervous, high-strung, or tense
49.   Has difficulty learning
60.   Apathetic or unmotivated
61.   Poor school work
62.   Poorly coordinated or clumsy
72.   Messy work
78.   Inattentive, easily distracted
80.   Stares blankly
92.   Underachieving, not working up to potential
100. Fails to carry out assigned tasks

Externalizing

Delinquent Behavior

26.   Doesn't seem to feel guilty after misbehaving
39.   Hangs around with others who get in trouble
43.   Lying or cheating
63.   Prefers playing with older children or youths
82.   Steals
90.   Swearing or obscene language
98.   Tardy to school or class
101. Truancy or unexplained absence
105. Uses alcohol or drugs for non-medical purposes

Aggressive Behavior

3.   Argues a lot
6.   Defiant, talks back to staff
7.   Bragging, boasting
16.   Cruelty, bullying, or meanness to others
19.   Demands a lot of attention
20.   Destroys his/her own things
21.   Destroys property belonging to others
23.   Disobedient at school
24.   Disturbs other pupils
27.   Easily jealous
37.   Gets in many fights

53. Talks out of turn
57. Physically attacks people
67. Disrupts class discipline
68. Screams a lot
74. Showing off or clowning
76. Explosive or unpredictable behavior
77. Demands must be met immediately, easily frustrated
86. Stubborn, sullen, or irritable
87. Sudden changes in mood or feelings
93. Talks too much
94. Teases a lot
95. Temper tantrums or hot temper
97. Threatens people
104. Unusually loud

Other Problems Not in the Main Scale Groupings

5. Behaves like opposite sex
28. Eats or drinks things that are not food — don't include sweets
30. Fears going to school
44. Bites fingernails
46. Nervous movements or twitching
47. Nightmares
55. Overweight
56. Physical problems without known medical cause
58. Picks nose, skin, or other parts of body
59. Sleeps in class
73. Behaves irresponsibly
79. Speech problem
83. Stores up things he/she doesn't need
91. Talks about killing self
96. Seems preoccupied with sex

99.   Too concerned with neatness or cleanliness
107.   Dislikes school
109.   Whining (continued)
110.   Unclean personal appearance
113.   Please write in any problems your child has that were not listed above

Appendix 2C

Supplemental Reference Information

Annotated Bibliography

Except for the Achenbach and McConaughy (1997) book described at the end of this Appendix, all the publications listed below can be ordered from: Child Behavior Checklist, 1 South Prospect Street, Burlington, VT 05401-3456; Fax: 802/656-2602; E-mail: Checklist@uvm.edu; Web: http://www/uvm/edu/~cbcl/

The following Manuals and the C-TRF Guide provide detailed information on the rationale, development, research basis, normative samples, and distributions of scores for each form. They also provide illustrations of applications in various settings, plus relations to other assessment procedures.

Achenbach, T.M. (1991b). Manual for the Child Behavior Checklist/4-18 and 1991 Profile.

Achenbach, T.M. (1991c). Manual for the Teacher's Report Form and 1991 Profile.

Achenbach, T.M. (1991d). Manual for the Youth Self-Report and 1991 Profile.

Achenbach, T.M. and Rescovla, L.A. (2000) A Manual for the ASEBA Preschool Forms and Profiles. Burlington, VT: Research Center for Children Youth, and families.

Achenbach, T.M. (1997). Guide for the Caregiver-Teacher Report Form for Ages 2-5.

Achenbach, T.M. (1997). Manual for the Young Adult Self-Report and Young Adult Behavior Checklist.

Berube, R., & Achenbach, T.M. (2001). Bibliography of published studies using the ASEBA: 2000 edition.

McConaughy, S.H. & Achenbach, T.M. (1994). Manual for the Semistructured Clinical Interview for Children and Adolescents.

Updated annually, the Bibliography lists 61 languages in which the forms have been translated, plus over 3,500 publications by over 7,000 authors, categorized by over 300 topics. Topics related to child and family work include:

Abuse
Adolescence
Adoption
African-American
Aggression
Alcoholism
Anger

Antisocial Conduct
Anxiety
At-Risk
Attention Deficit Disorder
Autism
Behavior Changes
Caregivers
Co-Morbidity
Conduct Disorder
Conflict
Corrections
Cross-Informant Program
Cruelty
Custody
Death
Delinquent Behavior
Depression
Developmental Changes
Developmental Disorders
Diagnosis
Diagnostic & Statistical Manual
Direct Observation Form
Disaster
Disruptive Behavior
Divorce
Emotional Disorders
Ethnicity
Family Functioning
Family Problems
Fire Setting
Follow-up
Forensic Applications
Foster Care
Gender Problems
Hispanic
Homeless
Hostility
HIV
Hyperactivity
Illness
Immigrant

Self Esteem
Separation
Sexual Abuse
Sexual Behavior
Sex Differences
Siblings
Single Parent
Social Competence
Socioeconomic Status
Special Education
Special Needs
Stress
Substance Abuse
Suicide
Teacher Perceptions
Teacher's Report Form
Temperament
Therapy
Treatment
Violence
Welfare
Youth Self-Report & Profile
Available from Sage Publications:

Achenbach, T.M., & McConaughy, S.H. (1997). *Empirically based assessment of child and adolescent psychopathology: Practical applications.* (2nd ed.). Thousand Oaks, CA: Sage.

This book illustrates a variety of practical applications of the empirically based assessment forms with a range of cases in a variety of settings. It also reviews findings on correlates of the empirically based syndromes. The book can be ordered from Sage Publications, 2455 Teller Road, Thousand Oaks, CA 91320-2218; phone 805-499-9774; fax 805-499-0871; E-mail order@sagepub.com. Price $18.95 paperback, plus shipping and handling.

Appendix 2D

Questions and Answers About the Forms

1. Who completes the forms?

    Birth parents, foster parents, & others who know the child well complete the CBCL and YABCL; youths and young adults complete the YSR and YASR; teachers complete the TRF; caregivers and preschool teachers complete the C-TRF; interviewers complete the SCICA; and observers complete the DOF.

2. Who scores the forms?

    Clerical workers, child and family workers, and other staff.

3. How long does it take to score a form?

    Two minutes by computer; 5 to 12 minutes by hand.

4. What does the social worker receive?

    A profile that compares the child with a normative sample of peers on each syndrome scale (such as, Aggressive Behavior, Attention Problems, and Somatic Complaints) and scores on each specific problem. For the CBCL/4-18, YSR, YASR, and TRF, an additional profile displays competencies or adaptive functioning.

5. How long does it take the worker to evaluate a profile?

    From 2 to 5 minutes.

6. How much do forms cost?

    For either hand scored or computer profile: 50¢ per rating form ($25 per package of 50).

7. What are the fastest ways to process the data?

    Either (a) Scannable "bubble" forms of the CBCL/4-18, YSR, & TRF which can be processed by reflective-read scanners, image scanners, and fax; or (b) a Client-Entry Program enables parents, youths, and teachers to enter their responses into a computer.

8. Have these forms been well researched?

    The Bibliography of Published Studies lists over 3,500 publications that report findings using these forms on many topics, such as Abuse, Adolescence, Adoption, African-Americans, Aggression, Alcoholism, Antisocial Conduct, Attention Deficit Disorder, Caregivers, Conduct Disorder, Corrections, Cruelty, Custody, Death,

Delinquent Behavior, Depression, Developmental Changes, Diagnosis, Disaster, Disruptive Behavior, Divorce, Emotional Disorders, Ethnicity, Family Functioning, Family Problems, Fire Setting, Follow-up, Forensic, Foster Care, Gender Problems, Hispanic, Homeless, HIV, Immigrant, Internalizing/Externalizing, Interviews, Life Events, Marital Problems, Migrant, Multiple Informants, Neglected, Obesity, Oppositional Disorder, Outcomes, Parent Characteristics, Parent-Child Relationships, Parent Management Training, Parent Perceptions, Parent Psychopathology, Parent Stress, Post-Traumatic Stress Disorder, Poverty, Pre-School, Puerto Rican, Refugee, Resilience, School Behavior, School Refusal, Self Esteem, Separation, Sexual Abuse, Sexual Behavior, Siblings, Single Parent, Social Competence, Special Education, Special Needs, Substance Abuse, Suicide, Teacher Perceptions, Violence, Welfare. Appendix C lists additional topics.

9. Where can ordering information be obtained?

For the Child Behavior Checklist:
ASEBA, 1 South Prospect St.
Burlington, VT 05401-3456
Fax: 802-656-2602; Tel: 802-656-8313 or −2608.
E-mail: ASEBA@uvm.edu
Web: http://aswba.uvm.edu

Questions and Answers About Using the Forms

1. What if no birth or foster parent is available to complete the CBCL?

Others who know the child well can complete the CBCL. Possibilities include relatives, adult siblings, and caregivers who are responsible for the child in an institutional setting. If no surrogate parent is available, the CBCL may be completed by child and family workers who first collate information from all available sources.

2. What if there are multiple parent figures who can complete the CBCL?

If both parents and/or multiple parent surrogates are available, each one should complete a separate CBCL rather than having them collaborate on a single CBCL. Having them complete separate CBCLs preserves potentially important similarities and differences in their perceptions of the child. The computer-scoring programs facilitate comparisons among multiple informants.

3. What if a parent or surrogate is not capable of completing the CBCL independently?

An interviewer provides the parent or surrogate with a CBCL while retaining a second copy. The interviewer says: "I'll read you the questions on this form and I'll write down your answers." Respondents who can read well enough usually begin answering the questions without waiting for the interviewer to read them aloud. Even when respondents have poor reading skills, it is helpful for them to see the format.

4. What if a parent or surrogate cannot read English but can read another language?

    Translations are available in 55 languages. Send requests for specific translations to the CBCL address or fax number provided earlier.

5. The forms request parent's type of work. How should this item be answered if this information is unknown or is difficult to answer because the child has lived with various parent figures?

    Parental occupation may be useful to know, and it is often used to score socioeconomic status for research purposes. Because it does not affect the scoring or interpretation of profiles, however, it can be omitted.

6. When a child has multiple teachers, which teacher should complete the TRF?

    If one teacher has significantly more contact with the child, that teacher is preferable. If multiple teachers have similar levels of contact, it is advisable to request a TRF from each teacher. The computer-scoring programs facilitate comparisons among multiple TRFs, the CBCL, and the YSR to identify similarities and differences among reports by different informants.

7. Many of the items on the forms refer to problems. How can the results be used in a strength-oriented program?

    The CBCL/4-18, TRF, YSR, and YASR have scales for competencies or adaptive functioning. Most of the forms also have open-ended questions that request the respondent to describe the "best things" about the child. The forms are thus designed to tap strengths as well as problems. Most children, however, who are candidates for services are at risk for problems or already display problems. To most effectively help these children, it is necessary to have a clear picture of their problems and their strengths. Bolstering their strengths is usually linked to reducing their problems.

8. How should information about individual items be used?

    In addition to contributing to scale scores, each item is important in its own right. To help social workers quickly spot scores for each competence and problem item, the profiles display the score for each item. Workers may also review informants' open-ended responses to obtain further details of how a child is viewed. Responses to particular items are especially helpful for alerting workers to strengths and interests, as well as to risks for harm to self or others, destructive behavior, somatic problems, information on substance use, and specific obsessions, compulsions, strange behavior, and strange ideas.

9. Are the standardized forms compatible with other assessment procedures?

The forms are inexpensive, are usually self-administered, require little staff training or time, and provide a wide range of information relevant to diverse situations. They are, therefore, compatible with nearly all other assessment procedures. When administered early in the evaluation of a case, they can highlight issues on which other assessment procedures can then focus. If, for example, a social worker reviews profiles from CBCLs, TRFs, and/or the YSR before conducting an interview, she can utilize the interview to further explore what is shown by the profiles and areas not tapped by the forms.

10. When forms are re-administered, how is improvement determined?

Appendix C lists the Manual for each form. In each Manual, there is an appendix that shows the standard error of measurement (SEM) for each scale. As a rough rule-of-thumb, changes that exceed twice the SEM shown for the relevant group on a particular scale may be statistically significant. As one example, the SEM is 1.98 on the Anxious/Depressed syndrome for 12-year-old referred boys. This SEM means that a decline of 4 points (2 x 1.98 rounded off to the nearest whole score) would approximate statistical significance. To evaluate the clinical significance of changes, it is important to consider whether the child's score is in the clinical, borderline clinical, or normal range. A drop from the clinical range to the normal range ordinarily would be more valuable than a drop of the same size within the low end of the normal range or within the high end of the clinical range. Thus, changes should be judged in relation to the broken lines on the profiles that demarcate the clinical, borderline, and normal ranges.

11. With whom should completed forms and profiles be shared?

Completed forms and profiles should be protected as would other confidential assessment data. With the appropriate permissions, however, they can be shared with other professionals whose work entitles them to confidential assessment data. These professionals include psychologists, psychiatrists, clinical social workers, and special educators, many of whom are familiar with the CBCL family of forms.

3

The Clinical Status of Children in State Custody

Craig Anne Heflinger and Celeste G. Simpkins

Introduction

For the past 25 years, child welfare workers have recognized that attention needs to be paid to the mental health needs of children in state care. In the 1970s, several articles appeared presenting data on the clinical status of children in foster care (e.g., Fanshel & Shinn 1978; Shah 1974; Swire & Kavaler 1977). A growing number of studies have documented the mental health needs of this population through a variety of mechanisms, including record review, clinical interviews and observations, and the use of standardized questionnaires (e.g., Chernoff et al. 1994; McIntyre & Keesler 1986; Blumberg et al.1995). The focus to date, however, has been on children in family foster care, although a larger population of children is in state care. The more than half a million children served in foster care each year (Rosenfeld, et al. 1997) swells to almost double that number when children in juvenile detention facilities and those in state custody residing in kinship care or other group placements are included. Few if any studies focus on this broader population of all children in state care. This study describes the clinical status of the full spectrum of children in custody of one state using standardized measures to document mental health status needs of this population.

Methods

This study was part of the Children's Program Outcome Review Team (C-PORT). The C-PORT, which was initiated in 1994, is an independent evaluation of the service system for children in custody of the State of Tennessee and is managed by the Tennessee Commission on Children and Youth (TCCY) (Tennessee Commission on Children and Youth 1997). The TCCY is an advocacy agency for policies and services that promote and protect the health, well-being, and development of all children and youth in Tennessee. The TCCY is responsible for monitoring and evaluating services to children in state custody. The C-PORT involves intensive case reviews on a stratified random sample that is representative of children and youth in state custody. It is guided by a structured interview protocol that yields child, family, and service system variables.

Instruments

The clinical status of children and youth in Tennessee state custody was examined by incorporating two standardized measures into the ongoing case review study: the Child Behavior Checklist (CBCL) and the Child and Adolescent Functional Assessment Scale (CAFAS).

The Child Behavior Checklist (CBCL)

The Child Behavior Checklist (CBCL) (Achenbach and Edelbrock 1991) is used as a measure of behavior problems of children 2–18 years old. Two versions of the CBCL were utilized in this study: the CBCL/2-3 and CBCL/4-18 for the respective age groups. The CBCL also includes measures of competencies, but the competency scores were not included in the C-PORT study. The CBCL relies upon parent/caregiver report of the child behavior and has been norm referenced for large populations (Achenbach and Edelbrock 1991; Zima, Wells & Freema, 1994). The instrument provides a Total Problem score indicative of clinical status, two broad-band scores (Externalizing and Internalizing), and scale scores for eight syndromes (Withdrawn, Somatic Complaints, Anxious/Depressed, Social Problems, Thought Problems, Attention Problems, Delinquent Behavior, and Aggressive Behavior). For the CBCL, high scores indicate a higher level of clinical behavior, and low scores indicate age-appropriate normal behavior. The cut points for borderline clinical and clinical range designations are based on T scores formed on a clinical population (Achenbach & Edelbrock 1991; Armsden, Pecora & Payne 1996; McConaughy & Achenbach 1988). Because the CBCL relies upon parent/caregiver report of child behavior, the caregiver must have known the child for 2 months or more to be eligible for the study.

The Child and Adolescent Functional Assessment Scale (CAFAS)

The Child and Adolescent Functional Assessment Scale (CAFAS) (Hodges 1990; Hodges & Wong 1996) is used to assess psychosocial functioning of children 3–18 years old. The CAFAS measures the degree of impairment in functioning in children and adolescents secondary to emotional, behavioral, or substance use problems (Hodges, 1990; Hodges & Wong, 1996). It is a structured interview consisting of 251 questions with closed-end response options. In this study, the CAFAS was completed by trained staff after they conducted interviews with caregivers, teachers, case managers, and other providers of services to the child. The CAFAS was based on the interview information and information contained in case records. If interview data with relevant persons was not available or if case records were incomplete, the case was considered ineligible for the CAFAS. In the C-PORT study, interviews were conducted by TCCY staff, volunteers with one of the departments or agencies serving children in state custody, and university research staff who were specially trained in the procedures. Case reviews upon which the CAFAS was based were conducted in one region per month throughout each year, with only one case review per child.

The CAFAS is multidimensional and provides a rating of average functioning or mild, moderate, or severe impairment for each of five areas: Role Performance, Thinking, Behavior, Moods and Emotions, and Substance Abuse. In all areas, the developmental level of the child is taken into account in scoring.

The Role Performance Scale of the CAFAS reflects the effectiveness with which the child fulfills the roles most relevant to his or her place in the community, specifically family, school, and job expectations. For instance, usual expectations in the family or current placement setting include age-appropriate self-care, chore responsibilities, and observance of rules. School expectations center on regular attendance, following rules, and completion of homework. Employed youths are expected to adhere to work schedules and manage their school and home responsibilities. The Thinking Scale examines age-appropriate expectations for rational thought and communication. It identifies illogical thinking, inability to communicate ideas, poor judgment, and poor decisionmaking related to impaired thought processes.

The Behavior Scale of the CAFAS measures the extent to which the child's daily behavior toward self and/or others is appropriate, acceptable, and understandable. Emphasis is placed on patterns of interpersonal interactions, with impairment defined as significant problems in more than one relationship. Also included are items that involve dangerous behavior toward self or others, risk-taking, and failure to consider consequences. The Moods and Emotions Scale focuses on Anxiety and Depression. Anxiety may be expressed as fear, worry, tension, or panic. Depression may be expressed as sadness, moodiness, feelings of worthlessness, irritability, or fatigue. Moodiness and irritability may be viewed as normal for some ages, but impairment in functioning and emotional difficulties are suggested when there is disruption of the activities in daily life. The Substance Use Scale focuses on maladaptive or inappropriate substance use by youths that is disruptive to normal functioning. Alcohol, marijuana, and other "street" drugs are commonly the substances of abuse.

The CAFAS has been adopted by several states for evaluating state-served children (Hodges & Gust 1995; Hodges & Wong 1996). The CAFAS authors recommend using total scores to indicate treatment needs, with severe functioning impairment (ratings of 70 or greater) indicating the need for long-term treatment; moderate impairment (ratings of 40-69) indicating periodic treatment; mild impairment (ratings of 20-39) indicating short-term treatment; and low levels of impairment (less than 20) indicating supportive intervention (Hodges, Wong, & Latessa 1998). As opposed to the CBCL, on which high scores indicate a higher level of clinical behavior and low scores indicate age-appropriate normal behavior, high scores on the CAFAS scales indicate greater impairment in functioning, and low scores indicate age normal functioning.

The Sample

From the total 1,258 children and youth (aged birth to 21 years) included in the 1995-96 C-PORT samples, 1,202 youth were age 2 through 21 years and, therefore, eligible for administration of either or both the CBCL and the CAFAS. These eligible youths were 56% male, 65% white, and 30% African American. Sixty-one percent were age 13 or older; 22% were 6–12 years old; and 17% were 2–5 years old. The majority (63%) had been adjudicated dependent, neglected, or abused, although 21% had an adjudication of delinquent and 16% of unruly. Almost 4 of every 5 children (79%) were in the custody of the Department of Human Services, and 17% were in the custody of the Department of Youth Development. Thirty-eight percent of these youths resided in foster homes, 35% in some type of group residence, and 27% in family or kinship settings.

Of the total 1,258 children and youths in the 1995-96 C-PORT sample, 1,189 youths were in the eligible age range (2-18 years old) to have either the CBCL/2-3 or the CBCL/4-18 completed. Caregivers who had known the youth less than 2 months (n=41) and those who overtly refused to participate (n=75) further reduced this number to 1,073. Of this number, 64% (685 of 1,073) actually completed the CBCL (See Table 3-1). This percent reflects the overall 2-year return rate. During 1995, the CBCL often was provided to caregivers (such as the foster parents or group home residential counselors) to be completed independently and returned by mail, and in that year, the return rate was 43%. In 1996, the procedure was changed to interviewer administration, and the rate increased to 87%. The groups of children with the lower response rates were those in family or kinship care (55%) and those adjudicated unruly, for which the overall return rate was 58%. The lowest response rate (50%) was for those children in family or kinship care who were also adjudicated unruly. CBCLs, however, were completed by caregivers in at least two-thirds of all eligible cases for children ages 6–12 years and 64% of those 13 and over (compared to 58% of those under 12), females (compared to 63% for males), children in foster care or group residences, and children who were adjudicated dependent/ neglected or delinquent.

Of the total eligible children, 1,191 were age 3 years and older and therefore age-eligible for completion of the CAFAS scales. Interview and case record information was incomplete for 112 of these children, leaving 1,079 children as the final eligible population for the CAFAS (Table 3-1). The CAFAS scale was completed for 1,014 (94% of those eligible). For 78% of the CAFAS sample (n=791), the Department of Human Services (the child welfare department in most states) was the custodial department. Eighteen percent (n=187) of the children were in the custody of the Department of Youth Development (the juvenile justice system department in most states); 3% (n=26) in the custody of the Department of Education; and 1% (n=10) in the custody of the Department of Mental Health and Mental Retardation.

Results

Child Behavior Checklist (CBCL) Scores

The CBCL provides information about problems at the global level, with three summary scales (Total Problems, Internalizing, and Externalizing) and information on 8–11 specific syndromes, depending upon whether the CBCL/2-3 or CBCL/4-18 is applicable. For both the CBCL/2-3 and the CBCL/4, –18, the Total Problem Score, Internalizing, Externalizing, Withdrawn, Somatic Complaints, Anxious/Depressed, and Aggressive Behavior scales are computed. For 2- to 3-year old children, sleep disorders and destructive behavior are also

Table 3-1. CBCL and CAFAS Sample

Demographics	CBCL (N=1073)			CAFAS (N=1079)		
	n	n with CBCL	%	n	n with CAFAS	%
Age Group						
Birth to 5 years	175	102	48%	86	84	98%
6-12 years	249	169	68%	264	251	95%
13+ years	649	414	64%	729	679	93%
Gender						
Female	465	307	66%	462	432	94%
Male	605	378	63%	614	582	95%
Race						
African American	321	201	63%	322	331	97%
Caucasian	691	448	65%	703	654	93%
Other	58	36	62%	51	49	96%
Residence						
Family Home	271	152	56%	276	264	96%
Foster Home	424	286	68%	388	366	94%
Group Residence	375	247	66%	412	384	93%
Adjudication						
Dependent/Neglected	694	451	65%	648	610	94%
Unruly	158	93	59%	188	179	95%
Delinquent	218	141	65%	240	225	94%
Total Completed	1,031	685	66%	1,076	1,014	94%

Demographics are reported from a total of 1,258 C-PORT cases. To be eligible for the CBCL, children had to be 2–18 years old and have a caretaker who had known them for at least 2 months. To be eligible for the CAFAS, children had to be ages 3–21 years and the interviewer had to be able to obtain sufficient information from interviews and case records. Children who were on runaway status and not available for direct interview, for example, were not rated on the CAFAS.

calculated. For 4- to 18-year-old children and youth, Thought Problems, Social Problems, Attention Problems, and Delinquent Behavior are also calculated.

Forty-one percent of the children in custody (see Table 3-2) were reported as having significant borderline clinical or clinical behavior problems. Almost one-third (30%) exhibited problems to such a great extent that their Total Problem scores were in the clinical range. When behavior problems are totaled to form the Internalizing, Externalizing, and Total Problems scores, the extent of the problems for a large number of these children becomes more apparent. Twenty percent of the children in custody had scores in the clinical range for Internalizing behaviors, and 30% scored in the clinical range for Externalizing behaviors.

The CBCL scores are based on the caregivers' ratings on the 113 items of the CBCL. On the problem behavior scales, 8% to 12 % of children received scores in the clinical range and, when scores in the borderline clinical range were included, the percentages increased to 19% to 26%. The areas of greatest difficulty for this population were reflected in the Aggressive, Delinquent, Social Problems, and Withdrawn scales. Overall, 31% of the children scored in the clinical range in at least one of the scales, and when scores in the borderline clinical range were included, the percentage of youths with significant mental health problems rose to 55%.

The middle age group (6–12 years) was more likely to have behavioral problems in the clinical range, with the youngest age group (under 6), the least likely to fall within the clinical range on the Total Problem scale, Externalizing, and aggression scales (X^2 with p values < .01). There were significant (X^2 with p values < .01) effects between type of residence and CBCL ratings on Internalizing, Externalizing, Social Participation, and Delinquency. Those living in family homes were more likely to have scores in the nonclinical range (72%) than those in foster homes (61%) or group homes (51%). Adjudication was significantly related (X^2 with p values < .05) to Social Problems. Children who had been adjudicated unruly or delinquent were judged more often to be within the clinical range than those adjudicated dependent, neglected, or abused. There were no significant relationships based on gender or race.

Children and Adolescents Functional Assessment Scale (CAFAS) Scores

The CAFAS was used to determine the current level of psychosocial functioning of children in state custody whose cases were reviewed through the C-PORT. On the total CAFAS Scale, over two-thirds of the children were rated as having some degree of impairment in functioning. Approximately half the children in the CAFAS sample (566 of 1,034 children) were rated as functioning in the average range for their age on 3 or more scales, while one-half demonstrated some level of impairment in one or more of the areas of functioning measured. Over half (57%) the children demonstrated at least mild impairment in Role Performance, with more than one-third (40%) showing moderate or severe problems in meeting the daily demands of family, school, or job expectations (see Table 3-3). This scale also received the highest mean score, indicating that overall, this group of children has the greatest difficulty and is in need of the most supportive services in the area of role expectations.

Seven percent of the children over age 5 in state custody showed at least mild impairment on the thinking scale, with 5% of this group showing moderate or severe impairment. This result indicated marked confusion and communication problems requiring assessment and treatment. Almost half of this group of children (44%) had some level of impairment, and almost one-quarter (24%) were rated as having moderate or severe impairment on the behavior scale. Forty-one percent of the children were rated as having at least mild impairment of Moods and Emotions.

The Substance Use scale focuses on maladaptive or inappropriate substance use by youth that is disruptive to normal functioning. Eighteen percent of the children over 12 years old

Table 3-2. Frequencies, Means, and Standard Deviations for the CBCL

Category	Applicable ages (years)	% of Children by Category (N = 685)			Total Number	Mean CBCL Scale Score	Standard Deviation
		Normal	Borderline Clinical	Clinical			
Withdrawn	2-18	78%	13%	9%	667	42.35	9.86
Somatic Complaints	2-18	80%	12%	8%	667	45.16	7.52
Anxious/ Depressed	2-18	81%	12%	7%	667	40.53	9.33
Social Problems	4-18	78%	14%	8%	630	42.76	9.22
Thought Problems	4-18	80%	10%	10%	630	45.66	8.74
Attention Problems	4-18	81%	9%	10%	630	40.96	10.76
Delinquent Behavior	4-18	74%	15%	11%	630	45.25	9.79
Aggressive Behavior	2-18	74%	14%	12%	667	42.26	10.89
Sleep Problems	2-3	83%	17%	0%	38	52.49	4.90
Destructive Behavior	2-3	72%	28%	0%	38	54.43	7.52
Total Problem Score	2-18	60%	11%	30%	683	55.06	13.29
Internalizing Scale	2-18	71%	9%	20%	683	52.47	11.99
Externalizing Scale	2-18	59%	11%	30%	683	55.86	13.24

CBCL scores are based on raw scores ranging from 0 to 236. The T scores themselves range from 23–100. For the Total Problem, Internalizing, and Externalizing Scales, scores of less than 60 are in the normal range; scores 60–63 are in the borderline clinical range; and scores 64 or higher are in the clinical range. For all syndrome scales, scores of 66 or less are in the normal range; scores 67–70 are in the borderline clinical range; and scores 71 or greater are in the clinical range [Achenbach & Edelbrock 1991].

showed at least mild difficulty in this area, with 11% of this group exhibiting moderate to severe problems.

The two domains with the most problems in functioning were Role Performance (the effectiveness with which the child fulfills the roles most relevant to his or her place in the community) and behavior toward self or others. Over two-thirds of the children (68%) were impaired in at least one area, and 53% were moderately to severely impaired in at least one area. Although 15% of the children had no apparent impairment in psychosocial functioning at all, 12% had moderate to severe impairments in 3 or more areas of functioning.

The effects of age, gender, race, type of residential placement (family home, foster home, or group residence), and adjudication (dependent/neglected, unruly, or delinquent) also were examined. Four independent variables (age, gender, residence, and adjudication) had significant ($p < .01$) relationships with the CAFAS scales after adjusting for multiple comparisons using the Bonferroni adjustment (see Table 3-4). There was a positive relationship between age and psychosocial functioning. The older the child, the greater the likelihood that he or she would be rated as impaired in the areas of Behavior Towards Others, Role

Table 3-3. Frequencies, Means, and Standard Deviations for the CAFAS

Scales	% of Children by Category (N=1,014)				Mean Score	Standard Deviation	Total Number
	Average	Mild	Moderate	Severe			
Role	43%	17%	10%	30%	12.78	12.78	1,002
Performance							
Thinking	93%	2%	4%	1%	1.39	1.39	911
Behavior	56%	21%	17%	7%	7.47	7.47	1,011
Moods	59%	22%	15%	4%	6.46	6.46	995
Substance Abuse	82%	7%	7%	4%	3.26	3.26	547
Total Score	32%	30%	23%	15%	29.5	29.5	1,014

For the total score, the authors of the CAFAS, Hodges and Wong [1996] recommend the following cutoffs: Average=0–19; Mild=20–39; Moderate=40–69; and Severe=70 and higher. For scale scores, the following scores apply: Average=0; Mild=10; Moderate=20; Severe=30.

Total Numbers differ because of eligibility for the scale. The Thinking scale was scored for children over 5 years old, and the Substance Abuse scale was scored for those over 12 years old. Other differences are the result of missing data for the scale.

Performance, Moods and Emotions, and on the total CAFAS score. Male youth had significantly higher impairment scores than females on Behavior Towards Others, Role Performance, and the total CAFAS score. Children living in group residences had significantly higher CAFAS scores on all scales, and those children living in foster homes had lower scores on five of the six scales (the one exception being the thinking scale). Children adjudicated dependent or neglected were less likely to have psychosocial impairments than those adjudicated as unruly or delinquent. Children who had been adjudicated as delinquent had significantly higher scores on the Role Performance and Substance Abuse scales. There were no significant differences in ratings based on race.

Relationship of the CAFAS to the CBCL

Two methods were used to examine the relationship between the CAFAS and the CBCL. First, correlations were performed between the six CAFAS scale scores and the CBCL three broadband and eight syndrome scale scores. Because each scale instrument purports to assess a child's mental health through behavioral measures, the scales from the two instruments should be highly related. Of the 66 correlation coefficients, only 2 were not significant at the $p < .05$ level. Fifty-eight of the 66 correlations were significant at or below the $p < .01$ level. The weakest correlation was between the CAFAS Substance Use sub-scale and the CBCL scales other than Aggressive and Delinquent Behavior.

The CAFAS scale for Behavior Towards Others had the highest correlation with the CBCL Aggressive Behavior scale ($r = .43$). The CAFAS Moods and Emotions scale was highly correlated with the CBCL scales for Anxiety/Depression (.36), Social Problems (.39) and

Table 3-4. Significant Means for the CAFAS Scales by Age, Residence, Adjudication, and Gender

CAFAS Scale	Age Group		
	3-5	6-12	13 +
Behavior Towards Others	3.45[a]	6.35	8.38[a]
Role Performance	4.70[a,b]	9.44[b,c]	15.02[a,c]
Mood and Emotions	2.77[a]	5.38[c]	7.32[a,c]
Substance Abuse	NA	1.09	3.42
Thinking	NA	1.22	1.46
Total CAFAS Scale	10.83[a,b]	22.31[b,c]	34.53[a,c]

	Residence		
	Family	Foster	Group
Behavior Towards Others	6.14[d]	5.48[f]	10.29[d,f]
Role Performance	11.46[d]	7.76[f]	18.47[d,f]
Mood and Emotions	5.33[d]	5.11[f]	8.52[d,f]
Substance Abuse	3.23	.69[f]	4.42[f]
Thinking	.74[d]	1.21	1.95[d]
Total CAFAS Scale	25.15[d]	19.45[f]	42.19[d,f]

	Adjudication		
	Dependent, Neglected, or Abused	Unruly	Delinquent
Behavior Towards Others	6.28	8.66	9.73
Role Performance	9.25[g,h]	15.88[h]	19.86[g]
Mood and Emotions	5.82[h]	7.44[h]	7.42
Substance Abuse	1.46[g]	3.43	5.78[g]
Thinking	1.40	1.53	1.27
Total CAFAS Scale	22.89[g,h]	36.26[h]	42.27[i]

	Gender	
	Male	Female
Behavior Towards Others	8.18[j]	6.50[j]
Role Performance	14.97[j]	9.85[j]
Mood and Emotions	6.56	6.34
Substance Abuse	3.51	2.90
Thinking	1.48	1.28
Total CAFAS Scale	32.65[j]	25.37[j]

All significance levels are <= p .01

[a] Age 3-5 significantly different from Age 13+

[b] Age 6-12 significantly different from Age 3-5

[c] Age 13+ significantly different from Age 6-12

[d] Family residence significantly different from Group

[e] Foster care significantly different from Family

[f] Group care significantly different from Foster

[g] Dependent/Neglected/Abused significantly different from Delinquent

[h] Unruly significantly different from Dependent/Neglected/Abused

[i] Delinquent significantly different from Unruly

[j] Males significantly different from Females

Internalizing Behaviors (.36). CAFAS Role Performance correlated to the CBCL Externalizing scale (.39), and the CAFAS thinking scale correlated to the CBCL thought disorder scales (.37). The highest correlation was between the total CAFAS and the CBCL aggression (.39) and Total Problems scales (.38).

The CBCL Total Problem scores were compared to CAFAS total scores to further examine the relationship between the two instruments' classification schemes (see Table 3-5). When examined by classification (normal, borderline clinical, and clinical versus average, mild, moderate, or severe impairment), only 9% (55 cases) were in clear dispute (clinical on the CBCL and average on the CAFAS or severe impairment on the CAFAS and normal on the CBCL). Forty percent of the cases were in clear agreement (clinical with severe impairment, borderline with mild/moderate impairment, nonclinical with average impairment, or low impairment on both scales). One-half (51%) of the cases were in the intermediate group where there was a high (clinical or severe) or low (normal or average) score on one scale and a "middle" score on the other scale.

In total, the CAFAS and CBCL appear to be correlated, but the overlap of the two is not so great as to indicate that either of the instruments could serve the purposes of both. Further evaluation continues on the contributions of each instrument.

The Mental Health Priority Population

Over half (58%) the children in the sample had a formal mental health diagnosis reported in their case record and documented in the C-PORT. An additional 28% of the sample did not initially have a formal mental health diagnosis but were classified within the clinical range on the CBCL Total Problems score. When the children with a formal mental health diagnosis were combined with the children with a CBCL Total Problems score in the clinical range and considered the "diagnosed group," 83% of the population had a mental health diagnosis either from the *Diagnostic and Statistical Manual (DSM – IV)* (American Psychiatric Association 1994) or the CBCL. Of this group of children, many also were rated with moderate or severe impairment in psychosocial functioning (as measured by the CAFAS). Based on the two-fold federal definition of serious emotional disturbance (SED)—which requires both a DSM diagnosis and evidence of impaired functioning (Federal Register 1993; Tennessee Department of Mental Health 1994)—40% of the children for whom the CAFAS was completed could be classified as SED (see Figure 3-1).

SED designation was related to age, with older children significantly (by X^2 analysis with $p < .01$) more likely to be designated as SED (48%) than younger children (30% of 6-12 year olds and 10% of those under 6 years). There were no significant differences in the percentages of children designated as SED based on race. Males were more likely to be designated SED (45%) than were females (33%). Children who had been adjudicated delinquent (compared to those adjudicated neglected or dependent or as unruly) and children assigned to the Department of Youth Development (54%) were more likely to be classified as SED (59%). The majority of the SED population (69%) were children in the custody of the Department of Human Services, the children generally considered the "typical" child welfare population. Children with SED were

Table 3-5. CAFAS Total Scores and CBCL Total Problems Scores Comparison

	CBCL Categories		
	Normal Range	**Borderline Clinical Range**	**Clinical Range**
Average	24.6% [a]	2.8%	4.6% [d]
Mild Impairment	19.5%	3.6% [a]	9.1%
Moderate Impairment	9.2%	2.8% [a]	9.2%
Severe Impairment	4.5% [d]	1.5%	8.6% [a]

[a] denotes agreement
[d] denotes disagreement
Note: All other percentages indicate "middle" on one score and high or low on the other.

likely to be placed in a group home residence (58%) and to have had 5 or more previous admissions (50%) to some type of residential program. The children designated as SED, however, had not been in custody longer than children not classified as SED.

Discussion

The CBCL and the CAFAS provide a wealth of information about the mental health status of children in state custody. This study provides one of very few representative samples of this population and provides needed descriptive information on evaluating and planning for mental health needs.

On the CBCL, slightly less (40%) of the children had significant behavior problems, as indicated by scores in the borderline or clinical range. The greater number of children were in the clinical range on the Aggressive and Delinquent Behavior scales.

The two CAFAS domains on which the greater number of problems in psychosocial functioning were identified were Role Performance (the effectiveness with which the child fulfills the roles most relevant to his or her place in the community) and Moods and Emotions. Over half of the children (53%) showed moderate to severe impairment in at least one of the 5 areas, with 40% showing impairment in two or more areas. Overall, the CAFAS total scores indicated that this sample of children and youth in state care had a range of treatment needs: 32% needed supportive intervention; 30% required short-term treatment (up to 6 months); 23% needed periodic treatment (over a 6–24 month period); and 15% required long-term treatment (1–5 years).

CAFAS scores were used to examine potential bias in the completed CBCL sample. CAFAS scores were examined for children with completed CBCLs and without completed CBCLs. When comparing children in the total CAFAS sample with or without a completed CBCL, there were no significant differences in total CAFAS score. Those children with a CBCL, however, were rated as significantly less impaired on the CAFAS scale for Substance Abuse, indicating that CBCL scores for this sample may under-represent the level of mental health

Figure 3-1. Mental Health Priority Population: Children with Impaired Functioning and MH Diagnosis

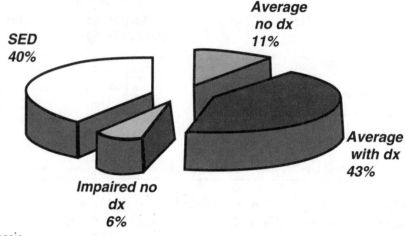

Note: dx=diagnosis

difficulties in the population of children in custody, especially for those over 12 years old with a substance abuse problem.

The correlations between the CAFAS scales and the CBCL scales were lower than the correlations in the .42 to .49 range found by Hodges and Wong (1996) in their studies of the psychometric properties of the CAFAS. The differences may be the result of sample differences, as this sample was of children in state custody and the Hodges and Wong (1996) sample was of military dependent children. While somewhat lower than found by Hodges and Wong, the correlations show reasonable agreement between the CAFAS and the CBCL for this population. Although these instruments differ in the way information is gathered, they are complementary in that the results inform treatment needs and document trends and changes that impact service delivery. The CBCL defines a probable clinical population, and the CAFAS identifies the depth of the impact of the problem behaviors on daily functioning of the child and the level intervention needed.

Taken together, the CBCL and CAFAS indicated relatively high levels of mental health problems and subsequent treatment needs. The proportion of children in custody who meet SED criteria in Tennessee has increased in each of the last three years (Heflinger & Simpkins 1997). The increase is attributable to the growth in the number of children with diagnoses recorded in their case records and in the number of children with interviewer-rated impairments.

It is important to document problem behavior and impairments in psychosocial functioning for children who come into custody, specifically with regard to their mental health needs and their delinquent or criminal behavior. The Department of Human Services (DHS) in Tennessee, which has responsibility for 80% of the children in state custody, has a clear need for such information. This study highlights the needs of these children: 40% had scores in the borderline clinical or clinical range on the CBCL Total Problems score and 57% had periodic or long-term treatment needs as identified by the CAFAS total score. Based on the total custody population in Tennessee of approximately 12,000 children and youth, the rate of significant mental health problems for children served by DHS (40% to 57%) translates into 4,800 to 6,840 children in need of mental health intervention. In addition, the finding that 40% of the children in custody met the criteria for SED indicates that assessment and treatment services, including special education intervention, are needed for some 4,800 children and youth.

These findings also have implications for training staff who care for children in state custody. It was found that staff did not necessarily document or identify children's mental health problems. One-quarter of the children had no formal mental health diagnosis in their case records but were rated in the clinical range on the CBCL or with moderate to severe levels of impairment on the CAFAS. Training social workers to recognize potential areas of difficulty and to seek needed assessment, support, and treatment is critical. Minimizing caseworker turnover and ensuring continuity in the assignment of social workers to children's cases would strengthen efforts to identify children's mental health needs and develop appropriate interventions.

The inclusion of the CAFAS and the CBCL provides much needed information about the functioning and behavior of the children and youth in state custody. These instruments are a relatively cost-effective method for assessing the level of functioning and treatment needs of children in state care. The results have high face validity and correspond to other evidence from family members and social workers who have described the problems and needs of these children.

Acknowledgment

This research was funded by a grant from the National Institute of Mental Health (M4 50101, Principal Investigator: Craig Anne Heflinger).

References

Achenbach, T.M., & Edelbrock, C. (1991). *Manual for the Child Behavior Checklist and 1991 Profile.* Burlington: University of Vermont Department of Psychiatry.

American Psychiatric Association (1994). *Diagnostic and Statistical Manual of Mental Disorders (4th ed.).* Washington, DC: American Psychiatric Association.

Armsden, G., Pecora, P.J., & Payne, V. (1996). *A profile of youth placed with the Casey Family Program using the Child Behavior Checklist/4-18 and the Teachers Report Form.* Seattle, WA: The Casey Family Program, Research Department.

Blumberg, E., Landsverk, J., Ellis-MacLeod, E., Ganger, W., & Culver, S. (1995). Use of the public mental health system by children in foster care: Client characteristics and service use patterns. *The Journal of Mental Health Administration, 23,* 389–405.

Center for the Study of Social Policy (1993). *Kids count data book.* Washington, DC: Center for the Study of Social Policy.

Chernoff, R., Combs-Orme, T., Risley-Curtiss, C. & Heisler, A. (1994). Assessing the health status of children entering foster care. *Pediatrics, 93,* 594–601.

Cheung, F. K. & Snowden, L. R. (1990). Community mental health and ethnic minority populations. *Community Mental Health Journal, 26,* 277–291.

Fanshel, D. & Shinn, E.G. (1978). *Children in foster care: A longitudinal investigation.* New York: Columbia University Press.

Substance Abuse and Mental Health Services Admininstration, Center for Mental Health Services, 58 Fed. Reg. 96, 29425 (May 20, 1993).

Heflinger, C.A., & Simpkins, C.G. (1997). *1996 Clinical findings regarding children in state custody.* Nashville, TN: Vanderbilt Institute for Public Policy Studies, Center for Mental Health Policy.

Hodges, K. (1990). *Child and Adolescent Functional Assessment Scale and Global Level of Functioning.* Unpublished scale. Eastern Michigan University, Ypsilanti, MI.

Hodges, K., & Gust, J. (1995). Measures of impairment for children and adolescents. *Journal of Mental Health Administration, 22,* 403–413.

Hodges, K., & Wong, M.M. (1996). Psychometric characteristics of a multidimensional measure to assess impairment: The Child and Adolescent Functional Assessment Scale. *Journal of Child and Family Studies, 5,* 445–467.

Hodges, K., Wong, M.M., & Latessa, M. (1998). Use of the Child and Adolescent Functional Assessment Scale (CAFAS) as an outcome measure in clinical settings. *Journal of Behavioral Health Services & Research, 25,* 325-336.

McConaughy, S.H., & Achenbach, T.M. (1988). *Practical guide for the Child Behavior Checklist and related materials.* Burlington: University of Vermont Department of Psychiatry.

McIntyre, A., & Keesler, T. Y. (1986). Psychological disorders among foster children. *Journal of Clinical Child Psychology, 15,* 297–303.

Rosenfeld, A. A., Pilowsky, D. J., Fine, P., Thorpe, M., Fein, E., Simms, M. D., Halfon, N., Irwin, M., Alfaro, J., Saletsky, R., & Nickman, S. (1997). Foster care: An Update. *Journal of the American Academy of Adolescent Psychiatry, 36,* 448–457.

Shah, C.P. (1974). Psychiatric consultations in a child welfare agency. *Canadian Psychiatric Association Journal, 19,* 393–397.

Swire, M.R. & Kavaler, F. (1977). The health status of foster children. *Child Welfare, 56,* 635–653.

Tennessee Commission on Children and Youth (1994). *Children's Plan Evaluation Report.* Nashville, TN: Tennessee Commission on Children and Youth.

Tennessee Commission on Children and Youth (1997, June). C-PORT 1996 Evaluation results summary. *The Advocate, 1,* 1–11.

Tennessee Department of Mental Health (1994). *Annual Plan for a Comprehensive System of Mental Health Services in Tennessee.* Nashville, TN: Tennessee Department of Mental Health.

Woodward, A. M., Dwinell, A. D. & Arons, B. S. (1992). Barriers to mental health care for Hispanic Americans: A literature review and discussion. *Journal of Mental Health Administration, 19,* 224–236.

Zima, B.L., Wells, K.B. & Freeman, H.E. (1994). Emotional and behavioral problems and severe academic delays among sheltered homeless children in Los Angeles County. *American Journal of Public Health, 84,* 260–264.

4

Demographic Differences in Children's Residential Treatment Progress

William A. Shennum, Debra C. Moreno, and JoAnna C. Caywood

Introduction

Residential treatment programs for children have garnered a variety of critics and sympathizers over the years (see Berrick 1993; McKenzie 1997). Most children in residential treatment today entered through the public child welfare or mental health systems. Many children are at the "high end" of the service continuum, having been abused, neglected, or diagnosed with psychiatric disorders. They present a myriad of emotional and behavioral problems and typically have complex family problems as well.

Unfortunately, the knowledge base concerning the effectiveness of residential treatment is diverse and fragmented. One reason is that to a great extent, the residential treatment industry is more advocacy-oriented than scientific. Neither critics nor supporters of residential care can produce definitive evidence of treatment effectiveness or ineffectiveness. Both groups often rely on polemics or political correctness to support their claims, and consequently, the credibility of assertions about residential care or other alternatives such as family preservation or treatment foster care are undermined. To the extent that research in the field is overshadowed by advocacy, advancement of knowledge is limited.

An important trend in residential treatment is the development of empirically validated measures of treatment outcomes. When program results can be measured with precision, claims about program effectiveness gain credibility. Furthermore, when different types of children's service agencies utilize comparable measures of treatment outcome, it is possible to make the cross-service comparisons necessary to evaluate "what works best for whom." The goals of the present study are to provide a set of findings on children's progress in residential treatment and to examine some of the group demographic factors that may mediate treatment progress.

What Is Known About Residential Treatment Effectiveness?

A number of literature reviews have been published that summarize studies on residential treatment. Bates, English, and Kouidou-Giles (1997) reviewed the literature on residential treatment and provided comparisons with literature on alternative forms of care, including family preservation, treatment foster care, and individualized services. They noted that the research in most of these areas suffers from methodological flaws, including lack of experimental controls and use of nonstandardized outcome assessments. In their review of the findings, the authors noted that there is little empirical evidence to support the claim that nonresidential approaches are superior to residential treatment.

Curry (1995) reviewed the current research on residential treatment and also concluded that methodological and resource obstacles hampered progress in this area. He was encouraged, however, by certain trends in research, such as the application of developmental psychopathology theories to treatment research. He stressed the importance of defining treatment components and the postdischarge environment.

Pfeiffer and Strzlecki (1990) conducted a meta-analysis of residential treatment outcome studies to determine factors that were consistently related to positive treatment outcomes. They found that positive outcomes were associated with several factors, including a supportive postdischarge environment, healthy family functioning, and presence of acute (as opposed to chronic) symptoms. McDonald, Allen, Westerfelf, and Piliavin (1996) conducted an extensive review of studies on adult outcomes for children who had been in out-of-home care. Their review included studies of foster care and residential group care. With certain exceptions, they noted that family foster care tended to produce better adult outcomes than did residential care. Many of the studies reviewed, however, did not control for problem severity, family income, and other key variables. Further, a number of their findings contradicted the notion that long-term foster placement is detrimental.

The United States General Accounting Office (GAO) (1994) also completed a study of residential care for high-risk youth. Investigators identified 18 prominent residential programs and reviewed the programs through site visits, interviews with professional staff, and program observation. The study team interviewed experts and program officials, identifying some of the positive attributes of residential treatment programs (e.g., removal of clients from dangerous environments) as well as some of the negative ones (e.g., disruption of family attachments). The GAO concluded that: "residential care appears to be a viable treatment option for some high-risk youth...however, few programs conduct rigorous evaluations to measure effectiveness or long-term outcomes" (1994, p. 4).

The Role of Agency-Based Research and Evaluation

There would seem to be general consensus that residential treatment programs provide a needed service within an array of intervention alternatives for troubled children and families (Duchnowski, et al. 1993). Clearly, however, residential treatment is more costly than less restrictive, community-based forms of care, and, as a result, may be viewed as diverting sorely needed funds from community-based services. Because of issues related to cost, it becomes all the more critical to understand the parameters of residential and other types of treatment. For whom and for what kinds of problems are various service alternatives most effective?

Agency-based research affords a promising approach for developing such information. In contrast to many fields in which the academic community provides much of the impetus for scientific development, in human services (including child welfare), applied research and program evaluation activities are producing a new body of knowledge about services for children. Most child welfare agencies already collect client outcome information, and the major agency accreditation bodies in the field (the Council on Accreditation of Services for Families and Children (COA) and the Joint Commission on Accreditation of Healthcare Organizations (JCAHO) require that accredited agencies carry out quality assurance and outcome data collection. Agencies, through meeting these accreditation requirements, add to the cumulative knowledge base about child treatment programs.

Funding for agency-based research, however, is a challenge for most agencies. The public agencies that refer children to residential treatment do not typically fund research or evaluation. Consequently, although agencies are required to collect data for accreditation, they generally are not funded sufficiently for research or evaluation (Pecora, Seelig, Zirps, & Davis} , and collected data frequently are underutilized. Agencies that have invested in the development of research and evaluation are in a better position to maximize the use of data and, through the development of a capacity for informed program improvement, can share their data with the general professional community.

The Study Method

This study was conducted at Five Acres—The Boys and Girls Aid Society of Los Angeles County, a private and nonprofit agency that has made an investment in research and program evaluation. The agency's research and evaluation department collects client outcome data on children and families served in its residential treatment and other programs, including family preservation, home-based services, and treatment foster care. It is responsible for conducting program evaluations, providing quality assurance data, and carrying out research studies (Shennum & Carlo 1995; Carlo & Shennum 1989).

The residential treatment facility studied had a capacity to serve 80 children aged 6–12. The program utilized a social learning approach to treatment that focused on individualized behavioral objectives, social skills development, and family reunification. The study examined CBCL data on the treatment progress of children in this program and compared different demographic groups of children served. The examination of client factors related to improvement was intended to identify those clients who were most and least successful in treatment and thus, to determine program strengths and weaknesses. This information was used to pave the way for quality improvement activities by illuminating the goodness (or poorness) of fit between services and client needs.

Subjects

Subjects in the study were 68 children placed in the residential treatment program at Five Acres. All children selected for the study sample were adjudicated by courts as dependent and were referred by the local public children's services bureau. Their average age at admission into the program was 9.6 years (SD = 1.5), with a range of 6.5 to 12.0 years of age. At the time of admission, 56% of the children (n = 38) were under age 10.0, while 44% (n = 30) were age 10.0 and older.

Sample selection criteria included all children in the agency's residential treatment program during 1995–96 who, at the time of selection, had been in the program for at least 16 months. A minimum stay of 16 months was used as a selection criterion because it represented the approximate median length of stay at the agency. The study focused on children's progress during the 16-month period. Data from assessments completed after the 16-month mark were not included.

Sixty percent (n = 41) of subjects were male. This percentage approximates the overall number of spaces available to boys in the agency's residential treatment program. The sample distribution was 48.5% (n = 33) African-American, 23.5% (n = 16) Caucasian, 19.1% (n = 13) Latino, and 8.8% (n = 6) others (see Table 4-1). This distribution is representative of the children and youth served by the primary referral source, the Los Angeles County Department of Children and Family Services (Digre & Rubenstein 1996).

Instruments

Three instruments were used in the study. Children's behavioral functioning and progress were assessed using the Child Behavior Checklist (CBCL) (Achenbach 1991). The CBCL assesses behavioral problems and competencies and provides standardized scores based on national norms. Second, the California Association of Services for Children Outcome Measure System (C.S.C.) (California Association of Services for Children 1995) was used to record demographic and placement history information. The system, developed by a voluntary state association of agencies to record outcomes and characteristics of children served, is implemented on a statewide basis among member agencies. This study utilized data from the C.S.C. that included client age at admission, gender, race/ethnicity, abuse history, and out-of-home placement history. Third, children's intellectual functioning was assessed with the Wechsler Intelligence Scale for Children-Revised (WISC-R) (Wechsler 1992).

Seventy-nine percent (n = 54) of the children had indications of physical abuse in their histories and 58.8% (n = 40) had indications of sexual abuse. Most children had previous out-of-home placements prior to their present stay in residential treatment. Only 11.8% (n = 8) had no previous placements. Forty-seven percent (n = 32) had previous placement in a residential treatment or psychiatric hospital setting (see Table 4-2). Additional placement history data included age at first placement, number of placements, and placement rate per year (see Table 4-3). On average, subjects experienced their first placement at age 5.6 years

Table 4-1. Gender and Race/Ethnicity Distribution of Subjects

	n	*Percentage*
Gender		
Males	41	60.3%
Females	27	39.7%
Race/Ethnicity		
African-American	33	48.5%
Caucasian	16	23.5%
Latino	13	19.1%
Other	6	8.8%

and had an average of 3.8 placements until the current placement at age 9.5. The average number of placements per year was 1.18 placements, an average that may be used as a measure of the overall rate of children's out-of-home placements. Results from the WISC-R indicated that sample functioning, in general, was in the low-average range. The average full-scale IQ score of the sample was 89.2 (*SD* = 11.6). Average verbal and performance IQ scores were 86.9 (*SD* = 13.4) and 91.5 (12.6), respectively.

Data Collection

Study data were drawn from research department files within the agency. No special procedures were used, and no direct contact with the sample was made. Agency scheduling for children's CBCL evaluations were linked to quarterly evaluations required by the public children's services bureau overseeing placements. A preliminary CBCL was completed one month after admission (not used in this study). An assigned child care worker subsequently completed a CBCL on each child at three-month intervals and then postadmission. For the present study, CBCL *T* scores were taken from the evaluations at months 4, 7, 10, 13, and 16 (referred to as Times 1 through 5). To achieve consistent assessments over time, the children's primary child care worker completed the CBCL during treatment. Staff turnover, at times, necessitated flexibility as to which staff member completed the CBCL at different points in time. The treatment team reviewed CBCL profiles and made any scoring adjustments deemed necessary. Most often, scoring adjustments include changes in item scores based on treatment team agreements. CBCL results were included in all quarterly reports sent to referral agencies and court officials.

Additionally, the CBCL was completed on the day of admission (intake) for most of the children. Because children were admitted from different types of placements (treatment facilities, group homes, foster homes, and homes of family members), consistency in informants was uneven. Often, these "intake" CBCLs were completed by caseworkers, rather

Table 4-2. Abuse History and Previous Placements of Subjects

	N	Percentage
Abuse History		
Physical	54	79.4%
Sexual	40	58.8%
Highest Level of Previous Placement		
No Previous Placements	8	11.8%
Foster Care	20	29.5%
Group Home	8	11.8%
Residential Treatment	19	28.0%
Psychiatric Hospital	13	19.1%
Total	68	100.0%

than the caregivers most familiar with the children's behavior. As a result, comparability of these "intake" assessment results to subsequent assessments could not be assured. Analyses of these assessments are presented in the Results section of this report.

Data Analysis Approach

Repeated measures analyses of variance (ANOVAs) were performed on CBCL scores to evaluate treatment progress. Relationships between demographic variables (gender, age, and race/ethnicity) and progress were studied with multiple regression analysis. First, treatment progress scores (dependent variables) were computed by subtracting Time 5 from Time 1 CBCL T-scores. Second, a restricted regression model was computed to account for initial differences in problem level (Time 1 CBCL scores), placement history (placements per year), and verbal IQ. Third, a full regression model was computed, which added a demographic independent variable set (age, gender, and race/ethnicity) to the restricted model. Any increase in proportion of variance accounted for by the full over the restricted model was attributable to demographic variables. The significance of this increase was evaluated with an F test (see Pedhazur 1973). Fourth, for analyses in which the demographic variable set contributed significant variance, beta weights for specific independent variables were examined to determine relationship to treatment progress.

The Results

Analysis of Baseline CBCLs

An initial series of analyses was carried out to compare two different baseline assessment points: Intake and Time 1. An accurate CBCL baseline is vital to the evaluation of treatment progress. Given the observational nature of the CBCL, residential treatment staff would not be expected

Table 4-3. Prior Placement Information

	M	SD
Age at Admission	9.55	1.46
Age at First Placement	5.61	3.17
Number of Prior Placements	3.79	2.08
Placement Rate/Year	1.18	1.41

to complete the CBCL accurately until a child had resided in the program for a period of time. Initial assessments of children were done on the day of admission (intake) by either the previous caregiver or a placement case worker. To examine the comparability of intake ratings with baselines obtained during the first months of treatment, Intake and Time 1 CBCL scores were compared. Results are found in Table 4-4. Results indicated that intake scores were higher (more deviant) for Total Problems and lower for the Activity Competency scales.

Assessments conducted at admission, however, pose methodological difficulties. The environments in which children had been observed were different, and the informants varied in degree of familiarity with the child. Additionally, placement caseworkers may have relied on second-hand information rather than the direct observation required by the CBCL. To examine informant differences, comparisons were made between children whose intake CBCLs had been completed by caregivers (such as parents or foster parents) and children who were rated by placement case workers. These results are found in Table 4-5. Findings indicate that caregivers made significantly higher ratings in Total Externalizing Problems, Delinquency, and Aggressive Behavior.

In summary, a number of differences were found across informants at the time of children's admission to treatment. Intake ratings tended to be higher (more deviant) than assessments conducted after admission. Children's CBCL scores obtained after children were admitted to the program were based directly on behaviors identified within the residential treatment setting. These CBCL scores were more uniform and relevant to the setting in which change was measured. Because of these methodological considerations, it was decided that the Time 1 assessments provided the most reliable baselines from which to record treatment progress.

Treatment Progress

Table 4-6 provides the mean CBCL scores over time for subjects. The 5 time periods indicated represent 3-month intervals (at 4, 7, 10, 13, and 16 months subsequent to admission). Main effects were tested with repeated measures ANOVAs. Significant effects were found for the Total Internalizing Problems scale ($F = 2.66, df = 4,268, p < .05$), Anxious/Depressed ($F = 2.63, df = 4, 268$), $p < .05$), Attention Problems ($F = 2.82, df = 4, 268, p < .05$) and School Competency ($F = 2.73, df = 4, 224, p < .05$). Marginally significant effects were noted for Withdrawn ($F = 2.04, df = 4, 268, p < .10$) and Total Competency ($F = 2.05, df = 4, 268, p < .10$). All of these effects were in the direction of improved behavioral functioning over time.

Table 4-4. Comparison of Intake and Time 1 CBCL T Scores

| | Timing of Baseline Measurement | | |
| | At Intake | At Time 1 | |
Problem Scales	*Mean (SD)*	*Mean (SD)*	*T (50)*
Total Problems	69.7 (6.5)	66.9 (9.8)	1.97**
Internalizing	66.8 (8.6)	65.5 (10.1)	<1.0
Externalizing	69.3 (7.8)	66.8 (12.0)	1.59
Withdrawn	66.5 (8.7)	67.8 (10.5)	<1.0
Somatic Complaints	56.8 (7.8)	55.2 (6.1)	1.40
Anxious/Depressed	68.9 (9.4)	66.5 (12.0)	1.26
Social Problems	64.7 (9.8)	66.3 (11.1)	1.0
Thought problems	62.9 (9.7)	60.2 (8.5)	1.34
Attention problems	67.2 (7.7)	64.3 (11.3)	1.62
Delinquency	69.2 (8.9)	68.1 (9.1)	<1.0
Aggressive Behavior	68.3 (10.1)	67.3 (13.2)	<1.0
Competency Scales			
Total Competency	37.9 (7.1)	39.0 (5.0)	1.10
Activities	43.6 (8.2)	47.2 (5.3)	2.43**
Social	34.8 (10.2)	35.7 (7.9)	<1.0
School	33.5 (7.8)	33.0 (6.9)	<1.0

** $p < .05$

Note: For Social and School DF = 42

Demographic Variables and Progress

The next analyses examined the relationships among demographic variables (age, gender and race/ethnicity) and progress. The dependent variables in these analyses were change in scores from Time 1 to Time 5 on each CBCL scale. First, restricted regression models were computed which contained independent variables of Time 1 CBCL scores (to account for initial level of severity of behavioral problem and to reduce regression to the mean effects); previous placements per year (to account for severity of placement and abuse history); and verbal IQ (to account for differences in intellectual levels among children). Second, a full regression model was computed which added the independent variable set including age at admission, gender, and race/ethnicity. An F test was carried out, which tested the significance of the increase in variance accounted for by the full model over the restricted model (see Table 4-7).

The restricted models accounted for a significant amount of variance in children's treatment progress (average squared multiple correlation coefficient was .34). Most of this effect was a regression to the mean artifact, whereby children with higher Time 1 scores (or lower, in the case of the Competency Scales) demonstrated greater improvement. Comparison of full model and restricted models indicated that the demographic variables increased the

Table 4-5. Comparison of Previous Caregiver and Caseworker Intake CBCLs

| | Person Completing Intake CBCL | | |
| | Previous Caregiver | Caseworker | |
Problem Scales	Mean (SD)	Mean (SD)	T (45)
Total Problems	72.1 (7.6)	69.2 (6.3)	1.25
Internalizing	66.5 (11.0)	67.2 (8.0)	<1.0
Externalizing	74.8 (8.8)	67.6 (7.2)	2.66**
Withdrawn	65.3 (9.1)	66.6 (8.0)	<1.0
Somatic Complaints	56.3 (6.8)	57.7 (8.2)	<1.0
Anxious/Depressed	69.9 (11.3)	68.9 (9.0)	<1.0
Social Problems	66.7 (10.8)	64.7 (9.6)	<1.0
Thought problems	63.4 (11.3)	63.0 (9.3)	<1.0
Attention problems	69.2 (8.7)	66.6 (7.7)	<1.0
Delinquency	74.7 (8.9)	67.8 (8.5)	2.27**
Aggressive Behavior	76.1 (13.3)	66.0 (8.5)	2.28**
Competency Scales			
Total Competency	38.5 (8.6)	37.8 (7.0)	<1.0
Activities	44.6 (7.7)	43.5 (8.4)	<1.0
Social	33.9 (13.1)	34.9 (9.7)	<1.0
School	33.4 (7.9)	33.6 (8.0)	<1.0

** $p < .05$
Note: For Social and School DF = 40

proportion of variance accounted for by an average of 10%. Significant increments ($p < .05$) in the proportion of variables accounted for were shown on the following scales: Total Problems, Total Internalizing Problems, Total Externalizing Problems, Thought Problems, Delinquency, Aggressive Behavior, and School Competency. Scales with marginally significant increases were: Withdrawn, Anxious/Depressed, and Social Competency. A review of the regression coefficients produced by the full models showed that age at admission was a significant predictor of improvement on five scales: Total Problems, Total Externalizing, Delinquency, Aggressive Behavior, and School Competency. In each case, older children (age 10 and older) showed greater progress than children under 10 years of age. Gender was a significant predictor only on the Social Competency Scale, with boys showing greater progress. Race/ethnicity was significant on 3 scales, with Latino subjects showing less progress in Total Internalizing, Withdrawn, and Thought Problems than African Americans and Caucasians.

Table 4-6. CBCL T Scores of Children in Residential Treatment Over Five 3-month Intervals

| | Time Since Admittance to Residential Treatment | | | | | |
	Time 1 Mean (SD)	Time 2 Mean (SD)	Time 3 Mean (SD)	Time 4 Mean (SD)	Time 5 Mean (SD)	$F_{(4, 268)}$
Problem Scales						
Total Problems	67.3 (9.3)	66.2 (10.0)	66.9 (11.3)	66.4 (10.2)	65.5 (9.7)	<1.0
Internalizing	65.0 (9.8)	63.9 (11.0)	64.2 (11.2)	63.5 (11.3)	60.7 (10.9)	2.66**
Externalizing	67.8 (12.0)	67.3 (11.4)	67.8 (12.3)	67.8 (11.1)	67.6 (10.0)	<1.0
Withdrawn	67.0 (10.3)	66.2 (10.0)	65.5 (10.6)	66.3 (10.5)	63.7 (9.4)	2.04*
Somatic Complaints	54.8 (6.1)	55.5 (7.2)	55.3 (8.2)	55.1 (8.1)	54.2 (6.0)	<1.0
Anxious/Depressed	66.1 (11.4)	65.3 (11.6)	66.0 (12.0)	64.5 (11.0)	62.2 (10.2)	2.63**
Social Problems	66.1 (10.8)	65.0 (11.1)	65.3 (11.6)	63.5 (10.9)	63.9 (10.8)	1.88
Thought problems	60.6 (8.7)	61.0 (10.0)	61.4 (8.9)	60.2 (10.4)	59.1 (10.0)	<1.0
Attention problems	64.5 (10.4)	64.4 (10.2)	64.2 (10.0)	64.0 (10.4)	61.4 (10.2)	2.82**
Delinquency	68.4 (9.1)	67.3 (9.8)	67.0 (9.7)	67.7 (8.6)	66.5 (8.9)	<1.0
Aggressive Behavior	68.8 (12.6)	68.5 (12.7)	69.7 (14.2)	68.6 (12.2)	67.9 (12.0)	<1.0
Competency Scales						
Total Competency	39.4 (4.9)	39.2 (4.9)	39.1 (5.6)	39.9 (5.8)	40.5 (5.8)	2.05*
Activities	47.6 (5.2)	47.3 (5.3)	47.1 (5.4)	47.2 (6.0)	47.4 (5.9)	<1.0
Social	36.6 (8.2)	37.1 (9.0)	37.6 (10.2)	38.0 (9.8)	39.2 (9.0)	1.13
School	33.2 (7.6)	33.2 (7.9)	32.2 (8.0)	33.6 (8.6)	35.1 (8.5)	2.73**

** $p < .05$ * $p < .10$

Note: For Social and School $DF = 4, 224$

Table 4-7. Multiple Regression Analyses of Children's CBCL Improvement Scores

	R^2 Restricted Model	R^2 Full Model	Increment in R^2	F (5, 59)
CBCL Problem Scales				
Total Problems	0.285	0.433	0.148	3.09**
Internalizing	0.396	0.497	0.101	2.35**
Externalizing	0.403	0.521	0.118	2.93**
Withdrawn	0.492	0.575	0.083	2.29*
Somatic Complaints	0.501	0.517	0.016	<1.0
Anxious/Depressed	0.512	0.589	0.077	2.2*
Social Problems	0.256	0.315	0.059	1.01
Thought problems	0.338	0.468	0.13	2.9**
Attention problems	0.31	0.388	0.078	1.5
Delinquency	0.305	0.426	0.121	2.48**
Aggressive Behavior	0.337	0.479	0.142	3.92***
CBCL Competency Scales				
Total Competency	0.241	0.312	0.071	1.22
Activities	0.4	0.415	0.015	<1.0
Social	0.229	0.345	0.116	2.1*
School	0.286	0.409	0.123	2.46**

$* p < .10$ $** p < .05$ $*** p < .01$

Note: Restricted Model includes Time 1 CBCL Score, Placements/Year, and Verbal IQ. Full Model additionally includes age, gender and dummy codes for race/ethnicity.

Discussion

This study produced a variety of findings concerning the effectiveness of residential treatment for children and factors related to treatment progress. It used a standardized outcome measure, the CBCL, in agency-based research and evaluation. Given the methodological limitations of the study, results permit a cautious conclusion that children demonstrated behavioral progress during treatment. For the sample as a whole, progress was limited to 3 areas: Internalizing Problems, Attention Problems, and School Competency. This finding, however, represents positive outcomes for the children and for the treatment program.

The CBCL appeared to be a useful instrument for tracking children's functioning in residential treatment. Some issues arose, however, in establishing accurate baselines or starting points from which to measure progress. Comparison of assessments done at admission with those conducted shortly afterward indicated that children displayed slightly less problem behavior initially than they did just prior to placement. Unfortunately, there was inconsistency among informants at the time of admission because of the variety of children's previous placements. When previous direct caregivers (such as parents and foster parents) were available, their CBCL assessments showed more deviancy for children than the assessments of placement case workers, most notably in Externalizing Problems. Had the intake baselines provided by previous caregivers been used, progress over time would have been significant for Externalizing Problems.

Because of the often haphazard manner in which children move through the children's services system, previous caregivers were not consistently available to complete the CBCL. It was not always possible to obtain a valid baseline of children's behavior prior to admission that represented the child's functioning at the time placement decisions were made. The most methodologically reliable baselines, consequently, were those provided by staff within the residential program, even though these assessments may have underestimated the frequency and severity of children's initial problems.

CBCL data are also useful in the analysis of child factors related to improvement and identification of program strengths and weaknesses. The analyses in this study, for example, showed that specific groups of children showed more improvement than others, a finding that corresponds with clinical intuition (that is, the sense that different treatment methods work better for different clients). CBCL scores in the area of Externalizing Problems showed that, despite baseline issues, children made no improvement during the 16-month study period. More detailed analyses, however, indicated that some children did demonstrate significant improvement. Although children in the 6–9 age group showed little progress in Externalizing Problems, children aged 10–12 did particularly well in this area. Such detailed information can assist program managers to develop hypotheses about why younger children may not respond to the treatment model in the desired way and to examine the developmental appropriateness of interventions.

When comparable data from programs that use alternative treatments are available, some of the mechanisms of therapeutic change can be illuminated. Agencies should look at outcomes in a nondefensive way, and rather than discounting negative results entirely (by blaming the assessment instruments, blaming the staff, or even worse, blaming clients for poor outcomes), they should adopt a more scientific attitude toward outcomes. Through identifying children who improve the least in residential treatment, agencies can develop effective treatment methods for clients with poor outcomes.

The present results suggest that demographic variables may account for about 10% of the variance in children's behavioral improvement. Age was the most consistent predictor, with younger children (under 10) displaying poorer outcomes in several areas. Clearly, developmental levels are important for treatment programming and provide the basis for many communities' avoidance of residential treatment for younger children. Gender and race/ethnicity, in general, had relatively weak effects compared to age, and these findings, in all likelihood, were not consistent enough to be reliable. The presence of negative outcomes on three CBCL scales for Latino children, however, is suggestive of cultural competency questions related to treatment and assessment. Are Latino children served equally well in the program compared to other children? Do staff complete the CBCL as well for Latino children? This study does not answer these questions. It does, however, suggest that if an applied research and evaluation study is to be useful to the agency in which it is conducted, the agency should identify the areas that need improvement and generate more specific questions.

Because this study was conducted within a single agency, its methodological limitations should be apparent. The number of subjects was relatively small, and the generalizability of findings to other agencies cannot be determined without closely comparing population and service characteristics. Also, treatment variations were neither introduced nor examined, and, as a result, it was not possible to link outcomes to specific interventions. This type of information would require cross-agency comparison or within-agency treatment variation. Further, although the longitudinal design employed in this study provided some useful findings, the unavailability of control/comparison samples does not permit the ruling out of obvious threats to validity of findings (such as maturation effects). The use of demographic comparisons, however, added some power to the design by providing information on differential progress of various client groups. Although these kinds of methodological limitations plague most agency-based research, they should not discourage programs from measuring outcomes, distinguishing between good and poor outcomes, identifying the characteristics of children associated with different outcomes, and attempting to use findings to improve effectiveness.

Conclusion

This study, conducted in a children's residential treatment center, was designed to respond to some of the current questions about the efficacy of residential treatment for children with emotional/behavioral problems. Utilizing a sample of 68 boys and girls aged 6–12, it evaluated behavioral progress over time as measured by the Child Behavior Checklist (CBCL). Results indicated that children as a whole made significant progress in several areas, including Total Internalizing Problems, Attention Problems, Anxiety/Depression and School Competency. Relationships between demographic variables and progress were also examined to determine if certain groups of children demonstrated greater progress than others. Results of multivariate analyses showed that, after children's initial levels of functioning were taken into account, demographic variables accounted for about 10% of additional variance in treatment progress. The strongest findings related to child age, where it was noted that older children (ages 10–12 at admission) showed greater improvement in Total Problems and Total Externalizing Problems than did children between the ages 6 and 9.

This study illustrates the value of applied evaluation research and the use of the CBCL in treatment planning and program improvement. For agencies providing services to children and families, evidence should be collected on the outcomes of their services. The field needs facts—not rhetoric—about the appropriateness of alternatives such as residential treatment, foster care, and community-based services. Outcome measures, compared across service categories, can help define the best fit between clients and programs. Soundly-developed measures such as the CBCL and other instruments provide important tools for outcome-based planning.

References

Achenbach, T.M. (1991). *Manual for the Child Behavior Checklist/4-18 and 1991 Profile.* Burlington: University of Vermont, Department of Psychiatry.

Bates, B.C., English, D.J., & Kouidou-Giles, S. (1997). Residential treatment and its alternatives: A review of the literature. *Child & Youth Care Forum, 26*(1), 7–51.

Berrick, J.D. (1993). Group care for children in California: Trends in the '90s. *Child & Youth Care Forum, 22*(1), 7–22.

California Association of Services for Children (1995). *CSC outcome measure system question booklet.* Sacramento: California Association of Services for Children.

Carlo, P., & Shennum, W.A. (1989). Family reunification efforts that work: A three year follow-up study of children in residential treatment. *Child and Adolescent Social Work, 6* (3), 211–216.

Curry, J.F. (1995). The current status of research in residential treatment. *Residential Treatment for Children & Youth, 12*(3), 1–17.

Digre, P. & Rubenstein, B. (1996). *Los Angeles County Department of Children and Family Services Statistical and Community Development Report.* Los Angeles: Department of Children and Family Services.

Duchnowski, A.J., Johnson, M.K., Hall, K.S., Kutash, K., & Friedman, R.M. (1993). The alternatives to residential treatment study: Initial findings. *Journal of Emotional and Behavioral Disorders, 1*(1), 17–26.

McDonald, T.P., Allen, R.I., Westerfelt, A., & Piliavin, I. (1996). *Assessing the long term effects of foster care: A research synthesis.* Washington DC: Child Welfare League of America Press.

McKenzie, R.B. (1997). Orphanage alumni: How they have done and how they evaluate their experience. *Child & Youth Care Forum, 26* (2), 87–111.

Pecora, P.J., Seelig, W.R., Zirps, F.A. & Davis, S.M. (Eds.). (1996). *Quality Improvement and Evaluation in Child and Family Services.* Washington, DC: CWLA Press.

Pedhazur, E.J. (1973). *Multiple Regression in Behavioral Research: Explanation and prediction* (2nd ed.). New York: Holt, Rinehart & Winston.

Pfeiffer, S.I., & Strzelecki, S.C. (1990). Inpatient psychiatric treatment of children and adolescents: A review of outcome studies. *Journal of the American Academy of Child and Adolescent Psychiatry, 29,* 847–853.

Shennum, W.A., & Carlo, P. (1995). A look at residential treatment from a child's point of view. *Residential Treatment for Children and Youth, 12*(3), 31–44.

United States General Accounting Office. (1994). *Residential Care: Some high-risk youth benefit, but more study needed* (GAO/HEHS Publication No. 94-56). Washington, DC: United States General Accounting Office, Health, Education and Human Services Division.

Wechsler, D. (1992). *Wechsler Intelligence Scale for Children-third Edition.* San Antonio, TX: Psychological Corporation.

5

Use of the Achenbach Child Behavior Checklist in a Longitudinal Study of Treatment Foster Care Outcomes

Mark E. Courtney and Andrew Zinn

Introduction

This chapter reports selected early results of the PATH Outcomes Study. This study is a longitudinal investigation of treatment foster care (TFC) services provided by the Professional Association of Treatment Homes (PATH), a private not-for-profit agency that operates foster homes in several Midwestern states. This chapter focuses on the use of the Achenbach Child Behavior Checklist (CBCL) (Achenbach 1991a) and examines:

- the association between CBCL scores reported by foster parents and subsequent discharge outcomes for youth in PATH care; and

- the relationship between CBCL scores reported by foster parents and Youth Self-Report (YSR) scores reported by a subset of youth in the PATH Outcomes Study (Achenbach, 1991b).

Early results provide support for the utility of the CBCL in longitudinal TFC research. Treatment foster care (also referred to as therapeutic foster care, foster family based treatment, and specialized foster care) has been promoted in recent years as a beneficial placement for children in the child welfare system who formerly may have been sent to group care facilities such as group homes or residential treatment centers (Hudson & Galaway 1989). By and large, these children and youth are abused, neglected, or delinquent and have been placed out of their homes by court order. TFC is one way for the child welfare system to provide mental health and other intensive social services to children in out-of-home care. Indeed, a recent review of research on TFC described it as a "service for meeting the needs of children and adolescents with serious emotional and behavioral disturbances and their families" (Meadowcroft et al. 1994, p. 565).

Surveys of TFC programs, the majority of which are administered by private, nonprofit agencies, reveal several key features (Hudson, et al. 1994). Foster parents working in TFC function as professional members of a treatment team. They are provided significantly more training and are compensated at higher rates than traditional foster parents. In addition and in contrast to traditional foster family care, the number of children placed in a given home is low, typically one or two. Caseloads tend to be smaller for TFC social workers (usually about 10 children per worker), and it is possible to give more attention to each case.

TFC is gaining acceptability as an alternative to group care placement for troubled youth. TFC is believed to be a more "normalizing" experience for troubled youth since they are placed in a "family-like" setting as opposed to an institutional environment (Hudson & Galaway 1989). This approach is consistent with the Adoption Assistance and Child Welfare Act of 1980 (P.L. 96-272), which mandates the "least restrictive" placement for youth in out-of-home care. Evidence suggests that TFC serves as an effective alternative to psychiatric hospitalization (Chamberlain & Reid 1991), residential treatment (Colton 1988), and correctional institutions (Chamberlain 1990). Moreover, the cost of TFC is far less than virtually all forms of group care, though it is more expensive than traditional foster family care. TFC is a rapidly growing sector of the child welfare system. A survey of 321 TFC programs operating in Canada and the United States found that most programs were relatively new, with 88% having been established since 1989 (Hudson et al. 1994).

Although there is excitement among providers regarding the value of TFC for children and families, the empirical literature on the outcomes of these programs is limited (Meadowcroft et al. 1994). In addition to the handful of experimental studies that show that TFC compares favorably with institutional care, several nonexperimental and quasi-experimental evaluations of TFC have demonstrated positive outcomes for children placed in such settings (Bogart 1988; Colton 1988; Hazel 1989; Fanshel et al. 1990). Yet, the gaps in knowledge about TFC are many and large (Hudson et al. 1994; Meadowcroft et al. 1994). Specifically, researchers and practitioners seek more information about which youth seem to fare best (or worst) in TFC, and which services and levels of service relate to program outcomes (Meadowcroft, et al. 1994).

This chapter analyzes data collected on 259 children whose progress is being followed by the PATH Outcomes Study. These children were placed in PATH care by child welfare and probation agencies between October 1995 and April 1997. All of the children experienced at least 3 months of PATH care and some had lived in PATH care for over 18 months. The first set of analyses concerns the correlates of discharge outcomes for 259 of the children. The second set of analyses compares CBCL and YSR scores for 148 of the children for whom paired data from these instruments were available. Each of these analyses is described below.

The PATH Outcomes Study

PATH has been in operation for over 25 years, making it one of the oldest TFC agencies in North America (Galaway 1978). PATH is relatively unique in that it was founded and continues to be governed predominantly by foster parents. As one of the largest TFC agencies, it operates more than 300 homes caring for over 500 children.

The PATH Outcomes Study was designed to examine changes in youths' status (e.g., behavior change, placement stability, and permanency outcomes) over a two-year period. The study involves 380 youth between the ages of 11 and 17 who entered PATH care in Minnesota and Wisconsin between October 1995 and August 1997. Youth became eligible for inclusion in the study if they had been in PATH care for 3 months. Although the results are not included in this report, data collection continued for this study through December 1999. A minimum of two years of follow-up data ultimately will be available on all youth, with youths' progress followed until discharge from the program or the completion of data collection.

Outcomes of interest in this study included behavior change in the children over time and various discharge outcomes of TFC (i.e., return home, placement in a more or less restrictive environment, running away from care, adoption, and emancipation to independent living). The study was designed to explore the degree to which these phenomena are affected by (a) characteristics of the child (e.g., age, gender, race/ethnicity, maltreatment history, disabilities, out-of-home care history, and behavior problems) prior to and during care; (b) characteristics of the child's family of origin (e.g., family structure, parental strengths and problems, and involvement of the parent(s) in the youth's treatment); (c) characteristics of the treatment foster home and agency environment (e.g., the education and experience of PATH foster parents and social workers, parenting style of foster parents, and number of children in the foster home); and (d) mental health and social services received by the child and family while the child is in PATH care. PATH hopes that the study ultimately will help the agency develop an efficient means of assessing agency practice and child and family outcomes on an ongoing basis.

There were several reasons for using the age range of 11–17 years in this study. The age range was intended to reduce the heterogeneity that would be introduced by including children younger than 11 years. The age range also acknowledged the different developmental tasks facing youth as they enter adolescence. Nationwide, the majority of children in TFC are 11–17 years old (Meadowcroft et al. 1994), and over 70% of PATH children were also in this age range. In addition, a single behavioral measure could be used with children in the imposed age range.

Children discharged from PATH before the 3-month mark—about 25%—were excluded from the study because personnel, including foster parents, generally were not in a position to know much about the youth in their care until they had spent a minimum of several weeks in the home (Urquiza et al. 1994). Instead, the study was limited to children who had remained in TFC long enough to "settle in" to their new homes, or, at least, had experienced a long "honeymoon" period. The identification of these children was facilitated by the PATH practice of convening a meeting of each child's treatment planning team at quarterly intervals after placement. The team for each child included some or all of the following: the youth, the referring social worker, PATH social worker, foster family, members of the youth's family of origin, therapist, school personnel, and medical personnel.

These meetings and the preparation leading up to the meetings provided PATH social workers with valuable information about a youth and the youth's family.

Data collected for the study came from PATH agency records and quarterly surveys completed by agency social workers and foster parents. Foster parents completed the CBCL as part of their quarterly survey. The primary advantage of using foster parents and social workers as sources of data is that they are the primary agents of treatment in the TFC environment. Foster parents, by virtue of their parenting role, are in the best position to comment on the characteristics and progress of children in their care. Beginning in May 1997, children in the study were invited to complete the YSR at the same time that foster parents completed their surveys and CBCLs.

A Competing-Risks Model of Exit from PATH Care

The PATH Outcomes Study examined change over time across several areas of child functioning. A particular outcome of interest was the transition out of PATH care. Which youth leave PATH care via "successful" exits through moves to a "less restrictive" or more permanent environment (such as home, kinship foster care, or nontreatment foster care)? Which youth experience "unsuccessful" exits through moves to a more restrictive environment (such as group care, incarceration, or psychiatric hospitalization) or running away from PATH? Which youth remain in long-term care? A competing-risks event-history analysis of the timing of discharge outcomes for the 259 children was conducted to explore these questions.

Successful and unsuccessful exits were clearly defined. Successful discharge outcomes were defined as discharge to the care of a parent, relative, or legal guardian ($n = 76$) or placement in a nontreatment foster home ($n = 3$). Unsuccessful outcomes were defined as discharge to another TFC home ($n = 5$), group home ($n = 18$), residential treatment center ($n = 4$), psychiatric hospital ($n = 2$), jail ($n = 7$), or other institution ($n = 5$), or running away from PATH care ($n = 15$). Nine youth were discharged to independent living, an exit that was treated as neither successful nor unsuccessful for the purposes of this study. Thus, of the overall sample of 259 children, 31% (79) experienced successful discharge outcomes, 22% (56) experienced unsuccessful outcomes, 4% (9) were emancipated, and 44% (115) remained in PATH care at the time of analysis.

This study relied on a competing-risk regression model of the hazard of exit from PATH care. Successful and unsuccessful exits were "competing" in the sense that children were considered to be "at risk" of each type of exit while they were in care, but they could experience only one type of exit. Intuitively, a hazard function can be thought of as the likelihood that something will happen (e.g., a youth will exit TFC placement) at any given point in time. The model estimated here shows the average effect over time of independent variables on the relative odds that a youth will experience, on the one hand, a successful exit from PATH care, or, on the other hand, an unsuccessful exit. Variables can increase the odds of both types of exits, decrease the odds of both types of exits, or increase the likelihood of one type of exit while decreasing the likelihood of the other.

The statistical model used in this study has the ability to make use of "censored" observations (Cox 1972; Yamaguchi 1991). Observations of children who did not exit PATH care by the end of July 1997 are censored in the sense that it is not known when they will leave PATH care. Leaving these observations out of the analysis would represent an enormous loss of information since nearly one-half of the sample did not exit care during the study period. The event histories of youth who were emancipated to independent living were also treated as censored at the point of exit because this transition out of PATH care is as much a function of a youth's age as a sign of successful or unsuccessful placement. For each of the two types of exits, data on youth who experience another type of exit are treated as censored at that point since the youth is no longer at risk of the exit of interest. In hazard rate regression models, subjects are generally considered "at risk" of an event until they either experience the event or are censored. This approach enables the researcher to construct unbiased estimates of the proportion of subjects remaining in a particular state at various points in time after having entered the initial state and to construct unbiased estimates of the effects of independent variables on the likelihood that subjects will exit the initial state (e.g., living in a PATH foster home).

In addition to CBCL internalizing and externalizing T scores, child characteristics included the youth's age at entry into care, gender, race/ethnicity, the number of distinct out-of-home care placements the youth had prior to entering PATH care, whether the youth had lived in a group care setting at any time prior to PATH, whether the child had run away, the primary reason for the youth's placement in out-of-home care, and the youth's permanency plan (see Table 5-1). Parental characteristics included the parents' marital status and the social worker's assessment of the level of parental involvement with the child since placement with PATH. Foster home characteristics included the total number of children living in the home (both foster and nonfoster children) and the total number of years of fostering experience of the foster parent. The independent variables were chosen because of their significance in previous foster care research and served as control variables for assessing the relationship between CBCL scores and exits from PATH. Independent variables were assessed at about the time of the first quarterly review done of the child's progress since intake to PATH care. Although findings with respect to all of the independent variables will be presented below, the discussion of findings will be restricted to the relationship between CBCL scores and exits from PATH care.

Findings

In general, PATH children exhibited a higher than normal level of behavioral disturbance as reported by their foster parents. Approximately 27% ($n = 71$) of children in this sample scored in the borderline-clinical range or higher on the Total Problems score of the CBCL. Slightly fewer (20%, $n = 53$) scored in the borderline-clinical range or higher on the Internalizing scale and just over 30% ($n = 78$) scored in the borderline-clinical range or higher on the Externalizing scale.

Table 5-2 shows the hazard ratio coefficients for the Cox models of "successful" and "unsuccessful" exits from PATH care. Hazard ratios, rather than log-odds coefficients, are

Table 5-1. Descriptive Statistics on the PATH Outcomes Study Sample (*N* = 259)

VARIABLE	Mean	Standard Deviation
CBCL Internalizing score (at first quarterly report)	58.201	10.866
CBCL Externalizing score (at first quarterly report)	62.127	11.265
Child age in years at entry to care	15.100	1.540
Years experience as foster parent	10.503	7.636
Number of children living in foster home	2.903	2.186
Number of prior placements	3.259	3.174
Level of parental involvement with child	1.456	1.031

VARIABLE	Frequency	%
Child's race/ethnicity		
Caucasian	195	75%
African American	14	5%
Native American	19	7%
Other race/ethnicity	31	13%
Gender		
Male	155	60%
Female	104	40%
At least one institutional placement:		
Yes	132	51%
No	127	49%
At least one runaway episode:		
Yes	128	49%
No	131	51%
Primary placement reason		
Parental abuse or neglect	62	24%
Parent-child conflict	85	33%
Child crime or truancy	75	29%
Other reason	37	14%
Permanency Plan		
Reunification with family	161	62%
Long-term foster care	39	15%
Emancipation/independent living	36	14%
Parental characteristics		
Parents married and living together	53	20%
Parents divorced or separated	106	41%
Parents never married	31	12%
Missing data on parental relationship	69	27%

presented because the former are more intuitively appealing (see Table 5-2). A hazard ratio greater than one indicates a higher risk for exit while a ratio of less than one implies a lower risk. For a continuous variable, the hazard ratio shows the multiplicative change in the likelihood of a particular exit owing to a one-unit increase in the value of that variable. For example, each one-unit increase in the CBCL externalizing score increases the estimated overall likelihood of unsuccessful exit by approximately 4% or a factor of 1.04. For a categorical variable, the risk ratio corresponds to the multiplicative change in the rate of exit associated with a particular value of the variable relative to the comparison category for that variable (comparison categories are listed in Table 5-2). For example, having a permanency plan of long-term foster care lowered a child's estimated probability of successful exit from PATH care by nearly three-quarters (a factor of .227) compared to the rate experienced by children with a permanency plan of family reunification. It is possible for a variable to increase *both* the likelihood of successful and unsuccessful exit. A history of running away from care, for example, increased the likelihood of both forms of exit from care.

CBCL scores were not found to be associated with successful moves from PATH care. Three other variables, however, exhibited a statistically significant association with the likelihood of successful discharge. Youth who had a history of running away from home or previous foster placements were more likely than other youth to experience a successful discharge. Youth placed for "other reasons" were more likely to experience successful discharge than youth whose primary reason for placement was parental abuse or neglect. Not surprisingly, youth whose permanency plan was either long-term foster care or emancipation were much less likely to experience successful exits from care than children whose plan was family reunification.

A number of youth characteristics were associated with the estimated hazard of unsuccessful exit from PATH care. Relatively higher CBCL externalizing scores were associated with significantly higher risk of unsuccessful exit from care. A one-unit increase in this CBCL sub-score corresponded to a 4% increase in the hazard of unsuccessful discharge. Caucasian youth were much less likely than children of "other" race/ethnicity (predominantly Latinos and Southeast Asian Americans) to experience unsuccessful exits. Female youth were about half as likely as male youth to leave PATH to a more restrictive environment or to run away. A history of running away from home or foster care increased a child's odds of unsuccessful discharge. In comparison to placement for reasons of parental abuse and/or neglect, placement because of parent-child conflict or for "other" reasons increased the likelihood of unsuccessful discharge. Youth with a permanency plan of long-term foster care were much less likely to experience undesirable discharge outcomes than children with a permanency plan of family reunification. Finally, higher levels of parental involvement corresponded to a reduced likelihood of unsuccessful exits.

The most consistent finding concerning the relationship between CBCL Internalizing and Externalizing scores and exits from PATH care was the lack of any relationship between Internalizing scores and the timing of exits. The hazard ratios for Internalizing scores for both types of exits were very small and statistically insignificant. Even at the bivariate level, there

Table 5-2. Cox Model of the Competing Risks of "Successful" and "Unsuccessful" Exits from PATH Care (*N* = 259).

VARIABLE	"Successful" Moves (79 events, 180 censored) Hazard Ratio	"Unsuccessful" Moves (56 events, 203 censored) Hazard Ratio
CBCL Internalizing score	.996	.997
CBCL Externalizing score	.986	*1.042
Child demographic characteristics		
Age in years at entry to care	1.076	1.014
Caucasian	n.a.	n.a.
African American	.716	1.292
Native American	.978	.723
Other race/ethnicity	.579	*2.921
Male	n.a.	n.a.
Female	.917	*.487
Foster parent/home characteristics		
Years experience as foster parent	.994	1.031
Number of children living in foster home	.940	.958
Child's history prior to PATH care		
Number of prior placements	.968	1.029
At least one institutional placement	1.329	.998
At least one runaway episode	**2.248	**2.403
Placement due to parental abuse/neglect	n.a.	n.a.
Placement due to parent-child conflict	1.416	*3.204
Placement due to crime or truancy	.651	1.749
Placement for other reason	*2.762	**4.542
Permanency plan at quarterly review		
Permanency plan of family reunification	n.a.	n.a.
Permanency plan of long-term care	**.227	*.310
Permanency plan of emancipation	**.255	.470
Parents divorced or separated	.920	1.900
Parents never married	.389	2.302
Missing data on parental relationship	.936	.751
Level of parental involvement with child	1.098	*.703

*$p < .05$; **$p < .01$

was no discernable relationship between Internalizing scores and the estimated hazard of successful or unsuccessful exits.

In contrast, CBCL Externalizing scores were strongly associated with the estimated hazard of unsuccessful discharge. This relationship was robust, holding up in a multivariate event-history model that included several variables shown in other research to be associated with placement failure (e.g., a history of running away, placement instability, and/or institutional placement). A one-standard deviation increase in the observed CBCL Externalizing score raised the estimated hazard of unsuccessful exit by over 40%. Similarly, 32% of youth who scored in the borderline-clinical range or higher on the Externalizing score experienced unsuccessful exits as compared to only 17% of children with lower scores.

Comparison of CBCL and YSR Scores for Children in the PATH Outcomes Study

The original design of the PATH Outcomes Study called for collecting data from foster parents and social workers only. Foster parents, in particular, were to provide comprehensive and ongoing information about child behavior by completing the CBCL on a quarterly basis. Because foster parents serve as surrogate parents for children in out-of-home care, they seemed a reasonable alternative to parents for obtaining CBCL scores. Nonetheless, from the outset of the study, the research team and PATH was aware of the limited research on the use of the CBCL by foster parents. There were concerns that foster parents, because of their ongoing work with troubled children, may be desensitized to certain child behaviors to a greater degree than nonsurrogate parents; or alternatively, they may view the youth in their care as more disturbed than others would perceive them to be to be and may over-report certain behaviors. In particular, the researchers and some PATH staff were concerned that foster parents would be more attentive to externalizing behavior problems than internalizing problems since "acting out" youth can pose more of a problem for managing a foster home than withdrawn or depressed youths.

In order to gain a comparative view of the behavior of children in TFC, PATH requested in May 1997 that youth in the study complete the YSR on a quarterly basis at approximately the same time that foster parents completed the CBCL. All youth who were then a part of the study and all new entrants to the study were asked to complete YSRs until the study was completed or they exited from PATH care. The youths' participation was voluntary, and they were paid for their time in completing the YSR. The study generated 148 CBCL/YSR paired observations for 148 children at the time of data analysis for this chapter (see Table 5-3). These observations were made across a mix of quarters since some youth had been in the study for a relatively long period and others had just entered the study. Table 5-3 shows the correlations between CBCL and YSR scores, mean CBCL and YSR scores, and the estimated probabilities that these means differ by chance alone. The pattern of correlations between YSR and CBCL scores was striking, with the Externalizing scale and its associated syndrome scales exhibiting somewhat higher positive correlations than the Internalizing scale and syndromes. In fact, the observed difference between the CBCL/YSR correlation coefficients for the Internalizing and Externalizing scales was statistically significant ($p < .05$), indicating a greater agreement between PATH foster parents and foster youth regarding Externalizing behaviors than for Internalizing behaviors. This pattern of results—higher agreement between informants on the Externalizing than Internalizing items—is similar to that reported by Sawyer (1990) in a comparison of YSR and parent-generated CBCL scores for an Australian general population sample.

Mean YSR scores for the 148 youth were lower than CBCL scores reported by foster parents for every CBCL scale except the Somatic Problems scale. The mean differences in scores were large in some cases, approaching one-half of a standard deviation for some scales. All of the differences were statistically significant except for the Somatic Problems scale. Thus, in general, the youth in PATH care appeared to see themselves as less behaviorally disturbed relative to their peers than did their foster parents.

There are a number of possible explanations for the systematic differences between YSR and CBCL scores. The experience of foster parents in caring for troubled youth may make them more attentive than other parents to problem behavior. Alternatively, because treatment foster care is intended to be an alternative to institutional placement, treatment foster parents may feel the need to view their charges as more disturbed than they actually are. Foster youth may tend to downplay their problems out of concern that honest answers may lead to unwanted attention from their foster parents or social workers. Finally, the scoring system for the CBCL and YSR may have contributed to the difference between CBCL and YSR T scores. The CBCL and YSR require judgments by caregivers and youth about the frequency of problem behaviors, judgments that may be framed to some extent by one's understanding of how common a particular behavior is in the general population. Children who live with emotionally disturbed children in out-of-home care may not perceive that they engage in a particular behavior "often" when they compare themselves to their peers. Such skewed perspectives may lead to the type of results reported here. At any rate, further research is needed before any one of these explanations can be favored over another.

Conclusion

One of the primary purposes of the PATH Outcomes Study was to develop concise measurements of treatment process and outcome that can be used on an ongoing basis within the organization. Inclusion of the CBCL as a core element of the study reflected the hope that it would serve as a useful measure of child behavior change over time, as a predictor of other important changes in child status (such as discharge outcomes), and as a useful clinical assessment tool. The study also was designed to identify possible areas for program refinement with ethnic minority children, males, and children who enter care as a result of parent-child conflict.

The results to date of the study provide some support for the use of the CBCL in ongoing monitoring of well-being for youth in out-of-home care and for clinical purposes, but the support is not unequivocal. On the one hand, at least in the case of youth in PATH care, CBCL Externalizing scores served as a good indicator of the relative risk of unwanted placement

Table 5-3. Comparison of CBCL and YSR Scores[a]: Correlation Coefficients and Comparison of Means (*N* = 148)

CBCL Scale	r for YSR/CBCL	CBCL Mean Score	YSR Mean Score	$p > \Omega t \Omega$
Total Problems	**.35	61.17	55.40	.001
Internal	**.20	58.66	53.40	.014
External	**.47	61.71	56.75	.001
Withdrawn	.14	60.43	55.20	.01
Somatic Problems	**.28	54.39	55.22	.36
Anxious/Depressed	**.31	60.39	56.89	.01
Social Problems	**.32	60.77	56.17	.01
Thought Problems	**.25	59.57	55.28	.01
Attention Problems	**.36	61.58	56.93	.01
Delinquent Behavior	**.44	64.03	60.29	.01
Aggressive Behavior	**.46	60.24	56.99	.01

* *p* < .05, ** *p* < .01.

[a]These matched pairs of CBCL and YSR scores were collected across all quarters of the study period. Only the first paired observation per child was used for this analysis. T scores were used for all comparisons except for computing of correlation coefficients for scales where raw CBCL and YSR scores were used.

disruption. To the extent that this information can be used to anticipate problems for some youth in TFC, it may provide the basis for altering youth and family treatment plans to prevent such problems or to expedite the smooth transition of children to more appropriate placements. Based on analysis to date of PATH Outcomes Study data, CBCL Externalizing scores are being incorporated into a brief assessment tool that will be used by PATH social workers to help identify youth who are at high risk of unsuccessful discharge from PATH care. The expansion of the PATH sample to its full size and the collection of a minimum of two years of follow-up data should improve knowledge of the relationship between externalizing problem behaviors and case status outcomes, and, in the process, enhance the usefulness of the CBCL in assessment and treatment planning.

Some support for the use of the Externalizing scale of the CBCL in studying foster care outcomes also was provided by the analysis of paired YSR and CBCL reports on youth in the PATH study. Cross-informant correlations for the Externalizing syndrome scales ranged from .44 to .46 and the correlation across measures was .47 for the overall Externalizing scale. There appeared to be a moderately high level of agreement between PATH foster youth and their foster parents in the rank ordering of the Externalizing scale, even if the foster parents tended to view the youth as somewhat more disturbed relative to their peers than did the youth themselves. Still, use of both the CBCL and YSR for assessing Externalizing behavior problems would improve the likelihood of meeting the mental health needs of youth in TFC in a timely manner.

On the other hand, CBCL Internalizing scores were not found to be related in any way to the timing of exits from PATH care. Of course, this finding does not imply that CBCL Internalizing scores are of no use in predicting other important dimensions of foster youth well-being or for assessment purposes in foster care practice. CBCL scores are commonly used to assess youth functioning and, in that sense, may serve as important outcome measures in and of themselves. Currently, PATH social workers make use of Internalizing scores to identify youth who may need further mental health assessment or services. Still, this study offers no evidence that CBCL Internalizing scores have value in trying to predict discharge outcomes from TFC.

An additional concern about the use of CBCL Internalizing scores in assessing this population is the relatively low level of agreement between YSR and CBCL Internalizing scores. The CBCL alone may not serve as a very good measure of internalizing problem behaviors for these children. Indeed, analysis of pairs of CBCL and YSR forms completed during the study found several cases where a youth reported a high level of internal distress that, based on the CBCL, was completely unknown to the foster parents. In terms of social work practice, this finding suggests that, at minimum, social work assessment in TFC should rely on both foster parent and youth reports of the internalizing behavior problems of youth. In fact, as a result of comparison of CBCL and YSR scores during training sessions and case conferences, PATH has decided to make the YSR an integral part of ongoing assessment of youth. This step was taken in the hope that data from the YSR could help alert foster parents and social workers to potential problems of which they would not otherwise be aware. Further research is needed to help clarify the potential uses of the CBCL Internalizing scale in foster care practice and outcome research.

References

Achenbach, T.M. (1991a). *Manual for the Child Behavior Checklist/4-18 and the 1991 profile.* Burlington: University Associates in Psychiatry.

Achenbach, T.M. (1991b). *Manual for the Youth Self-Report and the 1991 profile.* Burlington: University Associates in Psychiatry.

Bogart, N. (1988). *A comparative study of behavioral adjustment between therapeutic and regular foster care in the treatment of child abuse and neglect.* Unpublished doctoral dissertation, Memphis State University, Memphis, TN.

Chamberlain, P. (1990). Comparative evaluation of specialized foster care for seriously delinquent youths: A first step. *Community Alternatives, 2*(2), 21–36.

Chamberlain, P. & Reid, J.B. (1991). Using a specialized foster care community treatment model for children and adolescents leaving the state mental hospital. *Journal of Community Psychology, 19*(3), 266–276.

Colton, M. (1990). Specialist foster family and residential child care practices. *Community Alternatives, 2*(2), 1–20.

Courtney, M.E., & Zinn, A. (1997). *The PATH outcomes study: Preliminary results.* Madison, School of Social Work, University of Wisconsin.

Cox, D.R. (1972). Regression models and life tables. *Journal of the Royal Statistical Society, 34,* 187-202.

Fanshel, D., Finch, S., & Grundy, J. (1990). *Foster children in a life course perspective.* New York: Columbia University Press.

Galaway, B. (1978). PATH: An agency operated by foster parents. *Child Welfare, 57,* 667–674.

Hazel, N. (1989). Adolescent fostering as a community resource. *Community Alternatives, 1,* (1), 1–10.

Hudson, J., & Galaway, B. (Eds.) (1989*). Specialist foster family care: A normalizing experience.* New York: Haworth Press

Hudson, J., Nutter, R.W., & Galaway, B. (1994). Treatment foster care programs: A review of evaluation research and suggested directions. *Social Work Research, 18,* 198–210.

Meadowcroft, P., Thomlison, B. & Chamberlain, P. (1994). Treatment foster care services: A research agenda for child welfare. *Child Welfare, 73,* 565–581.

Sawyer, M.G. (1990). *Childhood behavior problems: Discrepancies between reports from children, parents, and teachers.* Unpublished Ph.D. dissertation. University of Adelaide, Australia.

Urquiza, A.J., Wirtz, S.J., Peterson, M.S., & Singer, V.A. (1994). Screening and evaluating abused and neglected children entering protective custody. *Child Welfare, 73,* 15–171.

Yamaguchi, K. (1991). *Event history analysis.* Newbury Park, CA: Sage Publications.

6

Follow-Up of Youth Returned to Home After Treatment in Residential Care

David B. Hickel

Introduction: The Agency Setting

The Sycamores, officially known as the Pasadena Children's Training Society, was established as an orphanage in 1902 and was the first children's home in the city. At the time of its founding, The Sycamores served both boys and girls. "Door-step" babies filled many pages of the admission books in the early days, with the infants' ages estimated by pediatricians if no notes containing such information were pinned to the blankets. If no names were available for the infants, they were often given the surname of Wilson, after the street on the west end of the campus.

As child welfare changed, so did the focus of The Sycamores. In 1964, the agency moved to its current site just north of Pasadena and gradually became a residential treatment facility. Between 1963 and 1965, the agency began to serve only boys and during this period, the campus housed 36 boys, ages 6–14. Agency capacity continued to grow, and currently, the agency treats at any one time 60 seriously emotionally disturbed boys between the ages of 6 and 14.

During the late 1980s and early 1990s, the nonpublic school component of the agency grew to nine classrooms and incorporated a therapeutic day treatment program. In 1991, The Sycamores applied for and received a Rate Classification Level (RCL) 14 rating from the State of California, which allows the agency to provide residential treatment services to youth who meet the following criteria:

- As a result of a mental disorder, the youth demonstrates substantial impairment in at least two of the following areas: self care; school functioning; family relationships; and community functioning; and either (a) the youth has been placed, or is expected to be placed, out of home; or (b) the mental disorder has been present for more than 6 months;

- The youth meets special education eligibility requirements; and

- The youth has received the current diagnosis within the past year.

The Sycamores implemented a strategic plan in the early 1990s that called for the development of a continuum of services for children. Plans were implemented to develop two to four additional group homes in the community; a Community Non-Public School/Day Treatment program; wraparound services; and foster family services. The Sycamores currently has over 200 employees and serves over 110 youth and families.

Approximately 10 years ago, the agency integrated cognitive behavioral therapy into all programs offered to youths. The agency trained teachers, clinicians, and milieu staff in cognitive behavioral techniques; applied cognitive behavioral techniques to family therapy; and educated families in the underlying principles of cognitive behavioral therapy. Youth and families were taught techniques that included problem identification and solving, self talk, thought stopping, cognitive imagery, cognitive planning such as "goal, plan, do, check" and "stop, think, and choose" (Meichenbaum 1989), and cognitive reframing of traumatic experiences. As youth, parents, child-care staff, teachers, and clinicians became more fluent in cognitive therapy, they received instruction in other techniques.

Following the implementation of cognitive behavioral therapy, the agency focused on an assessment of the efficacy of the treatment and the extent to which families were able to generalize the techniques in their home environments. The literature suggested that cognitive behavioral treatment was effective (Meichenbaum, 1989), but there was no research on the use of the treatment in out-of-home care nor research in agencies that utilized a wholly integrated approach. The Sycamores, consequently, began tracking some of the youth treated by the agency through the course of treatment and after they left the agency's care.

Method

The literature on child psychotherapy and treatment is vast and varied in form. Many of these written accounts laud the effects of particular methods of child therapy, although generally with no supporting data. Kazdin (1988) noted that of the 230-plus different forms of therapy used with youth, the great majority had not been evaluated empirically. The studies that have utilized an empirical approach have typically used one of three methods (Weisz & Weiss 1993). The first method involves the use of control groups and compares a treated sample of youth with a nontreated sample; the second method involves multiple treatment groups and compares the effectiveness of one treatment to another; and the third method includes only one group of youth, all of whom receive treatment. The third method, often used to evaluate the relative effectiveness of treatment, attempts to determine whether the group experienced any improvement and uses a case study approach. This study utilized this third method through a within-subjects repeated measures design and attempted to determine whether cognitive behavioral treatment in a residential setting was effective and if treatment generalized after the youth returned home.

The Child Behavior Checklist (CBCL) (Achenbach 1991) was chosen as an evaluation tool. The CBCL was used with two other related instruments, the Teacher's Report Form and

Youth Self Report, and consequently, multiple sources of data provided information on a youth's behavioral and emotional problems. The CBCL provides empirically derived and standardized information that is useful in treatment planning and goal setting, a particularly important benefit in cognitive behavioral treatment.

Profiles from the CBCL include eight syndrome constructs (Achenbach 1991). In addition, groupings are formed on two derived constructs of Internalizing and Externalizing behaviors as well as a Total Problem score. Raw scale scores and T scores based on national norms are produced for each of the syndrome scales and the Externalizing, Internalizing, and Total Problems scales. When making comparisons of youth in differing age samples, it is recommended that T scores be used (Achenbach 1991).

When using the CBCL, family involvement is an important consideration to ensure reliable and consistent informants who can provide preadmission-admission, discharge, and follow-Up data. In this study, 19 male youth with intact families (the total number of youth in the client pool who had consistent family involvement) were followed. In general, one-third of The Sycamores client population has consistent family involvement; a third has sporadic involvement; and another third has no involvement with family. The 19 boys in the study ranged in age from 6 to 13 at admission. By the end of follow-up data collection, 10 of the 19 boys had completed profiles that included admission, discharge, and follow-up information. Of those 10 boys, 7 had at least one birthparent, 2 were living in a relative's home, and 1 was living in a foster home. Ethnically, 2 were Latino, 3 were African American, and 5 were Caucasian. At the time of discharge from the agency, the boys' mean age was 11.4 years, with a range from 8.0 years to 14.1 years. The mean length of stay for these boys was 16.0 months, with a range of 11.2 to 20.2 months.

The parents were asked to complete the CBCL at intake, discharge, and approximately three months postdischarge. The 10 boys and their families received treatment from a team of professionals that included a therapist (masters level and above), psychiatrist, teacher, and cottage child care staff. Treatment included regular weekend and holiday home visits by the youth with their families. The purpose was to maintain strong familial involvement and the families were to practice the cognitive behavioral techniques they were learning in family therapy. At follow-up, all youth continued to live in their homes. Comparisons of the three separate time periods on the Externalizing, Internalizing and Total Problems Scales were done in a repeated measures using the Analysis of Variance design (ANOVA). To isolate the group or groups that differ from the others, a multiple comparison procedure (Tukey test) was used.

To provide more information regarding the subjects' level of functioning, clinicians completed for each boy the Global Assessment of Functioning (GAF) (American Psychiatric Association 1994) at intake and discharge. The GAF scale, which assumes that psychological, social, and occupational functioning is on a hypothetical continuum of mental health to mental illness, rates overall psychological functioning on a scale of 0 to 100. The higher the GAF rating, the better the individual's level of functioning. At follow-up, parents were introduced to the GAF scale and asked to rate their youth.

Results

Achenbach (1991) recommends that T scores of 60 be used as a demarcation point between clinical and normal samples on the Total Problem Scale. For the 10 boys at admission, the mean Total Problem Scale T score was 72.2 (see Figure 6-1). By discharge, all but 3 boys' scores were below the clinical cutoff, and the mean Total T score was 62.2 (see Figure 6-1). At the 3 month follow-up, the Total T score mean had risen slightly to 63 with slightly more scatter among the individual scores (5 boys were above 60). Both Internalizing and Externalizing T scores showed a similar pattern (see Figure 6-1).

Some differences in Total Problem T scores between measurements (treatments) were significant ($p < .01$; Table 1). Follow-up comparisons indicated that there were significant differences among the endorsed behavioral and emotional problems indicated by the Total T scores between Intake and Discharge and Intake and Follow-Up. There was no significant difference between Discharge and Follow-Up.

Some differences in Externalizing T scores between measurements (treatments) were also significant ($p < .05$; Table 1). Follow-Up comparisons indicated that there was a significant difference between Intake and Discharge but not between Intake and Follow-Up or between Discharge and Follow-Up.

Some differences in Internalizing T scores between measurements (treatments) were also significant ($p < .05$; Table 1). Follow-Up comparisons indicated that this significance was not maintained when comparing individual measurement periods. When Intake was compared with Discharge, Intake with Follow-Up, and Discharge with Follow-Up, significance was not maintained. This result suggests that although there seemed to be an overall change or improvement in functioning, it was much less dramatic than the effect of treatment on the externalizing behaviors.

GAF scores at intake were in the 40s and 50s, rose to the 60s at Discharge, and were in the 70s at Follow-Up (see Figure 6-2). A separate Paired-Sample T test analysis of GAF scores revealed that there were no significant differences between Intake and Discharge or Discharge and Follow-up. There was a significant difference between Intake and Follow-up (see Table 6-2).

Discussion

Behaviors and symptoms, as measured by the CBCL Total Problems scale, improved significantly by discharge and had not changed at the 3-month follow-up. This finding suggests that treatment was successful and that treatment gains "held" for at least the following 3-month period. Such a result is surprising given the small sample size, but it is balanced by the fact that a 3-month period is a fairly short period of time. The outcomes would have more impact if follow-up had been repeated at 6 and 12 months.

Analysis of the Externalizing scales suggested that behavior improved significantly by

Figure 6-1. Mean Direction of Change for All Subjects: Child Behavior Checklist Total Problems, Internalizing, and Externalizing T Scores

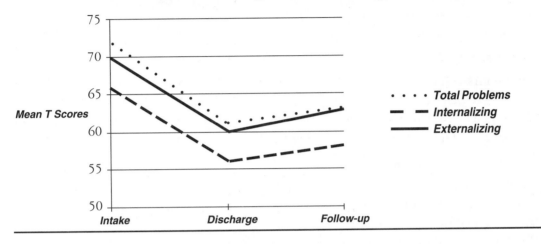

discharge and did not worsen significantly by the end of the 3 months. Lack of a strong significant difference among the Internalizing scores indicated that treatment was most effective with behaviors that were readily observable. The lack of significant difference between Intake and Follow-Up scores on the Externalizing scale alludes to a slight trend for the Externalizing scores to return to pre-treatment levels.

Rising GAF scores lend support to the improvement found in the CBCL scores. These GAF scores are intended to give an estimate of overall level of functioning, and hopefully these scores will improve as treatment progresses (it is an expected outcome of treatment that GAF scores rise as the benefits of treatment become more apparent). The fact that GAF scores continued to rise after the boys had left the agency may, in part, be explained by having a nonclinically trained person evaluate the youth's level of functioning as nonclinical observers may overrate progress.

Conclusion

It is important for residential treatment agencies to evaluate their methods and approaches to treating children placed in their care The data collected and analyzed in this study show that the effectiveness of such programs can be evaluated. Although this small study is by no means conclusive, it does suggest that evaluation is possible with a small investment in time and money. The data gathered in the study were useful to The Sycamores treatment staff because the data helped them recognize that they were doing excellent work with regard to the behaviors readily observed by others (such as externalizing behaviors) but that they needed

Table 6-1. ANOVA Comparison

Total T Scores   **p < .05**

Between Assessments	Yes	$p = .004$
Intake vs. Discharge (Tukey)	Yes	
Intake vs. Follow-Up (Tukey)	Yes	
Discharge vs. Follow-Up (Tukey)	No	

Externalizing T Scores

Between Assessments	Yes	$p = .018$
Intake vs. Discharge (Tukey)	Yes	
Intake vs. Follow-Up (Tukey)	No	
Discharge vs. Follow-Up (Tukey)	No	

Internalizing T Scores

Between Assessments	Yes	$p = .049$
Intake vs. Discharge (Tukey)	No	
Intake vs. Follow-Up (Tukey)	No	
Discharge vs. Follow-Up (Tukey)	No	

Figure 6-2. Mean Direction of Change for all Subjects: GAF Scores

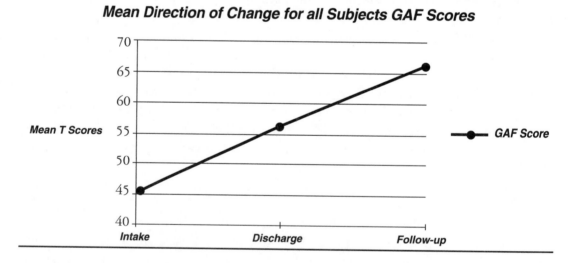

Mean Direction of Change for all Subjects GAF Scores

Table 6-2. Paired Sample T test Comparison of Intake, Discharge, and Follow-Up GAF Scores

	Discharge	*Follow-Up*
Intake	p = .007	p = .004
Discharge		p = .034

to put forth more effort on youths' internal problems. Staff could develop new goals, based on decreasing items or symptoms identified on the Internalizing scales and maintaining the treatment gains as measured by the Externalizing scales.

Further refinements of this outcome evaluation are needed. Specifically, in further studies, families should be more involved in completing the Child Behavior Checklist; other measures should be included; children should be followed for longer periods of time after they leave the agency; tools should be utilized to evaluate specific treatment strategies; and control groups should be used.

References

Achenbach, T.M. (1991). *Manual for the Child Behavior Checklist/4-18 and 1991 profile.* Burlington: University of Vermont Department of Psychiatry.

American Psychiatric Association. (1994). *Diagnostic and statistical manual of mental disorders* (4th ed.). Washington, DC: Author.

Kazdin, A.E. (1988). *Child psychotherapy: Developing and identifying effective treatments.* Elmsford, NY: Pergammon.

Meichenbaum, D. (1989, June 7). Paper presented for discussion to staff at The Sycamores, Altadena, CA. On file with The Sycamores. (?)

Weisz, J.R., & Weiss, B. (1993). Assessing the effects of clinic-based psychotherapy with children and adolescents. *Journal of Consulting and Clinical Psychology, 57*(6), 741–746.

7

Children Born to Drug-Using Mothers: A Longitudinal Perspective on Maternal Care and Child Adjustment

Sydney Hans, Victor Bernstein, and Linda Henson

Children born to women who abuse drugs during pregnancy are widely believed to be at developmental risk. Most scientific research on offspring of substance-abusing women has focused on the possible teratological effects of prenatal drug exposure on children's physical health and neurobehavioral development. In contrast, public policy related to drug-using parents has largely focused on the possible detrimental effects on parenting when substance abuse is present. Policy often has presumed that parental substance abuse, in and of itself, is evidence of a parent's unfitness to raise a child, with the implementation of initiatives such as mandatory referral of drug-exposed neonates to child protective services (see Besharov 1994; Hawley & Disney 1992; English 1990). Yet, data on the quality and continuity of care that children receive from their substance-abusing parents remain limited, and data on how such care affects child outcomes are even more limited.

A growing literature suggests that drug-exposed children are more likely than other young people to experience disruptions in parental care and to be raised by nonmaternal caregivers. A number of sources have reported an increase in American children raised by grandparents during the 1980s, with parental substance abuse emerging as the primary reason for grandparents assuming care (Burton 1992; Burton & Dilworth-Anderson 1991; Minkler et al. 1992; Minkler et al. 1994). In most urban settings, a majority of young children in foster care placement have a birthparent involved with drugs (Simms 1991; Wulczyn 1994; Barth et al. 1994). Among children who have already entered the child welfare system, those with drug-abusing parents appear to have less connection to their parents. Fanshel (1975), for example, reported that among New York City children in foster care, those with addicted mothers entered the system at younger ages, were more likely to become "locked into" the foster care system, and if they left the system, were more likely than other children to be discharged to persons other than their mothers.

Studies of substance-abusing women have found that a high proportion of their children experienced disruptions in maternal care. Studying 178 pregnant women enrolled in a methadone maintenance program, Regan and associates (1987) found that 40% of the women had at least one child in foster care or placed with relatives. Prospective data on the caregiving experiences of children with histories of prenatal drug exposure also suggest frequent changes in caregivers. Rodning and colleagues (1991), for example, followed a sample of 46 infants identified at birth as prenatally exposed to PCP and cocaine. By the time the children were 15 months of age, 20 children were in the regular daily care of their birthmothers, 11 were in the care of extended family members without their mothers' involvement, and 7 were in nonkinship foster care. Of the 20 cared for by their mothers, 13 lived in multiple-family households. Fiks and colleagues (1985) followed from birth a sample of 57 children born to women in methadone treatment and found that only 75% of the methadone women were a primary caregiver of their child by the child's third birthday, compared to 91% of women in a non-drug-using comparison group. In a sample of 64 children born to untreated heroin addicts and women involved in methadone treatment, researchers (Wilson 1989; Lawson & Wilson 1980) found that a high percentage (36%) of the drug-involved women abandoned contact with their infants before their first birthdays, although these were predominantly women from the untreated heroin group. Wasserman and Leventhal (1993) found that during the first 24 months of life, 20% of a group of 47 children whose mothers were cocaine dependent had experienced changes in placement compared to 2% in a case-matched comparison group.

Although developmental theory would suggest that disruptions in care have a negative impact on child development, this issue has received only limited attention in research on children born to substance-abusing women (Bernstein & Hans 1994). This chapter examines the relationship between child behavior and continuity in maternal care over the first 10 years of life in a group of children born to opioid dependent women and a comparison group. Child behavior problems and competence were assessed using the Child Behavior Checklist (CBCL) (Achenbach 1991a) administered to children's primary caregivers and the Teacher Report Form (TRF) (Achenbach 1991b) administered to children's classroom teachers.

Method

Sample

Seventy-seven African American children (mean age = 10.0 years, range 8.9 years–11.8 years) participated in the 10-year follow-up of a longitudinal study begun in 1978 (for details on sample recruitment and retention see Jeremy & Hans 1985; Hans 1989; Bernstein & Hans 1994; Grattan & Hans 1996). Thirty-six of the children had a documented history of prenatal exposure to opioid drugs; 41 were not exposed to opioids prenatally. At the time of recruitment into the study during the mothers' pregnancies, all families were living in inner-city neighborhoods and were of low to very-low socioeconomic status. Siblings were included in the sample if mothers gave birth to more than one child during the period families were recruited for the sample.

Opioid Drug Group

The opioid-group families were recruited at an urban research hospital from a special high-risk obstetrical clinic for drug-abusing women. The women enrolled in the study were identified on clinic records as users of methadone and/or other opioid drugs; did not appear to have major mental disorder (such as schizophrenia) or to be mentally retarded; were between the ages of 18 and 35; and consented to participate in the research for a period of 2 years. The methadone-using women were all involved in low-dose methadone-maintenance programs. Most of the methadone-maintained women occasionally used other drugs in addition to methadone, most commonly heroin, marijuana, diazepam, and pentazocine, and less commonly, cocaine and alcohol. All but four of the opioid group mothers were enrolled in methadone treatment. The other women were users of "T's and Blues", a combination of Talwin and an antihistamine widely used by intravenous drug-users in Chicago in the early 1980's as an inexpensive substitute for heroin (Chasnoff et al. 1983; Schnoll et al. 1985). Forty opioid-using women were recruited for the sample. During the recruitment period, these women gave birth to 46 infants (including one set of twins and 5 non-twin sibling pairs). Data were available at middle childhood for 36 of the children.

Comparison Group

A comparison group was recruited at the same hospital from a prenatal clinic for low-income, medically low-risk mothers. Mothers were excluded from the comparison group if they showed evidence of ever having used opioid drugs, engaged in more than light consumption of alcohol, displayed symptoms of thought disorder, had mental retardation, or were not between the ages of 18 and 35 years. Fifty women were recruited for the comparison group. They gave birth to 54 infants (including one set of twins and 3 non-twin sibling pairs). Data were available at the middle-childhood assessment for 41 of the comparison children.

Procedure

Data in this study were derived from assessments conducted during three sessions when the children were approximately 10 years old. At that time, the children's mothers or other primary caregivers were interviewed about family matters, including custody and household composition arrangements. Among the instruments administered was the CBCL (Achenbach 1991a). The instrument was read aloud to caregivers except for those who requested they be allowed to complete it independently. Fully completed CBCL data were available for 74 children.[1] For 22 of the children, caregivers other than birthmothers acted as respondents. The children's classroom teachers were mailed the Teacher Report Form (TRF) (Achenbach 1991b) to complete. TRF data were available for 76 children.[2]

Results

Involvement with Mother Over Time

At the end of the first 2 years of life, only one of the 77 children in the sample was not in the daily care of his birth mother. That child, whose mother was using illicit drugs, was not in contact with his mother and was being raised by a paternal aunt. By age 10, however, a high proportion of the children were no longer residing with their birth mothers. This proportion was higher for the children whose mothers had used opioid drugs during pregnancy: 17 of the prenatally drug-exposed children (47%) were not being cared for by their mothers compared to only 8 (20%) of the comparison children ($X^2(1) = 6.71, p < .001$). Table 7-1 presents the numbers of children being raised by their mothers and by different combinations of caregivers.

Twenty-two of the 25 children who at age 10 were not living with their mothers were residing with family members. Of these, 9 were living with maternal family members and 13 with fathers or paternal kin. Whether children were living with maternal or paternal kin was unrelated to history of prenatal drug exposure, but did differ by sex of child ($X^2(2) = 3.32, p = .07$), with boys more likely than girls to live with paternal kin. Of the 12 girls in the sample living with kin other than mother, 5 (42%) were living with father or paternal kin, and 7 (58%) were living with maternal kin. Of the 10 boys living with kin other than mother, 8 (80%) were living with father or paternal kin, and only 2 (20%) were living with maternal kin.

For the vast majority of the 25 children not living with their mothers, families had made the custody arrangements. In a number of cases, the state was involved in legalizing the families' guardianship arrangements, but in only three cases were the children under public guardianship (one comparison group, two drug group children). The comparison group child was in residential treatment for emotional difficulties, and his mother's inability to parent him was the result of her own mental health problems. Of the two drug-group children under public guardianship, one resided with a non-kinship foster mother after her mother abandoned her to the care of others, and the second child was placed with a relative after being taken away from her mother because of neglect.

For the 25 children outside of their mothers' care at age 10, the mothers' lack of involvement was primarily attributable to an inability or unwillingness to care for their children because of ongoing or recurring drug use (including four children in the comparison group whose mothers became drug involved). Other reasons that children were not in their mothers' care were death of the mother (three women, with all of the causes related to drug use), family economic problems, and child medical problems requiring special care. Table 7-2 identifies the primary reasons children were not in the care of their birth mothers.

Children who did not live with their mothers had varying levels of contact with them. Eleven of the children had no ongoing contact with their mothers. These children had mothers either who had died or who had permanently abandoned them. Eight knew where their mothers were and had regular personal or phone contact with them. Six had sporadic, often disruptive contact with their mothers. For these children, the mothers were generally absent from their lives but would reappear at unpredictable intervals.

Some of the 52 children in the sample who resided with their mothers at age 10 had not lived with their mothers continuously throughout their lives. Children whose mothers used drugs during pregnancy were less likely to have been in the continuous care of their mothers throughout their lives ($X^2(1) = 11.78, p < .001$). For the 19 children of drug-using women who were in the care of their mothers at age 10, only 13 (68%) had been in the care of their mothers

Table 7-1. Residential Caregivers of Children at Age 10

	Comparison	*Drug*
Mother and Father	17	4
Mother and Maternal Kin	2	5
Mother Alone	14	10
Total with Mother	33	19
Other Maternal Kin	2	7
Father and Paternal Kin	4	3
Father Alone	0	4
Other Paternal Kin	1	1
Residential Treatment	1	0
Godmother	0	1
Non-Kin Foster Mother	0	1
Total without Mother	8	17

throughout their lives. These 13 children represented 36% of the entire sample of children whose mothers had used drugs during pregnancy. By contrast, 100% of the 33 comparison group children who were residing with their mother at age 10 had been in the care of their mothers throughout their lives.

Child Behavior Problems

Tables 7-3 and 7-4 report summary scores for the Problem Behavior and Competence sections of the CBCL (completed by the primary caregiver) and the TRF. Means are reported separately for children whose mothers used drugs during pregnancy and those whose mothers did not. Problem Behavior syndromes, because their t scores are truncated at the lower end, are reported as raw scores. Competence Scales (CBCL), Academic and Adaptive Functioning Scales (TRF), and Internalizing, Externalizing, and Total Problems scores (CBCL) are reported in terms of t scores standardized for sex and age of child. Probability levels for statistical analyses are reported for two-tailed tests with no adjustments made to protect for testing of multiple hypotheses. Significance levels were set a priori at $p < .05$, but because of the risk of Type II errors in this relatively small sample, analyses with p values $< .10$ are reported as trends.

The children in the sample showed considerable variability in their scores. Problem Behavior Scale scores, as reported by caregivers and teachers, did not differ greatly from those in the normative sample. Competence Scale scores, as reported by caregivers, and Academic and Adaptive Functioning scale scores, as reported by teachers, were lower than in the normative sample by about three-quarters of a standard deviation, with the lowest compe-

Table 7-2. Reasons for Mother Not Residing with Child at Age 10 Years

	Comparison	Drug
Mother's Death	0	3
Mother's Drug Involvement	4	12
Mother's Mental Disorder	1	0
Economic Issues	0	2
Child Special Needs/Problems	1	0
Unknown Circumstances	2	0
Total	8	17

tence t scores in terms of the academic scales (School scale on the CBCL and Academic Performance scale on the TRF).

T-tests were computed on each of the CBCL and TRF scores shown in Table 7-3 and 7-4. There were statistically significant differences between the prenatally exposed children and comparison children on only three summary scales. Caregivers reported drug-exposed children to have more sexual problems ($t(71) = 2.89$, $p < .01$), and teachers reported comparison children to be more withdrawn ($t(71) = 2.04$, $p < .05$) and to behave more appropriately in the classroom ($t(73) = 2.97$, $p < .01$).

Comparisons were made of CBCL and TRF scores between children who were living with their mothers at age 10 and children who were not, and between those who had been in the stable care of their mothers throughout life and those who had not. None of these comparisons revealed statistically significant differences or trends.

Comparisons were made of CBCL and TRF raw scores (unstandardized for sex) for boys and girls separately. Based on caregivers' reports on the CBCL, boys were less competent academically (boys' mean=4.2, SD=1.1; girls' mean=4.8, SD=0.9, $t(71)$=2.19, $p < .05$) and had more attention problems (boys' mean=4.6, SD=3.7; girls' mean=2.5, SD=2.9, $t(71)$=2.19, $p < .01$). There was a trend for boys to show more delinquent behavior (boys' mean=2.5, SD=2.8; girls' mean=1.4, SD=2.1, $t(71)$=1.81, p = .07). Based on teacher reports on the TRF, boys had more attention problems (boys' mean=16.4, SD=9.6; girls' mean=10.6, SD=10.0, $t(74)$=2.56, $p < .05$). There was a trend for boys to be less competent academically (boys' mean=2.1, SD=0.9; girls' mean=2.4, SD=0.7, $t(74)$=1.78, p = .08) and show less appropriate behavior at school (boys' mean 3.2, SD=1.70; girls' mean=3.9, SD=1.4, $t(74)$=1.88, p =.07).

The remaining analyses explored correlates of the Total Competence, Internalizing, Externalizing, and Total Problems scales from the two instruments. Table 7-5 presents the intercorrelations between these summary scores for the CBCL and TRF. The cross informant correlations were low for Competence/Adaptive Functioning (r =0.10) and Internalizing Behavior (r =.12), but moderately high for Total Problems (r =.37) and Externalizing Behavior (r =.47).

Table 7-3. CBCL Scores by Maternal Drug Use during Pregnancy

Primary Caregiver Report	Comparison Group Mean (*SD*)	Drug Group Mean (*SD*)	Comparison Group Clinical or Borderline Clinical	Drug Group Clinical or Borderline Clinical
	T score	*T score*	*% T score < 33*	*% T score < 33*
Activities	45.63 (5.47)	46.30 (7.61)	2%	9%
Social	43.34 (7.11)	42.52 (7.44)	2%	6%
School	43.84 (7.69)	40.97 (7.89)	11%	16%
Total Competence	43.68 (7.45)	41.66 (5.67)	3%	6%
	raw score	*raw score*	*% T score > 67*	*% T score > 67*
Withdrawn	2.27 (1.94)	2.15 (2.44)	2%	3%
Somatic Complaints	1.42 (1.36)	1.42 (1.46)	0%	3%
Anxious/Depressed	2.59 (2.42)	3.12 (3.79)	2%	9%
Social Problems	2.34 (2.05)	2.36 (2.30)	10%	9%
Thought Problems	0.56 (0.84)	0.94 (3.91)	2%	15%
Attention Problems	3.34 (3.28)	3.91 (3.43)	7%	12%
Delinquent Behavior	1.66 (2.25)	2.49 (2.82)	10%	18%
Aggressive Behavior	8.24 (6.16)	7.94 (6.12)	7%	3%
Sex Problems*	0.05 (0.22)	0.52 (1.18)	0%	12%
	T score	*T score*	*% T score > 67*	*% T score > 67*
Internalizing Score	51.27 (8.43)	51.09 (10.24)	5%	9%
Externalizing Score	50.88 (10.62)	51.88 (11.13)	7%	9%
Total Problems Score	51.56 (8.35)	52.15 (10.63)	2%	12%

* $p < .05$, two-tailed

Behavior of Children Not Living with Birthmothers

Further analyses examined whether for the 25 children not living with their mothers at age 10, CBCL and TRF scores were related to history of prenatal drug exposure, sex of child, or type of caregiving experience. Table 7-6 presents mean CBCL and TRF scores for these children grouped by other risk factors. Findings suggest that teacher reports of Internalizing ($t(19)=2.23, p < .05$), Externalizing ($t(19)=2.19, p < .05$), and Total Problems ($t(19)=2.0, p = .06$) were greater if children were living with paternal rather than maternal kin. These differences between children residing with paternal and maternal family remained significant

Table 7-4. TRF Scores by Maternal Drug Use during Pregnancy

Teacher Report Form Clinical	Comparison Group Mean (*SD*)	Drug Group Mean (*SD*)	Comparison Group Clinical or Borderline Clinical	Drug Group Clinical or Borderline
	T score	*T score*	*% T score < 40*	*% T score < 40*
Academic Performance	40.23 (6.62)	40.19 (6.07)	63%	59%
Working Hard	43.48 (8.45)	43.92 (8.10)	55%	50%
Behaving Appropriately*	46.60 (8.04)	41.60 (6.27)	25%	53%
Learning	43.10 (7.89)	43.71 (8.63)	40%	44%
Happy	46.56 (7.49)	45.38 (6.99)	21%	21%
Total Adaptive Functioning	43.23 (8.13)	42.18 (8.15)	43%	50%
	raw score	*raw score*	*% T score > 67*	*% T score > 67*
Withdrawn*	4.43 (4.49)	2.42 (2.74)	20%	6%
Somatic Complaints	1.23 (2.84)	0.81 (1.97)	10%	11%
Anxious/Depressed	6.28 (7.42)	4.28 (4.81)	20%	11%
Social Problems	3.88 (5.39)	3.33 (3.45)	20%	11%
Thought Problems	0.75 (1.34)	0.64 (1.31)	15%	6%
Attention Problems	14.33 (10.44)	13.03 (9.90)	15%	17%
Delinquent Behavior	2.40 (3.32)	2.39 (2.85)	18%	11%
Aggressive Behavior	9.70 (13.48)	11.72 (10.10)	20%	17%
	0.05 (0.22)	*T score*	*% T score > 67*	*% T score > 67*
Internalizing Score	57.85 (13.60)	52.89 (10.96)	25%	11%
Externalizing Score	54.98 (13.68)	59.33 (9.58)	20%	17%
Total Problems Score	57.90 (13.52)	58.08 (10.58)	25%	19%

* p < .05, two-tailed

even after controlling for the sex of the child. The data also suggested a trend for teacher reports of Internalizing ($t(23) = 1.75, p = .09$) and Total Problems ($t(23) = 1.96, p = .06$) to be lower for those children who no longer had contact with their birth mothers.

Discussion

Data from this prospective longitudinal study of children whose mothers were dependent on opioid drugs during pregnancy echo findings of other investigations (Fiks et al. 1985; Lawson

Table 7-5. Intercorrelations of CBCL and TRF Summary Scores

	1	2	3	4	5	6	7
1. CBCL Total Competence							
2. CBCL Total Problems	-0.26						
3. CBCL Internalizing	-0.10	0.80					
4. CBCL Externalizing	-0.30	0.88	0.52				
5. TRF Total Adaptive *Functioning*	0.10	-0.11	0.03	-0.12			
6. CBCL Total Problems	-0.20	0.37	0.14	0.41	-0.61		
7. TRF Internalizing	-0.13	0.22	0.12	0.23	-0.37	0.81	
8. TRF Externalizing	-0.27	0.41	0.16	0.47	-0.47	0.88	0.58

& Wilson 1980; Rodning et al. 1991; Wasserman & Leventhal 1993; Wilson 1989). Children whose parents use drugs are at very high risk of experiencing disruptions in caregiving arrangements and losing their birthmothers as primary caregivers. At age 10, only 53% of the children born to drug-using women were residing with their mothers, and only 36% had been in the continuous care of their birthmothers since birth. This outcome contrasts with 80% of the children whose mothers did not use drugs during pregnancy and who had been cared for by their birthmothers on a continuous basis since birth. Half of those mothers in the comparison group who did not provide continuous care for their children became involved in drug use after the birth of their children, a factor that contributed to their inability to care continuously for their children.

Figures related to continuity in maternal care might be even more stark in other populations of drug-abusing women because the women in this study were a relatively stable group. The large majority of mothers were in methadone maintenance programs during their pregnancies; they all were discharged from the hospital with custody of their infants; and they all agreed to participate for two years in a research study. It is notable that all but one of the drug-using mothers were major caregivers throughout the first two years of their children's lives, suggesting that even when relationships with their children are well-established, drug-using women remain vulnerable to problems that prevent them from fulfilling their role as a parent.

Compared to the CBCL and TRF normative group, all children in the present sample showed somewhat low levels of academic competence. Yet, despite dire predictions that have been made about the long-term development of children prenatally exposed to drugs (Hopkins 1990; Kantrowitz 1990; Toufexis 1991), the children in the present sample whose mothers used drugs during pregnancy differed little in their behavior from other children of similar socioeconomic background. Compared to other children at age 10, they were more

Table 7-6. Mean (*SD*) CBCL and TRF Summary Scores for Children Not Residing with their Birth Mothers at Age Ten Years, Grouped by Prenatal Exposure History, Child Sex, Child Residence, and Child Contact with Biological Mother at Age 10 Years

	n	CBCL Total Competence	CBCL Internalizing Score	CBCL Externalizing Score	CBCL Total Problems
Prenatal Opioid Exposure	17	44.1 (5.0)	48.8** (7.7)	48.9 (9.5)	49.1 (8.0)
No Prenatal Exposure	8	41.2 (4.3)	54.5 (7.2)	52.5 (7.8)	54.4 (5.6)
Male	11	43.8 (3.9)	52.6 (6.3)	50.0 (7.2)	52.7 (5.4)
Female	14	42.9 (5.6)	49.0 (8.9)	50.2 (10.5)	49.4 (9.0)
Residing Maternal Kin	9	42.8 (5.4)	48.5 (8.6)	52.0 (9.4)	50.1 (8.9)
Residing Paternal Kin	13	43.7 (5.0)	52.4 (5.9)	49.5 (6.8)	51.7 (4.8)
Never Sees Birth Mother	11	42.8 (5.3)	48.8 (10.2)	48.2 (10.2)	48.9 (8.9)
Sees Birth Mother	14	43.7 (4.6)	52.0 (5.7)	51.4 (8.1)	52.4 (6.4)
		TRF Total Adaptive Functioning	TRF Internalizing Score	TRF Externalizing Score	TRF Total Problems
Prenatal Opioid Exposure		41.7 (6.7)	52.5 (11.1)	59.1 (9.5)	57.7 (11.2)
No Prenatal Exposure		47.1 (10.7)	56.0 (15.2)	54.6 (11.0)	55.9 (14.1)
Male		43.0 (9.4)	59.9* (12.7)	59.6 (9.6)	61.1 (10.7)
Female		43.6 (7.7)	48.2 (9.1)	56.2 (10.4)	53.8 (12.1)
Residing Maternal Kin		45.2 (9.6)	46.9* (9.4)	53.4* (8.3)	51.8** (10.6)
Residing Paternal Kin		41.8 (8.0)	58.1 (12.3)	61.8 (8.9)	61.6 (11.2)
Never Sees Birth Mother		45.6 (7.7)	49.0** (8.1)	54.3 (9.5)	52.3** (11.6)
Sees Birth Mother		41.6 (8.6)	57.4 (14.0)	60.7 (9.8)	61.2 (10.8)

* *p* < .05, two-tailed
** *p* < .10, two-tailed

likely to be rated by their caregivers as having sexual problems, more likely to be rated by their teachers as behaving inappropriately, and less likely to be rated by their teachers as being withdrawn. Although these few findings with multiple dependent indicators may be spurious, the sexual problems ratings are of particular concern. Closer examination of the four children whose caregivers reported sexual problem scores in the clinical range indicated that two of these children had been involved in precocious sexual activity: a girl who engaged in extreme self-stimulating behavior and a boy who engaged in sexual fondling of male and female younger children. The other two children, both girls, were thought by their parents to act or wish to be like the opposite sex.

Disruption in the care provided by the children's birthmothers (measured by whether mothers resided in the same household as their 10-year-old children) was not associated with child behavior problems or diminished social and academic competence. Yet, this lack of association should not lead to a conclusion that caregiving arrangements were unimportant in the lives of children. The role of caregiving is too complex to be captured by a single index such as residing with mother. In this sample, disruptions in maternal care occurred for a variety of reasons and at different times in children's lives and carried different meanings for children. Sometimes, the loss of or separation from a mother was a sudden, traumatic deprivation of a stable and caring parent figure. By contrast, the loss of or separation from a mother, although a difficult experience, sometimes relieved the child of the burden of coping with an unpredictable, difficult, or even abusive parent. For some children, a new living situation provided the child with a safe, stable, and loving environment, and for other children, the new living situation was complicated by stresses to which another child only added one more burden. In some cases, the new living situation was expected to be a permanent caregiving arrangement, and in other cases, the new living situation was intended to last only until the mother was able to or wanted to care for her child.

In examining the residence patterns of the 25 children no longer living with their mothers at age 10, the most striking observation was that for the vast majority of children whose mothers were unable to care for them, members of the family (fathers, maternal, and paternal kin) stepped in to assume care of the child. Most of these arrangements were initially made without intervention from the child welfare system. Another key observation was that the sex of the child was associated with the type of placement. Boys were more likely to be living with fathers and paternal kin, and girls more likely to be living with maternal kin. This gender bias in living arrangements may reflect family assumptions that boys are particularly likely to need the care of a male figure, especially their father, or it may reflect fathers' greater comfort raising boys without the help of a maternal figure. The fact that the children raised by fathers or paternal kin were more likely to be perceived by teachers as having internalizing and externalizing problems, even after controlling for the sex of the child, could suggest that fathers and their families provide less adequate care of the children. It also might reflect, however, a bias for placing children who are experiencing difficulties with their fathers and paternal relatives. Finally, a third observation was that those children whose teachers reported them to have the fewest internalizing and externalizing behaviors were those who no longer had contact with their birthmothers. This finding must be treated cautiously because of the small number of families involved in the analyses and because of its varied possible interpretations. It may be that children whose mothers cannot care for them thrive best if they make a "clean break" from their mothers. It may be, however, that caregiving arrangements in which mothers play a secondary or peripheral role reflect adaptations to other risk factors in the family system such as economic hardship, ongoing maternal substance abuse, maternal mental disorder, or behavior problems of the child.

Conclusion

There is a paradox in discourse on the welfare of children with substance-abusing parents. On the one hand, developmental theory suggests that disruptions in patterns of parental care are not in the best interest of the child (Bowlby 1973, 1980), and the child welfare establishment has generally adopted a position of nonintervention whenever possible to protect children from potential emotional harm caused by separation from family. On the other hand, considerable public policy has been based on the assumption that being raised by a mother who abuses substances is not in the best interest of the child, and many state laws equate prenatal substance exposure with child abuse.

The data presented in this chapter, using CBCL and TRF scores as indicators of child well-being, do not support either of these positions. Simply knowing whether parents abuse drugs or whether they can provide continuity of care reveals little about the quality of care experienced by a child either from a birthmother or substitute caregivers. Numerous factors other than substance abuse influence a parent's capacity to care for a child (Belsky & Vondry 1989). Substance-abusing parents vary greatly in their capacities to nurture children (Jeremy & Bernstein 1984; Bernstein et al. 1986; Bernstein & Hans 1994) as do potential foster care providers. The critical issue to consider in addressing issues of child welfare is not whether a parent uses drugs or whether a child is separated from a parent, but the quality of care a child receives. Policy and practice decisions related to placement of children need to be based on assessments of the capacity of caregivers in the family of origin and in potential foster families to nurture the child.

Endnotes

1. Two CBCL forms were not completed because of examiner oversight. One CBCL was not completed because of the mother's passive refusal to participate in all three research sessions.
2. After frequent written requests, one classroom teacher did not complete the TRF form.

Acknowledgments

This research was supported by grants (R18DA-01884 and R01DA-05396) from the National Institute of Drug Abuse. We acknowledge the major contributions of Joseph Marcus, Rita Jeremy, and Carrie Patterson to the conception and execution of this study and to Karen Freel in the collection of the data at the 10-year follow-up.

References

Achenbach, T.M. (1991a). *Manual for the child Behavior Checklist/4-18 and 1991 profile.* Burlington: University of Vermont Department of Psychiatry.

Achenbach, T.M. (1991b). *Manual for the Teacher's Report Form and 1991 profile.* Burlington: University of Vermont Department of Psychiatry.

Barth, R.P., Courtney, M., Berrick, J., & Albert, V. (1994). *From child abuse to permanency planning: Pathways of children through child welfare services.* New York: Aldine De Bruyter.

Belsky, J. & Vondra, J. (1989). Lessons from child abuse: The determinants of parenting. In D. Cicchetti & V. Carlson (Eds.), *Child maltreatment: Theory and research on the causes and consequences of child abuse and neglect* (pp. 153–202). Cambridge: Cambridge University Press.

Bernstein, V. J. & Hans, S. L. (1994). Predicting the developmental outcome of two-year-old children born exposed to methadone: The impact of social-environmental risk factors. *Journal of Clinical Child Psychology, 23,* 349–359.

Bernstein, V. J., Jeremy, R. J. & Marcus, J. (1986). Mother-infant interaction in multi-problem families: Finding those at risk. *Journal of the American Academy of Child Psychiatry,* 25(5), 631–640.

Besharov, D. J. (1994). *When drug addicts have children: Reorienting child welfare's response.* Washington, D.C.: Child Welfare League of America and American Enterprise Institute.

Bowlby, J. (1973). *Separation: Anxiety and anger.* New York: Basic Books.

Bowlby, J. (1980). *Loss: Sadness and depression.* New York: Basic Books.

Burton, L.M. (1992). Black grandparents rearing children of drug-addicted parents: Stressors, outcomes, and social service needs. *The Gerontologist, 32,* 744–751.

Burton, L.M., & Dilworth-Anderson, P. (1991). The intergenerational family roles of aged Black Americans. *Marriage and Family Review, 16,* 311–330.

Chasnoff, I.J., Hatcher, R., Burns, W.J., & Schnoll, S. H. (1983). Pentazocine and tripelennamine ('T's and blues's'): Effects on the fetus and neonate. *Developmental Pharmacology and Therapeutics, 6,* 162–169.

English, A. (1990). Prenatal drug exposure: Grounds for mandatory child abuse reports? *Youth Law News, 11,* 3–8.

Fanshel, D. (1975). Parental failure and consequences for children: The drug-abusing mother whose children are in foster care. *American Journal of Public Health, 65,* 604–612.

Fiks, K.B., Johnson, H. L., & Rosen, T. S. (1985). Methadone maintained mothers: Three year follow-up of parental functioning. *International Journal of the Addictions, 20,* 651–660.

Grattan, M.P., & Hans, S. L. (1996). Motor behavior in children exposed prenatally to drugs. *Journal of Occupational and Physical Therapy in Pediatrics, 16,* 89–109.

Hans, S. L. (1989). Developmental consequences of prenatal exposure to methadone. Prenatal abuse of licit and illicit drugs, In D.E. Hutchings (Ed.), *Annals of the New York Academy of Sciences, 562,* 195–207.

Hawley, T. L., & Disney, E.R. (1992). Crack's children: The consequences of maternal cocaine abuse. *Social Policy Report: Society for Research in Child Development,* 6(4), 1–23.

Hopkins, E. (1990, October 18). Childhood's end. *Rolling Stone,* pp. 66–72, 108–110.

Jeremy, R.J., & Bernstein, V.J. (1984). Dyads at risk: Methadone-maintained women and their four-month-old infants. *Child Development, 55,* 1141–1154.

Jeremy, R.J., & Hans, S.L. (1985). Behavior of neonates exposed in utero to methadone as assessed on the Brazelton scale. *Infant Behavior and Development, 8,* 323–336.

Kantrowitz, B. (1990, February 12). The crack children. *Newsweek,* pp. 62–63.

Lawson, M., & Wilson, G. (1980). Parenting among women addicted to narcotics. *Child Welfare, 59,* 67–79.

Minkler, M., Roe, K.M., & Price, M. (1992). The physical and emotional health of grand-mothers raising grandchildren in the crack cocaine epidemic. *The Gerontologist, 32,* 752–761.

Minkler, M., Roe, K.M., & Robertson-Beckley, R.N. (1994). Raising grandchildren from crack-cocaine households: Effects on family and friendship ties of African-American women. *American Journal of Orthopsychiatry, 64,* 20–29.

Regan, D.O., Ehrlich, S.M., & Finnegan, L.P. (1987). Infants of drug addicts: At risk for child abuse, neglect, and placement in foster care. *Neurotoxicology and Teratology, 9,* 315–319.

Rodning, C., Beckwith, L., & Howard, J. (1991). Quality of attachment and home environments in children prenatally exposed to PCP and cocaine. *Development and Psychopathology, 3,* 351–366.

Schnoll, S.H., Chasnoff, I.J., & Glassroth, J. (1985). Pentazocine and tripelennamine abuse: T's and blues. *Psychiatric Medicine, 3,* 219–231.

Simms, M.D. (1991). Foster children and the foster care system, Part II: Impact on the child. *Current Problems in Pediatrics, 21,* 345–369.

Toufexis A. (1991, May 13). Innocent Victims. *Time, 137*(19), 56–60.

Wasserman, D.R., & Leventhal, J.M. (1993). Maltreatment of children born to cocaine-abusing mothers. *American Journal of Diseases of Children, 147,* 1324–1328.

Wilson, G. S. (1989). Clinical studies of infants and children exposed prenatally to heroin. *Annals of the New York Academy of Science, 562,* 183–194.

Wulczyn, F. (1994). Drug-affected children in foster care in New York City. In R.P. Barth, J.D. Berrick, & N. Gilbert (Eds.), *Child welfare research review* (pp. 146–184). New York: Columbia University Press.

8

Professor Achenbach Meets Mick Jagger: Using the Child Behavior Checklist in Foster Care

Roger D. Phillips

"...You can't always get what you want.
But, if you try sometime,
you might find,
you get what you need..."
from "You can't always get what you want,"
Let It Bleed
Mick Jagger and Keith Richards (1969). ABCKO Music Inc.

Introduction

Five programmatic questions regarding the use of the Child Behavior Checklist (CBCL) (Achenbach 1991) in the foster care programs at Pinebrook Services for Children and Youth motivated the research described in this chapter. These questions, specific to Pinebrook's work but also broadly applicable to the use of the CBCL in many child welfare settings, are:

- What is the extent of behavioral difficulties shown by children in foster care?

- Are children in foster care today more behaviorally disordered than children in foster care in the past?

- Does the CBCL discriminate among children entering different foster care programs?

- Is there value in readministering the CBCL at brief intervals while a child is in foster care?

- To what extent do behavioral difficulties at entry into foster care influence children's discharge dispositions?

As the following discussion illustrates, some of these questions have been addressed by empirical research, but other questions have not been studied to any extent.

What Is the Extent of Behavioral Difficulties Shown by Children in Foster Care?

There is ample evidence that children who enter foster care display substantial behavioral difficulties at or shortly after placement (Hochstadt et al. 1987; Hornick et al. 1989; Pardeck 1983, 1984; Pilowsky 1995; Thompson & Fuhr 1992). Children in foster care also are overrepresented in populations of children using mental health services and among children enrolled in special education programs (Cantos et al. 1996; Garland et al. 1996; Goerge et al. 1991). Not all research, however, has reported elevated levels of psychopathology among children in foster care (Benbenishty & Oyserman 1995; Colton, Aldgate & Heath, 1991; Phillips 1998). Some of the inconsistent findings may be attributable to the use of suspect or nonequivalent measures of behavioral difficulties. Even when studies have used the CBCL, they have yielded mixed evidence (e.g., Hornick et al. 1989; McIntyre & Keesler 1986; Phillips 1998; Urquiza et al. 1994).

Are Children in Foster Care Today More Behaviorally Disordered than Children in Foster Care in the Past?

Based on clinical impressions, Pinebrook staff raised the possibility that children who more recently entered foster care are more behaviorally disordered than children who entered foster care in the past. A systematic evaluation of the level of behavioral disorder among children entering care, however, had not been undertaken at Pinebrook since CBCL data collection had begun at the agency five years earlier. A review of the research revealed no empirical evidence related to potential cohort differences among children in foster care.

Does the CBCL Discriminate Among Children Entering Three Different Foster Care Programs?

Pennsylvania offers three different foster care programs that are designed, in principle, to meet the range of needs of children who enter the child welfare system: regular foster care, specialized foster care, and intensive treatment foster care. These programs provide services in response to a gradient of social, emotional, and/or behavioral difficulties presented by the children assigned to the program. It was not known whether the CBCL would yield distinguishable profiles for children in each of the three foster care programs. Some research has found qualitative or quantitative behavioral differences in children entering foster care versus group homes, residential care, or family support services (Berrick et al. 1993; Hornick et al. 1989). There has been little empirical research, however, examining such differences with the foster care systems.

Is There Value in Readministering the CBCL at Brief Intervals While a Child Is in Foster Care?

Pinebrook staff believed that the CBCL, because of its superior psychometric and clinical status, might serve as a tool to measure the meaningful progress made by children during their stays in foster care. The extent to which the CBCL could serve this purpose, however, was not clear. The CBCL was administered at 6-month intervals after children entered care at Pinebrook, a task that came to be viewed by foster parents as, at best, burdensome. However, the data had not been analyzed to determine the value of this practice. At the same time, little guidance could be obtained from the empirical foster care literature.

To What Extent do Behavioral Difficulties at Entry into Foster Care Influence Children's Discharge Dispositions?

The behavioral difficulties of children in foster care have been related to a variety of outputs, such as placement maladjustment and disruption and returns to foster care (Iglehart 1993; Lawder et al. 1986; Pardeck 1983, 1985; Proch & Taber 1985; Stone & Stone 1983), and outcomes [e.g., school-related problems (Colton et al. 1995; Heath et al. 1989; Smucker et al. 1996)]. This study explored the extent to which initial behavioral difficulties might be related to two discharge dispositions: restrictiveness of living environment and goal attainment during placement.

The Pinebrook research used the CBCL: (1) to describe the behavioral status of a large sample of children in three Pinebrook foster programs from 1993 to the present; (2) to examine the relative value of repeated, brief-interval administrations of the CBCL; and (3) to predict dispositional outputs for children in Pinebrook foster care. One proviso is in order: although the third goal of the research resembles a program-evaluation goal, the project was not organized as such. The questions, sample, and methods were conceived and implemented as a descriptive study without the explicit controls necessary for a formal evaluation of the effectiveness of Pinebrook's foster care program. As a result, the results of the study should not be construed as answering program-evaluation questions.

Methods

Organization and Program Descriptions

Pinebrook Services for Children and Youth is a traditional, private, nonprofit child welfare agency that provides foster care services to county children and youth agencies. Referrals for foster care come from the local counties for children and youth who have been adjudicated as dependent by the court because of alleged physical, sexual, or emotional abuse; neglect; or other parenting breakdowns, such as inadequate supervision and inability to control the child's behavior. The primary direct services that caseworkers provide to children in all foster care programs is casework and case management. The caseworker to child ratio is generally 1 to 12. During the span of this study, Pinebrook's daily census of children in its various foster programs was approximately 150 to 170 children and youth.

Like many foster care providers in Pennsylvania, Pinebrook operates three main types of foster care programs that provide varying levels of casework services. Regular foster care (RFC) is designed for children who are healthy, well-functioning, and do not require extraordinary programming within or outside the foster home. Casework for children in RFC is provided on a regular but modest basis, and case management is used to ensure that ongoing developmental needs and opportunities of children are met within the foster home and surrounding community. Specialized foster care (SFC) provides individually designed treatment programs for children who have emotional, behavioral, social, or developmental problems. Casework is more frequent for children and foster families in SFC and is tailored toward specific therapeutic goals. Ancillary services (such as psychotherapy, supportive educational services, psychological evaluations, and medication monitoring) are provided as needed and, in fact, are fairly common in SFC. Historically, approximately 80% of the children in foster care at Pinebrook have been placed in SFC. Intensive treatment foster care (ITFC) is provided by foster parents who have been trained extensively to care for children whose functioning is too maladaptive to be managed in SFC. Casework, case management, and supportive ancillary services (such as specialized educational placements, psychiatric evaluations, wraparound services, and respite) are provided to children and foster families more frequently and intensely.

Sample

CBCL data were available from approximately 40% of the total population of children in Pinebrook foster care between 1993 and early 1997, with greatest representation at the initial CBCL administration ($n=297$). Sample sizes diminished at the second ($n=107$) and third ($n=42$) CBCL administrations as a result of discharges from care or operational breakdowns (such as foster parents not completing CBCLs). All children in the second CBCL subsample were represented in the initial-CBCL sample, and all children in the third-CBCL subsample were represented in both the initial- and second-CBCL samples.

Table 8-1 displays descriptive information regarding the sample, which was comparable to the larger population of children in Pinebrook's care. The sample was fairly evenly split between males and females and spanned ages from 4 to 18 years with comparable percentages within age groups across CBCL administrations. Most of the data were collected from 1994 to 1996, with less data from 1993 and 1997. The children were served in all three foster programs, but most children were in SFC.

There was substantial attrition in the sample from the initial to the third CBCL administration (see Table 8-1). Unfortunately, it was impossible to determine definitively the reasons for this attrition. Some attrition was caused by discharges from care (average length of placement during this time period was 14 to 17 months), and some was a function of noncompliance in foster parents' completion of the CBCL. Preliminary analyses, however, found no significant, systematic differences in CBCL scores as a result of discharge status or the characteristics of children who remained in the samples versus those who did not.

Measures

Besides the CBCL, this study also measured discharge destination and goal attainment during care. Discharge destinations were coded using the Restrictiveness of Living Environments Scale (Hawkins et al. 1989) in which a number is assigned to living environments based on the restrictiveness imposed on the child. The scale ranges from 1 for independent living,

Table 8-1. Sample Descriptive Statistics

Variable	Admin1 (n=297)	Admin2 (n=107)	Admin3 (n=42)
Sex (%)			
Female	52	51	49
Male	48	49	51
Age Group (%)			
4–5 yrs	13	11	12
6–8 yrs	23	20	19
9–11 yrs	21	32	35
12–14 yrs	25	17	23
15–18 yrs	18	20	12
Year (%)			
1993	7	1	0
1994	31	18	5
1995	24	43	61
1996	23	37	30
1997	15	1	5
Foster Program (%)			
RFC	13	9	9
SFC	77	79	74
ITFC	8	12	16

through mid scores for foster care (9 for regular foster care, 10 for specialized foster care, and 12 for foster family-based treatment home care), to 25 for incarceration. Destinations were recorded as less, same, or more restrictive relative to the child's foster care program at discharge. Children's attainment of goals specified in their Individualized Service Plan (ISP) were scored (none, some, most, all) by an independent rater based on reading the child's discharge report.

Procedure

Pinebrook foster parents completed initial CBCLs on children 45 to 60 days after entry into care and then at subsequent intervals of 6 months (+1 month). The foster parent ratings then were computer-scored via the standard CBCL software. Discharge destination and goal attainment were collected by independent raters directly from the final report after a child exited Pinebrook's care.

Results

Initial Levels of Behavioral Difficulties

On average and across the entire sample at the initial administration, all broad- and narrow-band CBCL scores fell in the upper-end normal range, except for aggressive behaviors which fell in the lower-end borderline range (see Table 8.2: read Time 1 values under All column). These reasonably benign results based on CBCL mean T scores were cast in a somewhat different light, however, when clinical-range CBCL scores were examined (see Figure 8-1). Percentages of the sample with scores reaching the clinical level were greater than would have been expected in the general population, which is consistent with the significant histories of abuse and neglect, problematic behaviors, and family dysfunction for most children who entered Pinebrook's care.

Separate one-way ANOVAs on initial CBCL T scores, using year as the grouping variable, provided information about the initial behavioral status of children then in care versus those in care in the recent past. Year of entry into care did not influence any CBCL scores, suggesting that the children then in foster care were not evidencing greater psychopathology than those children entering Pinebrook 5 years previously. On average, CBCL T scores were quite comparable across all 5 years, even diminishing slightly (total problems range: 59–62, total internalizing range: 55–57, total externalizing range: 60–63; similar ranges for narrow-band scores).

Levels of Behavioral Difficulties Across Foster Programs

Separate one-way ANOVAs on CBCL T scores with foster care program as the grouping variable were used to determine if scores differed by foster care program. Children in different foster programs yielded significantly different CBCL profiles (see Table 8-2: read across RFC, SFC and ITFC columns). This finding was consistently true for total problem behaviors, total externalizing, aggressive, and delinquent behavior, and social, thought, and attention problem scales. Program differences were insubstantial for broad- and narrow-band internalizing difficulties. The pattern of differences across programs was fairly stable during the initial and second CBCL administrations. Children in RFC and SFC produced comparable scores in the upper end of the normal range, which were less than those obtained by children in ITFC. The scores for children in IFTC fluctuated almost entirely within the borderline and clinical ranges. At the third CBCL administration, the number and size of significant program differences decreased, probably as a result of the smaller sample size. The pattern of results across foster care programs was comparable when percentages of children yielding wide- or narrow-band CBCL scores in the clinical range were evaluated.

Levels of Behavioral Difficulties Across Repeated CBCL Administrations

Separate repeated-measures ANOVAs were used to test effects of readministrations on CBCL T scores. No significant differences were found on CBCL broad- or narrow-band scores using two- or three-administration models in the analyses. In fact, the comparability of scores was quite striking (see Table 8-2: read down All column). When foster care program was added

Figure 8-1. Percentages of Children Obtaining CBCL Scores in the Clinical Range (*N* = 297)

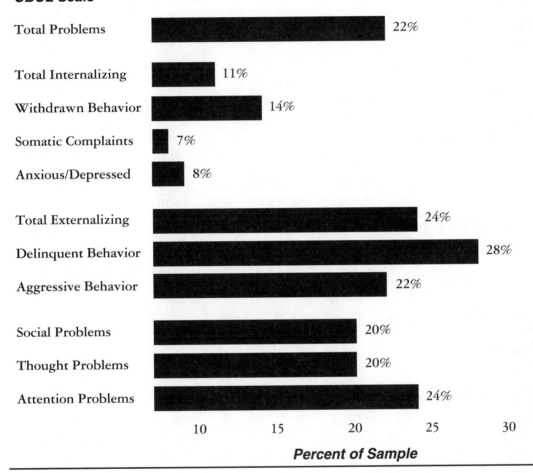

CBCL Scale

Percent of Sample

post hoc to the ANOVA model as a between-subjects factor, it prevailed as the only significant effect and without significant interactions, suggesting that the CBCL was unchanged across time for children regardless of their foster care program (see Table 8-2: read down RFC, SFC and ITFC columns). Once again, percentages of children obtaining clinical-range scores were elevated compared to estimates for the general population and were statistically equivalent across the three CBCL administrations.

Initial Behavioral Difficulties As Predictors Of Discharge Dispositions

Stepwise regression analyses were used to explore the contribution of initial behavioral difficulties at entry to the prediction of dispositional outputs from foster care, restrictiveness of discharge destination, and goal attainment during care. The initial regression analysis for each dependent variable included as predictors the age of child, length of placement, foster

Table 8-2. Mean CBCL T Scores (and Standard Deviations) by Foster Program and CBCL Administration

CBCL Score	Foster Program			
	All	RFC	SFC	ITFC
Total Problems				
Time 1	63(11)	58(13)	61(10)	71(9)****a
Time 2	63(10)	54(9)	61(10)	73(5)****a
Time 3	65(9)	61(8)	61(8)	73(4)***a
Total Internalizing				
Time 1	58(11)	56(10)	56(11)	61(10)
Time 2	56(10)	51(8)	56(10)	62(7)*b
Time 3	56(10)	52(10)	54(10)	63(6)
Total Externalizing				
Time 1	63(12)	57(13)	61(11)	72(8)****a
Time 2	64(12)	55(10)	62(11)	75(9)****a
Time 3	67(10)	65(9)	62(10)	74(6)*c
Withdrawal				
Time 1	61(10)	61(12)	58(9)	63(12)*c
Time 2	60(10)	57(11)	59(10)	63(10)
Time 3	60(9)	59(14)	58(10)	63(7)
Somatic Complaints				
Time 1	56(7)	56(6)	55(8)	56(7)
Time 2	55(6)	51(2)	55(6)	59(6)**b
Time 3	54(5)	52(2)	53(5)	56(4)
Anxiety/Depression				
Time 1	59(8)	56(7)	58(8)	62(10)*b
Time 2	57(9)	53(4)	57(9)	61(8)
Time 3	57(8)	53(3)	56(8)	63(5)
Delinquent Behaviors				
Time 1	63(9)	59(8)	62(9)	69(10)****a
Time 2	63(10)	55(5)	63(9)	71(12)****e
Time 3	65(9)	64(4)	62(9)	69(10)

Aggressive Behaviors

Time 1	65(11)	60(11)	62(11)	73(11)****a
Time 2	64(12)	58(9)	62(11)	78(12)****a
Time 3	68(11)	65(11)	62(10)	77(8)**c

Social Problems

Time 1	62(10)	59(9)	61(10)	66(10)*a
Time 2	62(10)	54(4)	62(10)	69(7)***d
Time 3	64(10)	58(12)	61(10)	72(8)*c

Thought Problems

Time 1	62(10)	59(9)	60(10)	68(13)***a
Time 2	61(10)	56(6)	60(9)	67(11)*a
Time 3	62(8)	60(8)	58(7)	69(6)**c

Attention Problems

Time 1	64(11)	62(12)	63(10)	68(10)
Time 2	63(10)	56(6)	62(10)	70(8)***a
Time 3	65(11)	60(18)	61(8)	75(11)**c

Only foster-program differences were found and are reported here: $*p < .05$, $**p < .01$,
$***p < .001$, $****p < .0001$.

a: (RFC=SFC)<ITFC
b: RFC=SFC SFC=ITFC RFC<ITFC
c: RFC=SFC RFC=ITFC SFC<ITFC
d: RFC<(SFC=ITFC)
e: RFC<SFC<ITFC.

---

care program, and CBCL total behavior problems T score. CBCL predictors were then expanded, if warranted, in subsequent analyses. If CBCL total behavior problems T score was a significant predictor of goal attainment in the initial regression, for example, a subsequent analysis would predict goal attainment from the same set of variables but would substitute Total Externalizing and Total Internalizing T scores for the Total Problems score. If either of those CBCL scores yielded significant relations with goal attainment, then it would be replaced by the appropriate narrow-band scores in a subsequent analysis. These analyses were exploratory, based on a smaller sample ($n=126$) of children for whom there were CBCL and discharge data. The results were not adjusted for Type 1 error inflation due to multiple tests and, thus, they should be considered as tentative. Preliminary analyses indicated no significant differences on any initial CBCL scores between the discharged subsample and those children remaining in care.

CBCL scores contributed significantly and most strongly to predicting both restrictiveness of discharge destinations and goal attainment, although the type of foster care program typically entered in a significant second step (see Table 8-3). Those significant initial predictive relations with Total Problems were carried only by Externalizing Problems in more focused analyses and, specifically, by Aggressive Behaviors for discharge-destination restrictiveness and Delinquent Behaviors for goal attainment.

Figure 8-2 depicts the patterns among the CBCL Total Behavior Problems T scores and foster care program as illustrative of all the findings for restrictiveness of discharge destination. CBCL scores for children in RFC increased dramatically and to clinical levels for children who moved from less to same restrictiveness destinations (although the latter cell (n=2) was very small). No child in RFC was discharged to a more restrictive setting. Children in both SFC and ITFC who were discharged to less restrictive destinations were in the normal CBCL range compared to their peers who were discharged to same or more restrictive settings. No ITFC child was discharged to a same restrictive environment.

The patterns of CBCL scores across foster care programs for goal attainment were nearly the inverse of those obtained for discharge destinations, given the opposite scaling of this variable. Figure 8-3 depicts the pattern for total problems as prototypical of the findings for all CBCL variables. Children in RFC scored significantly lower on the CBCL as their goal attainment increased from "some" to "all." CBCL scores were higher and in the borderline range for children in SFC who attained none or only some of their goals as compared to their peers who attained most or all of their ISP goals. Those ITFC children who attained some of their goals were notably higher on CBCL total problems when compared to those who attained all of their goals.

Discussion

The findings of this study raise seemingly contradictory and difficult to reconcile ideas regarding the use of the CBCL in foster care. First, on average, children in foster care at Pinebrook scored within or close to the normal range on all CBCL dimensions across all five years of data collection. The percentages of children obtaining clinical-level scores, however, were higher than population estimates. Second, the CBCL differentiated children who entered the three foster care programs designed to meet varying levels of social, emotional, and behavioral needs (RFC, SFC, ITFC), but the differences in CBCL scores were not always as expected. Third, repeated ratings on the CBCL across the first 16–18 months of care, regardless of foster care program, provided no new information on the children, but the impact of selective attrition on this finding seemed likely. Finally, despite these issues, the CBCL provided compelling information about the children who left care "successfully" versus those who left "unsuccessfully."

The modest mean levels of psychopathology found in this study are at odds with the substantial clinical histories that most children bring into Pinebrook foster care, the reports of staff and foster parents attesting to the difficulties of many of these children, and the weight of previous research. Nonetheless, the results suggest that because the population of children in foster care is so variable, assumptions about children's behavioral difficulties should not be made without substantiating evidence, including the use of psychometrically grounded instruments such as the CBCL.

Table 8-3. Stepwise Regression Analyses for Discharge Destination and Goal Attainment (*N* = 126)

CBCL T Score	Coefficient	r	r²	F
Discharge Destination				
1. Total Problems	.035	.408	.166	23.7****
Foster Program	.380	.440	.194	4.0*
2. Total Externalizing	.031	.366	.134	18.4****
Foster Program	.405	.406	.165	4.4*
3. Aggressive Behavior	.031	.347	.120	16.3****
Foster Program	.440	.397	.158	5.23*
Goal Attainment				
1. Total Problems	-.023	.290	.084	10.86***
Foster Program	-.413	.348	.121	4.87*
2. Total Externalizing	-.029	.365	.133	18.14****
Length of Placement	-.008	.403	.162	4.01*
3. Delinquent Behaviors	-.031	.343	.117	15.70****
Foster Program	-.415	.395	.156	5.30*

1 = First analysis (predictors: age of child, length of placement, foster program, CBCL Total Problems).

2 = Second analysis, if CBCL Total Problems was significant in #1 (predictors: as above, but substituting CBCL Total Externalizing and Total Internalizing for Total Problems).

3 = Third analysis, if either CBCL summary score was significant in #2 (predictors: as above, but substituting Aggressive Behavior and Delinquent Behavior for Total Externalizing).

*p<.05, **p<.01, ***p<.001, ****p<.0001.

The findings of modest levels of psychopathology may be the result of a number of factors. It may be that foster parents are a unique group of raters of children's behavior. Because they have fairly extensive experience with many challenging children, they may base their ratings of children on generous internal baselines despite the CBCL's clear instructions and may resist changing their subsequent ratings of the same children. Alternatively, the CBCL may not measure the gnarly minutiae of daily behavior that foster parents face and which they must address.

In fact, the CBCL may be tapping the more intractable, structural features of psychopathology. This feature of the CBCL may account for repeated CBCL administrations revealing little change during the first 16–18 months of care for the children in this study, both across

Figure 8-2. Mean CBCL T Total Problems Score by Foster Program and Restrictiveness of Discharge Destination (*N*=126)

Mean Total Problems T Score

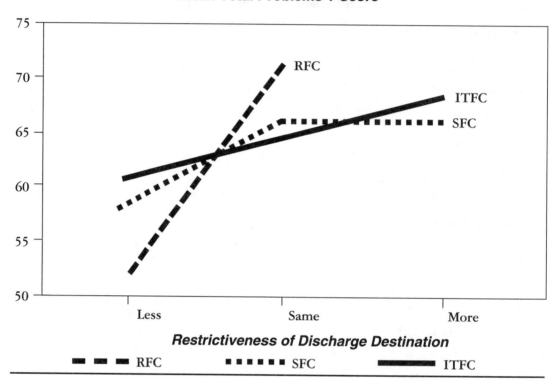

Restrictiveness of Discharge Destination

■ ■ ■ RFC   ■■■■■■ SFC   ▬▬▬ ITFC

and within foster care programs. Although it may have been assumed that the CBCL would operate like a symptom inventory that is sensitive to small behavioral fluctuations across small units of time, the present findings based on CBCL *T* scores do not support such a conclusion. That assumption also was not supported by additional analyses that were undertaken to approximate a symptom inventory by using only the total number of endorsed CBCL items. Those analyses produced identical findings, suggesting that child welfare researchers may be better served by true symptom inventories, diaries, or daily checklists of specific behaviors when trying to answer many questions about behavioral change.

These considerations, however, still beg important questions about the nature and unit of time. It is not clear, for example, whether change on the CBCL should be expected within six-month intervals. Are six-month intervals sufficiently long to allow for enduring changes in behavior? Or, are such intervals too long, diluting the fluctuations in symptomatic behavior? Do six-month intervals correspond to meaningful phases or transitions in interventions, or even in the development of children? As these questions suggest, finding little change across time in CBCL scores does not mean that change does not occur. The unit of time may be inappropriate relative to how change occurs in behavioral disorders, foster care, or children's development.

Figure 8-3. Mean CBCL T Total Problems Score by Foster Program and ISP Attainment (*N*=126)

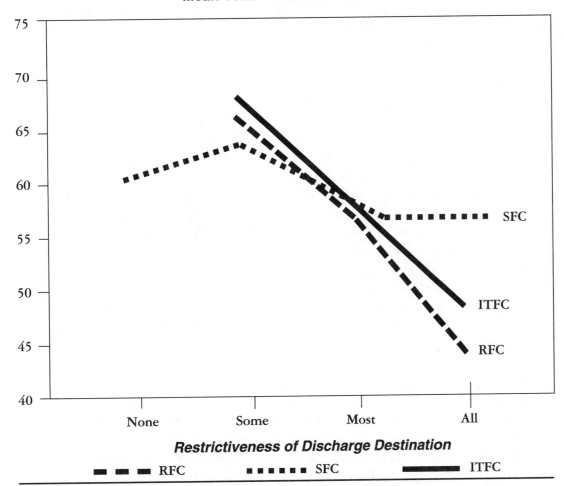

Implicit in this vague sense of time is an unmoored model of foster care as a fairly passive intervention, which may account for the sometimes marginal findings in the field. Programmatic innovations and evaluation research occur most effectively when theory provides a model for the intervention as well as its measurement (e.g., Cowen et al. 1990; Henggeler et al. 1994; Olds & Henderson 1989; Patterson et al. 1989). Many, however, have tried to fit or have been required to fit the CBCL into programs without regard to the original question: What is the model of intervention and change that links foster care with CBCL-measurable psychopathology?

A critical related question is: What theory informs the CBCL? The instrument's theoretical framework seems to be a fairly traditional view of psychopathology as originating from and centered in the individual, which is not problematic in and of itself. The difficulty may be, however, when the theoretical framework is transported to child welfare settings in which the evident pathology emerges from breakdowns in transactional processes of care, nurturance, development, and adaptation among children, caregivers, and social structures and systems. As a result, the CBCL may be limited in measuring all that is important or even relevant to understanding individual change or outcomes in foster care, as well as program effectiveness in child welfare.

Conclusion

The potency of the CBCL seems undeniable in describing important, clinically related characteristics of children. In this study, it effectively discriminated children who entered different foster care programs, with children in ITFC evidencing more clinical-level behavioral difficulties, especially externalizing behaviors, than children in RFC or SFC. Initial CBCL scores captured important information about these children that also was related meaningfully to their discharge status. Similar to the findings of Courtney and Zinn (this volume), children who were discharged to less restrictive environments or who achieved most or all of their ISP goals had lower initial CBCL scores than did children discharged to more restrictive environments or who achieved none or some of their ISP goals.

Thus, the value of the CBCL for child welfare may be in its powerful descriptive, diagnostic contribution, which the field must harness productively. CBCL behavioral difficulties at entry into foster care, for example, were more important in determining how the child left care than were the child's age, length of placement, and foster care program. A more extensive data set than the present one, however, will be needed in order to test fully an *a priori* model of how behavioral difficulties at entry into care interact with foster care interventions to affect immediate program outputs and short- and long-term program outcomes.

It also will be prudent to adopt a multi-measurement strategy for assessing behavioral difficulties in children in foster care. The CBCL may not capture desired information, such as daily functional behaviors, or there may be important reasons to obtain information from observers other than foster parents. The CBCL may be less amenable to answering some questions, such as change across short periods of time, and other measures may be more appropriate. It seems short-sighted at best for the field to place all its "eggs" in one measurement "basket," whether that be the CBCL or another measure. The questions that remain in child welfare are too varied and numerous, and it is unlikely that one measure will provide the perfect answer to all questions. There continues to be a need for well-grounded measures that are consistent with theoretical models of change and development in foster care to contribute to effective program evaluation.

References

Achenbach, T.M. (1991). *Manual for the Child Behavior Checklist and 1991 profile.* Burlington: University of Vermont, Department of Psychiatry.

Benbenishty, R., & Oyserman, D. (1995). Children in foster care: Their present situation and plans for the future. *International Social Work, 38,* 117–131.

Berrick, J.D., Courtney, M., & Barth, R.P. (1993). Specialized foster care and group home care: Similarities and differences in the characteristics of children in care. *Children and Youth Services Review, 15,* 453–473.

Cantos, A.L., Gries, L.T., & Slis, V. (1996). Correlates of therapy referral in foster children. *Child Abuse and Neglect, 20,* 921–931.

Colton, M., Aldgate, J. & Heath, A. (1991). Behavioral problems among children in and out of care. *Social Work and Social Sciences Review, 2,* 177–191.

Colton, M., Heath, A., & Aldgate, J. (1995). Factors which influence the educational attainment of children in foster family care. *Community Alternatives: International Journal of Family Care, 7,* 15–36.

Cowen, E.L., Wyman, P.A., Work, W.C. & Parker, G.R. (1990). The Rochester Child Resilience Project (RCRP): Overview and summary of first year findings. *Development and Psychopathology, 2,* 19–35.

Garland, A.F., Landsverk, J.L., Hough, R.L., & Ellis-MacLeod, E. (1996). Type of maltreatment as a predictor of mental health service use for children in foster care. *Child Abuse and Neglect, 20,* 675–688.

Goerge, R.M., Van Voorhis, J., Grant, S., Casey, K., & Robinson, M. (1991). Special education experiences of foster children: An empirical study. In A. Algarin & R.M. Friedman (Eds.), *4th Annual Research Conference Proceedings: A System of Care for Children's Mental Health: Expanding the Research Base* (pp. 335–345). Tampa, FL: Research and Training Center for Children's Mental Health, Florida Mental Health Institute, University of South Florida.

Hawkins, R.P., Almeida, M.C., & Samet, M. (1989). Comparative evaluation of foster-family-based treatment and five other placement choices: A preliminary report. In A. Algarin, R. M. Friedman, A. J. Duchnowski, K. Kutash, S. E. Silver, & M. K. Johnson (Eds.), *2nd Annual Research Conference Proceedings: A System of Care for Children's Mental Health: Expanding the Research Base* (pp. 91–111). Tampa: Research and Training Center for Children's Mental Health, Florida Mental Health Institute, University of South Florida.

Heath, A., Colton, M., & Aldgate, J. (1989). The educational progress of children in and out of care. *British Journal of Social Work, 19,* 447–460.

Henggeler, S.W., Schoenwald, S.K., Pickrel, S.G., Rowland, M.D., & Santos, A.B. (1994). The contribution of research to the reform of children's mental health services: Multisystemic family preservation as an example. *Journal of Mental Health Administration, 21,* 229–239.

Hochstadt, N.J., Jaudes, P.K., Zimo, D.A., & Schacter, J. (1987). The medical and psychosocial needs of children entering foster care. *Child Abuse and Neglect, 11*, 53–62.

Hornick, J. P., Phillips, D. M., & Kerr, N. (1989). Gender differences in behavioral problems of foster children: Implications for special foster care. *Community Alternatives: International Journal of Family Care, 1*, 35–52.

Iglehart, A. P. (1993). Adolescents in foster care: Predicting behavioral maladjustment. *Child and Adolescent Social Work Journal, 10*, 521–532.

Lawder, E.A., Poulin, J.E., & Andrews, R.G. (1986). A study of 185 foster children 5 years after placement. *Child Welfare, 65*, 241–251.

McIntyre, A. & Keesler, T. Y. (1986). Psychological disorders among foster children. *Journal of Clinical Child Psychology, 15*, 297–303.

Olds, D. & Henderson, C. (1989). The prevention of maltreatment. In D. Cicchetti & V. Carlson (Eds.), *Child maltreatment: Theory and research on the causes and consequences of child abuse and neglect* (pp. 722–763). New York: Cambridge University Press.

Pardeck, J.T. (1983). An empirical analysis of behavioral and emotional problems of foster children as related to re-placement in care. *Child Abuse and Neglect, 7*, 75–78.

Pardeck, J.T. (1984). Multiple placement of children in foster family care: An empirical analysis. *Social Work, 29*, 506–509.

Pardeck, J.T. (1985). A profile of the child likely to experience unstable foster care. *Adolescence, 20*, 689–695.

Patterson, G.R., DeBaryshe, B.D., & Ramsey, E. (1989). A developmental perspective on antisocial behavior. *American Psychologist , 44*, 329–335.

Phillips, R. D. (1998). What can the Child Behavior Checklist tell us about children in foster care? In C. Liberton, K. Kutash, & R. Friedman (Eds.), *The 10th Annual Research Conference: A System of Care for Children's Mental Health: Expanding the Research Base* (pp. 321–324). Tampa: Research and Training Center for Children's Mental Health, Florida Mental Health Institute, University of South Florida.

Pilowsky, D. (1995). Psychopathology among children placed in family foster care. *Psychiatric Services, 46*, 906–910.

Proch, K. & Taber, M.A. (1985). Placement disruption: A review of research. *Children and Youth Services Review, 7*, 309–320.

Smucker, K.S., Kauffman, J.M., & Ball, D.W. (1996). School-related problems of special education foster-care students with emotional or behavioral disorders: A comparison to other groups. *Journal of Emotional and Behavioral Disorders, 4*, 30–39.

Stone, N. M. & Stone, S. F. (1983). The prediction of successful foster placement. *Social Casework, 64*, 11–17.

Thompson, A.H. & Fuhr, D. (1992). Emotional disturbance in fifty children in the care of a child welfare system. *Journal of Social Service Research, 15*, 95–112.

Urquiza, A.J., Wirtz, S.J., Peterson, M.S., & Singer, V.A. (1994). Screening and evaluating abused and neglected children entering protective custody. *Child Welfare, 73,* 155–171.

9

A Profile of Youth Placed with Casey Family Programs Using the Child Behavior Checklist/4-18 and the Teacher's Report Form

Gay Armsden, Peter J. Pecora, Vincent Payne, and Charles Joyce

A substantial number of America's children are in foster care. In 1995 alone, the U.S. foster care population had an average daily census of 483,000 children and the system was estimated to have served an annual total of 710,000 children and adolescents (Tatara 1997). Demands on the foster care system in relation to the number of children served may increase in the near future as a result of welfare reforms that reduce family income supports (Courtney 1995). Costs associated with child welfare also are substantial. In 1997, close to $12 billion was spent on public agency child welfare (Committee on Ways and Means 1996; Lipner & Goertz 1996). In light of increasing costs, state and county governments are purchasing child welfare services (including foster care) from private agencies. They also are making significant efforts to economize, efforts that may result in more restrictive and less adequately funded programs and further accentuate the state of child welfare as both big and troubled. Despite the challenges facing child welfare, agencies lack adequate data about *who* is being served, toward what *outcomes*, with what mix of *interventions*, and at what *cost* (Paul 1967, Pecora, Massinga, & Mauserall 1997, Kluger, Alexander, & Curtis 2000).

Recognizing the lack of data, child welfare agencies must search for practical measures to support assessment, case planning, and program evaluation. A number of social service agencies are now using the Child Behavior Checklist (CBCL) and Teacher's Report Form (TRF) developed by Achenbach and Edelbrock (1983). In 1991, Casey Family Programs began using the CBCL and TRF to assess the competencies and behavior problems of children at three points while in the program: during the intake study and before admission; one year after admission to the program; and at age 18 or discharge from the program, whichever occurred first. The main purpose of the study was to document the behavior problems and competencies of children on entry into long-term foster care with Casey Family Programs.

This chapter presents CBCL and TRF data that were obtained for children as part of the admission study for Casey Family Programs between 1991 and 1993 and which represent a subset of findings from a larger study (Armsden et al. 1997). CBCL and TRF *T*-score and clinical-range findings are presented and are compared with one another and with the findings from other studies of children in family foster care and residential treatment. The chapter also includes the implications of the patterns of the Casey children's scores for clinical and program planning and identifies some questions to be addressed by further research. The specific questions on which this chapter focuses are:

1. How do Casey children at intake compare with CBCL normative and clinically referred samples (Achenbach 1991a, 1991b, 1991c)?

2. How do Casey children compare with other children in foster care or residential treatment?

3. How do reports by caregivers compare with reports by teachers?

4. What are the implications of the findings for clinical practice and program planning?

This chapter does not report on findings from the larger Casey study that examined differences between children accepted into the program and children not accepted and the children's changes in behavioral functioning after one year in the program (Armsden et al. 1997).

A Literature Review

CBCL Studies

Although children in foster care long have been reported to show elevated rates of behavior problems (e.g., Fanshel & Shinn 1978; Swire & Kavaler 1978), researchers more recently have employed standardized tests to document the behavioral and emotional functioning of these children. A number of published studies on children in foster care have reported scores on the CBCL, which facilitates comparison among samples. Studies using the CBCL have shown that children in long-term foster care evidence rates of psychological problems in excess of the normative sample of nonclinically referred children.

In one of the earliest CBCL studies of children in care, McIntyre and Keesler (1986) found that their sample of 4- to 18-year-olds in foster care was almost 9 times more likely than children in the CBCL normative sample to evidence clinically significant problem behaviors. Glisson (1994) found that 70% of a sample of adolescents entering state custody in Tennessee scored in the clinical range—7 times the normative rate. Dubowitz and colleagues (1993) reported that for a primarily African American sample of children and adolescents living in kinship care in Maryland, there was an almost 5 times greater overall risk of clinical-range levels of total problem behaviors compared with children in the CBCL normative sample. As part of a study of 267 children in foster care in 3 counties in California, Landsverk and associates (in press) found that children in care for 2 to 4 months experienced behavioral problems in the borderline or clinical range at 2.5 times the rate expected in a community population.

Studies of children in regular or treatment foster care (Evans et al. 1994; Glisson 1994; Hornick et al. 1989) and residential treatment (Friman et al. 1993; Hornick et al. 1989) have uniformly reported mean CBCL Total Problem scores that fall within the clinical range. The samples in these studies were either exclusively or predominantly adolescents. One study of younger children (ages 4 to 8) entering foster care reported a mean CBCL Total Problems score that fell within the borderline clinical range (T scores of 60–63) (Hulsey & White, 1989). The children in this study were reported to have significantly more behavior problems than the comparison group of children who were not in foster care.

Across studies of children in foster care, patterns on the CBCL profiles show that children's behavior problems are more commonly of an externalizing nature (i.e., delinquent and/or aggressive behaviors) than of an internalizing nature, with attention and social problems also more prevalent (Dubowitz 1994; Friman et al., 1993; Glisson 1994; Hoffart & Grinnell 1994; Hornick et al. 1989; McIntyre & Keesler 1986). Although Aggressive Behaviors and Attention Problems are among the more frequently occurring problems among CBCL normative samples, Delinquent Behaviors are among the more prevalent problems for clinically referred children (Achenbach 1991b).

Several studies of children in regular foster care or kinship care have reported gender differences in CBCL scores, but results are difficult to interpret. McIntyre and Keesler (1986) found no gender differences in the number of children with one or more problem scores in the clinical range. Patterns in their findings suggest that adolescent females may have been at greater risk than adolescent males in several behavioral areas, but differences in scale composition across age and gender groups on the pre-1991 CBCL make testing these apparent differences problematic. The findings of Hornick and colleagues (1989) also suggest that adolescent girls in foster care evidence more behavior problems than boys the same age, but statistical tests were not applied. Dubowitz and colleagues (1993), in their study of slightly younger children in kinship care, found the reverse pattern. Boys were significantly more likely to score in the clinical range on CBCL summary scales.

Two studies with relatively narrow age ranges noted no age differences in CBCL scores (Glisson 1994; Hulsey & White 1989). McIntyre & Keesler (1986) also reported no age-group differences in the proportions of children scoring in the clinical range on one or more problem scales. Comparison of the relative risk ratios for individual scales, however, reveals that on comparable scales (scales assessing Somatic Complaints, Withdrawal/Depression, Hyperactivity; and for boys only, Aggressive and Delinquent Behavior), children 12–16 years old showed 1.5 to 12 times the risk of disorder than did children 6–11. Preadolescent girls, however, appeared to be at a higher risk than adolescent girls of Aggressive Behavior (3 times higher) and Delinquent Behavior (1.5 times higher). Older children in the 1993 study by Dubowitz and colleagues were more likely to score in the clinical range for Internalizing Behavior, but the pattern of results suggests this finding was dramatically more marked for boys.

TRF Studies

Children in regular or treatment foster care also have been reported to exhibit behavior problems in the school environment (Fanshel & Shinn 1978). Only a few studies have reported

TRF scores for children in regular or treatment foster care. In one study (Glisson 1994), the mean total problems scores for the sample studied were in the borderline-clinical range, and in another study (Evans et al. 1994), the mean total problem scores was in the clinical range.

Longitudinal Studies

Glisson (1994, p. 13) followed youth 12–18 years old who entered state custody and found, after one year, that the sample showed "small but significant improvements" on most summary scales of the CBCL and TRF. Most youth, however, continued to score in the clinical range. Glisson also found that the older the child, the greater the improvement shown on TRF Externalizing Scores, and that girls showed significantly greater improvement on that score than did boys. Clark and colleagues (1994) reported significant improvements in both externalizing and internalizing scores of children in specialized foster care after 18 months in the program.

Summary

The CBCL and TRF research data collected thus far indicate that children in various forms of foster care experience fairly high levels of certain behavioral or emotional problems. This finding is an expected consequence of abuse or neglect that may be exacerbated by placement in foster care, depending upon the placement circumstances. Findings regarding sex and age differences in CBCL problem scores are not consistent across studies. Differences in sample type and age range studied and whether scales or summary scales were examined may account for the discrepancies in results.

Method

Measures

The instruments used in the Casey Family Programs study were the Child Behavior Checklist/4-18 (CBCL) (Achenbach 1991b) and the Teacher's Report Form (TRF) (Achenbach, 1991c). Descriptions of these instruments and a summary of their reliability and validity are presented in Chapter 2 of this volume.

Sample

In this study, the CBCL and TRF were administered at least 3 times during a child's stay in Casey Family Programs: at the time of intake; after the child had been in the program for 1 year (in late 1997, the follow-up period was changed from 1 year to 2 years); and at age 18 or case closure, whichever occurred first. The sample on which this report is based consists of children for whom both CBCL and TRF intake scores were obtained during the intake process prior to admission to Casey Family Programs. The sample represents 75% of all intake evaluations conducted between January of 1991 and December of 1993, as not all children who entered the program had TRFs that were available or could be scored. Intake findings were reported for 362 children who were eventually accepted into the program. Most of the children had been in foster care for 2 years or more prior to entering the Casey program. One-year follow-up findings were analyzed for 111 children who had intake and first-year CBCL data and are reported elsewhere (see Armsden et al. 1997). As Table 9-1 demonstrates, the characteristics of the accepted children whose intake CBCL and TRF data were examined are very close to those of all Casey children who were being served during this time period.

Respondents

The characteristics of the persons who completed the CBCL and TRF are presented in Tables 9-2 and 9-3. The respondents were those individuals most familiar with the child, typically in a family foster care setting (for the CBCL) or school setting (for the TRF).

Data Analysis

Scoring

The CBCL and TRF results are most commonly reported in terms of T scores and whether the T scores fall into two clinically significant ranges: "clinical" or "borderline clinical." The clinical range of scores indicates severe emotional and behavioral difficulties or low competence level. Scores in the clinical range are above approximately the 98th percentile for Problem Behavior scales and below the 2nd percentile for Competence and Academic/ Adaptive Functioning scales. Clinical-range problem behavior summary (broad-band and total) scores are above the 90th percentile, and for competence and Academic/Adaptive Functioning summary scores, they are below the 10th percentile. The borderline-clinical range of scores spans about the 95th to 98th percentiles for individual Problem Behavior scales, and the 2nd to 5th percentile for Competence and Academic/Adaptive Functioning scales. For the Summary scales, scores between the 83rd and 90th percentiles for Problem Behaviors are borderline-clinical, and scores between the 10th and 17th percentiles for Competence and Academic/Adaptive Functioning are in the borderline-clinical range. In this report, data analyses generally combined the borderline-clinical range and clinical-range cases into one category of cases, referred to as scoring in the "combined clinical range."

Statistical Analyses

Multivariate statistical tests, such as multivariate analysis of variance (MANOVA), were used wherever possible. For the problem behavior scales, three MANOVAs were conducted with the three internalizing scales, the two externalizing scales, and the three remaining scales (Social Problems, Attention Problems, and Thought Problems scores were sufficiently intercorrelated to suggest the use of MANOVA [Bartlett test of sphericity, $p < .0001$]). An additional MANOVA was performed on the three CBCL Competence section scales. These groupings of scales represent a statistical compromise between conservatively testing all scales in one or two MANOVAs and possibly "missing" a clinically relevant finding, and utilizing many univariate tests at the increased risk of Type I errors.

Table 9-1. Youth Demographic Data

Variable	Casey 1993 CBCL Sample[a] (N = 362)	Casey Family Programs[b] (N = 1087)
Age in years at intake	**Mean (SD)**	
	10.5 (3.1)	10.9
Sex	**n (%)**	
Female	201 (56%)	54%
Male	161 (44%)	46%
Primary ethnic identification		
African American	25%	27%[c]
Asian	1%	2%
Caucasian	47%	43%
Hispanic/Latino	12%	11%
Native American	10%	14%
Polynesian/Pacific Islander	5%	4%

[a]CBCL sample consists of children who were accepted into the Program during 1991–93 and who had both CBCL and TRF scores.
[b]Program-wide statistics are from the December 1993 Child Care Report for the children in the foster family care program component [The Casey Family Program 1993].
[c]Totals > 100% due to rounding.

Because of the exploratory nature of this research as well as the number of comparisons that were planned a priori, a more stringent level of statistical significance ($p < .01$) was used for most of the univariate test results. In a few cases, univariate results which met less stringent criteria ($p < .05$) are reported because of their possible clinical significance. Differences between age groups were analyzed, using the groupings made by the CBCL instruments (6–11 years and 12–18 years). Preadolescents (under 12 years) were compared with adolescents (12–18 years) in a number of analyses. Gender comparisons also were made.

Reference Samples

The mean scale scores for demographically matched normative and clinically referred samples are reported in the CBCL and TRF manuals (Achenbach 1991b; 1991c). T-score data are reported separately for four age/sex groups. In order to provide general comparisons between the average CBCL/TRF profiles for Casey children and those of the reference samples, it was necessary to combine the data on the four age/sex groups for each type of reference sample. (The mean T scores of the age/sex groups in each sample differed almost entirely by only one or two points). Data combination was done by calculating, for each scale, the mean of the

Table 9-2. Characteristics of CBCL Respondents

Characteristic	Percentage
Relation to the child	
Foster mother	59%
Other relative	21%
Staff member[a]	6%
Other[b]	4%
Referring caseworker	4%
Foster father	3%
Former foster parent	2%
Birth/stepparent	1%
Ethnicity	
Caucasian	60%
African American	24%
Native American	7%
Hispanic/Latino	5%
Polynesian/Pacific Islander	3%
Asian	<1%

[a]Staff member includes social service staff at shelter or group care facilities where the child is placed at intake.
[b]Includes school counselor and Casey social worker.

average score for the four age/sex groups, each score weighted according to group size. Average profiles for both the normative and clinically referred samples were generated. Each of these two reference profiles was based on a sample of 2,110 children ages 4–18 years old, 57% of whom were under 12 years and 51% of whom were girls. In terms of age and sex, this sample composition is quite similar to the characteristics of the Casey sample (see Table 9-1). Nevertheless, because the Casey sample is not strictly demographically matched to the reference samples, statistical comparisons are not appropriate, although some general comparisons can be made.

Findings and Practice Implications

The CBCL

CBCL Problem Behaviors of Children at Intake

As seen in Table 9.4, none of the average CBCL problem behavior scores for the sample of Casey children were in the borderline clinical or clinical range (even though many individual

Table 9-3. Selected Characteristics of Persons Who Completed the TRF Assessment Form

Respondent	Percentage
Teacher	97%
School counselor	3%

Ethnicity	Percentage
Caucasian	82%
African American	7%
Hispanic/Latino	5%
Asian	3%
Polynesian/Pacific Islander	1%
Native American	1%
Middle Eastern	<1%

Casey children had elevated scores). On average, Casey children scored above the normative (nonclinically referred) sample but below the clinically referred sample (Achenbach 1991a) in occurrence of behavior problems. The Casey children's profile of scores indicated a similarity to clinically referred children (Achenbach 1991a) in relative prevalence of problems, although at a lower level of occurrence.

The mean Total Problems T score for Casey children at intake was consistently lower than for other samples of children in foster care or residential treatment, most of whom were served as part of a shorter-term placement. The pattern of results is congruent with other samples, however, in terms of the behavior problems occurring most frequently (Externalizing Problem Behaviors, Attention Difficulties, and Social Problems).

Children on average received significantly higher Externalizing summary scores than Internalizing summary scores [$M(SD)$=55.6 (12.2) versus 53.6 (11.7); paired $t(361)$=3.30, p=.001]. For individual scales, the percentage of children falling into the CBCL borderline clinical or clinical range (combined clinical range) extended from 8 % (Somatic Complaints) to 25 % (Delinquent Behavior). Fifteen percent of children under 12 years of age scored in the combined clinical range on the Sex Problems scale (see Table 9.4). The normative rate is 5% of children in the combined clinical range on these scales (17% for summary scales).

CBCL Competence Profile of Children at Intake

None of the average CBCL competence profile scores for the sample of Casey children was in the borderline clinical or clinical range (see Table 9.5). Nevertheless, many individual children had scores in clinical ranges. Although the level of participation in activities (such as sports and jobs) for Casey children was virtually equivalent to the normative group (reference sample score = 48–49), school performance and social competence were dramatically weaker. Average school performance, as reported by caregivers, was well below normal. Weaknesses in such competency areas would appear to go hand in hand with the attention

Table 9-4.CBCL Problem Behavior Scores of Casey Children at Intake (N=362)

Scale	T score M (SD)	Percentage of children in borderline range[a]	Percentage of children in clinical range[a]	Total % in combined clinical range[b]
Internalizing				
Withdrawn	56.9(7.9)	8%	6%	14%
Somatic Complaints	55.0(6.6)	5	3	8
Anxious/Depressed	56.8(9.0)	6	9	14
Other[c]				
Social Problems	58.1(9.2)	10	9	19
Thought Problems	57.1(8.7)	12	5	17
Attention Problems	59.1(9.6)	11	10	22
Sex Problems (< 12 yr.)	55.4(9.4)	4	11	15
Externalizing				
Delinquent Behavior	59.0(8.9)	10 •	15	25
Aggressive Behavior	58.0(9.6)	9	11	20
Summary Scores				
Internalizing	53.6(11.7)	11	20	31
Externalizing	55.6(12.2)	10	28	38
Total Problems	55.9(12.1)	10	30	40

[a]Borderline clinical range includes scores between 67-70 for individual scale scores and 60-63 for summary scale scores. Clinical range includes scores 71 and above for individual scale scores and 64 and above for summary scale scores.

[b]Total percentage of children in borderline or clinical range. May be different from the sum of borderline and clinical percentages due to rounding. Normative rates are: 5% for scale scores and 17% for summary scale scores.

[c]These scales do not statistically cluster with each other or in either of the other scale groupings.

and social problems found among these children.

Individual scale items can lend added insight into behavioral functioning. Almost a quarter of the Casey sample at intake was rated as above average in getting along with parents. Caregivers reported about the same number of children as making above average grades in school. These two groups, which largely overlapped [$\chi^2(1)=13.53, p<.001$], appeared to be coping well with the negative consequences of their past life experiences and placement.

Demographic and Respondent Differences in CBCL Scores.

A set of four 2-way multivariate analyses of variance (MANOVA) were conducted to examine whether gender or age group (preadolescents versus adolescents) contributed to differences

Table 9-5. CBCL Competence Scores at Intake (*N*=362)

Scale	T score M (SD)	Percentage of children in borderline range[a]	Percentage of children in clinical range[a]	Total % in combined clinical range[b]
Activities (*n*=340)	47.8(6.4)	2%	1%	3%
Social (*n*=322)	41.8(8.6)	11	9	20
School (*n*=301)	39.2(9.5)	16	19	35
Total Competence (*n*=279)	42.4(8.9)	21	27	48

[a]Borderline-clinical range includes scores between 30-33 for individual scale scores and 37 - 40 for summary scale scores. Clinical range includes scores 29 and below for individual scale scores and 36 and below for summary scale scores.

[b]Total percentage of children in the borderline or clinical range. Normative rates are: 5% for scale scores and 17% for summary scale scores.

in CBCL scores. Separate analyses of Competence scales, Internalizing scales, Externalizing scales, and the remaining Problem scales revealed a significant age-group effect ($p<.05$) for the Internalizing scales [$F(3,356)=2.87$, $p=.03$]. Follow-up univariate analyses indicated that adolescents ($n=144$) were rated higher than preadolescents on Anxiety/Depression ($n=218$) [$M=58$, $SD=10$ versus $M=56$, $SD=8$; $F(1, 358)=6.05$, $p=.014$. Analyses of summary scores showed an age-group trend for Internalizing behaviors[$F(1,358)=6.26$, $p=.013$; adolescents; $M=56$, $SD=12$, pre-adolescents: $M=52$, $SD=12$]. No other results approached the .01 significance level.

Using the chi-square test, differences in the prevalence of clinical range scores by gender and by age group were examined. First, more males than females scored in the clinical or borderline clinical range on Social Competence [27% versus 15%; $\chi^2(1)=6.26$, $p=.012$]. Second, preadolescents were almost twice as likely as adolescents to evidence clinically significant Delinquent Behavior [31% vs. 15%; $\chi^2 (1)=9.88$, $p=.002$.] Because any occurrence of certain delinquent behaviors can be serious, item scores were examined. More preadolescents than adolescents received non-zero scores (ratings of "sometimes" or "often") on "steals at home" (24% versus 12%; $\chi^2[1] = 7.54$, $p = .02$). There also was some evidence of more "lying or cheating" among preadolescents (58% versus 46%; $\chi^2[1] = 4.45$, $p = .04$) and a trend toward more reports of "steals outside the home" (16% versus 9%; $\chi^2[1] = 3.64$, $p = .06$). These findings were unexpected and deserve careful future study. Although older youth might be expected to act out more in these areas, it may be that the types of behaviors characterized as delinquent were occurring differently for younger as opposed to older children. The findings may reflect a combination of more troubled, older youth not being accepted into the program and an aging factor in which some middle or late adolescent youth move away from delinquent behavior. Although these findings resulted from multiple tests and may have occurred by chance, they nonetheless may signal important clinical issues, including the presence of conduct disorders or attachment issues.

Tests were not conducted for differences in CBCL scores for children from various ethnic backgrounds. The sample sizes for most ethnic groupings were too small for meaningful analysis.

According to ANOVA's and Tukey HSD multiple comparison tests [$p<.05$], respondents who were related to the children, when compared with foster parents and professional caregivers, rated the children higher on Anxiety/Depression [$F(2,359)=3.50$, $p=.031$], Somatic Complaints [$F(2,359=5.99$, $p=.003$] and Aggressive Behavior [$F(2,359)=3.02$, $p=.050$], but also rated them higher in Social Competence [$F(2,276)=4.73$, $p=.010$]. These comparative findings should be viewed with caution as multiple tests were conducted, raising the risk of Type I error.

Practice Implications for CBCL Problem Behavior and Competence Items.

At the time of admission to the Casey program, children did not score, on average, in the borderline clinical or clinical range for any scale or summary score. Reliance on average scores may be misleading, however, in that a substantial number of children scored in the borderline clinical or clinical range for various problem-behavior or competence scales, especially with respect to the Externalizing, Attention Problems, Social Problems, and School scales. It is interesting that the general profiles of the problem behavior and competence scales closely parallel that of the clinically referred sample. This finding is expected, however, given the serious forms of child maltreatment these children had suffered and the emotional challenges faced by them as they coped with the partial or total loss of contact with their birth families. The Behavior Problem data indicate that as children enter the program, they need social skills development, school-based and other work focusing on attention problems, and that cognitive-behavioral and multi-systemic strategies that directly address delinquent behaviors are indicated (see Henggler et al. 1998).

The TRF

TRF Problem Behaviors at Intake.

As was true for the CBCL, average TRF Problem Behavior scores for Casey children at intake were above scores for the normative sample and below scores for the clinically referred sample (Achenbach 1991b). None of the average TRF problem behavior scores for Casey children were in the borderline clinical or clinical range, even though many individual children had elevated scores (see Table 9.6). Although the TRF scores reflected somewhat below-average functioning, the average Total Problems score (54.9) was lower than scores published for two other samples of children entering care, indicating better adjustment (Glisson 1994: $M=63$; Evans et al. 1994: $M=71$). In contrast to age and gender differences on the CBCL, no age group or gender differences were found in TRF problem scores.

The highest TRF scores at intake were found for Anxious/Depressed, Social Problems, and Aggressive Behavior. Lowest scores were found for Thought Problems and Somatic Complaints. School personnel reported that children showed significantly more Externaliz-

Table 9-6. TRF Problem Behavior Scores of Casey Children at Intake (N=362)

Scale	Mean T score (SD) range[a]	Percentage of children in borderline range[a]	Percentage of children in clinical range[a]	Total % in combined clinical range[b]
Internalizing				
Withdrawn	55.8(7.9)	4%	4%	9%
Somatic Complaints	52.8(5.6)	2	1	3
Anxious/Depressed	56.9(8.0)	10	5	15
Other[c]				
Social Problems	56.8(7.4)	10	3	13
Thought Problems	54.7(7.1)	7	2	10
Attention Problems	56.1(6.9)	6	3	9
Externalizing				
Delinquent Behavior	55.8(6.7)	7	2	9
Aggressive Behavior	57.4(8.0)	5	6	10
Summary Scores				
Internalizing	53.3(11.0)	9	20	29
Externalizing	55.3(9.7)	17	9	36
Total Problems	54.9(10.2)	14	20	34

[a]Borderline clinical range includes scores between 67-70 for individual scale scores and 60-63 for summary scores. Clinical range includes scores 71 and above for individual scale scores and 64 and above for summary scale scores.

[b]Total percentage of children in borderline or clinical range. May be different from the sum of borderline and clinical percentages due to rounding. Normative rates are: 5% for scale scores and 17% for summary scale scores.

[c]These scales do not statistically cluster with each other or in either of the other scale groupings.

ing problem behaviors than Internalizing problem behaviors [$M(SD)$=55.3 (9.7) versus $M(SD)$=53.3 (11.0); paired $t(361)$=3.56, $p<.001$]. The percentage of children scoring in the combined clinical range on the TRF was also examined. For individual scales, the percentage of children falling into the borderline clinical or clinical range ranged from 3 % for Somatic Complaints to 15 % for Anxious/Depressed. These data indicate that a substantial proportion of Casey children at the time of admission were having difficulties in the school setting as compared to the general population of children in the United States.

TRF Academic and Adaptive Functioning.

Average TRF academic and adaptive functioning scores for Casey children at intake fell below scores for the normative sample and above those for the clinically referred sample. Although this portion of the TRF offers less than the problem behavior section in the way of clinically useful information, it does indicate that children's functioning, on average, was not in the borderline clinical or clinical range (see Table 9.7). All the same, the scores of many individual children were within the clinical range. Average academic functioning was well below normal. Adolescent girls in this study were more than twice as likely as adolescent boys to score in the combined clinical range on Academic Performance [42% versus 19%; $c^2(1)=6.41$, $p=.011$]. As with scores on the CBCL school scale, the TRF academic functioning scales indicated that serious difficulties in school performance existed at intake for many Casey children. As listed in Tables 9.5 and 9.7, the total percentage of children in the clinical or borderline clinical range was 35% for the CBCL and 33 % for the TRF.

Many children who scored in the combined clinical range for school performance were also experiencing clinically significant levels of behavior problems. Fully 52% of these children were in the clinical ranges for the CBCL Total Problems summary score, and 58% for the TRF Total Problems summary score. Youth reported to have clinical levels of certain behavior problems (Attention, Anxiety or Depression, and Social Problems were 3 to almost 10 times as likely to have clinical level difficulties in their school work (see Armsden et al. 1997).

Practice Implications.

Teachers noted in the TRF some serious difficulties concerning children's Anxiety/Depression and Social Problems. These difficulties indicated a need for continued or, in some cases, increased emphasis on interventions designed to alleviate depression, increase self-esteem, develop social skills, and teach more positive ways of interacting with others. One service response was a special "Quality Services Redesign" project undertaken by certain Casey Divisions to provide more work group opportunities for children. Gains were reported in the areas of depression, self esteem, and social skills, but these interventions must be formally evaluated. The type of staff and foster parent training or coaching that is needed to more fully address these needs has yet to be determined.

A substantial percentage of children had clinical range scores for Anxiety/Depression, Social Problems, and Aggressive Behavior on the TRF. In many ways, these percentages provide a more clinically useful profile of Casey children at intake than the average T scores. They better illustrate the types of challenges that these children present for teachers as well as foster parents and staff at the point of entering the program.

Comparison of CBCL and TRF Data

Comparison of CBCL and TRF intake profiles indicates that fewer behavior problems were reported for children in the classroom setting than in nonschool settings (see Table 9.8). Compared with school personnel, caregivers on average rated Casey children as functioning less well, particularly in the areas of Delinquent Behavior [paired $t(361)=6.51, p<.001$] and Attention Problems [paired $t(361)=5.83, p<.001$]. Caregivers also rated children as having more Somatic Complaints [paired $t(361)=5.18, p<.001$], more Thought Problems [paired $t(361)=4.47, p<.001$], and more Social Problems [paired $t(361)= 2.52$, p=.012]. Agreement between caregivers and teachers with respect to Problem Behavior scales was modest (below

Table 9-7. TRF Academic and Adaptive Functioning Scores at Intake

Scale	Mean T score (SD) range[a]	Percentage of children in borderline range[a]	Percentage of children in clinical range[a]	Total % in combined clinical range[b]
Adaptive Functioning (N=340)	45.6(7.6)	14%	14%	28%
Academic Performance (N=342)	46.0(8.9)	9	24	33

[a]Borderline clinical range includes T scores between 37-40. Clinical range includes scores that are 36 and below.

[b]Total percentage of children in borderline or clinical range. Normative rate is 5%.

30% agreement). On broader indices of behavioral functioning (the Internalizing and Externalizing scales) and on academic functioning, however, there was a moderate amount of agreement between the two groups of raters (40–50% agreement).

A better understanding is needed of the implications for clinical interventions when children exhibit fewer difficulties—for example, they behave less aggressively—in school than in nonschool settings. Does the added structure or supports of a school setting help some children? Or is the difference in scores the result of teachers' reduced sensitivity to such behavior because they are working with many students, differences in where the behavior occurs (on the school grounds, for example, but not in the classroom), or the differences in types of behaviors rated on the TRF versus the CBCL? Discussions with social workers, children, foster parents and school personnel are needed to further explore these issues.

Measurement and Data Utilization Issues

Limitations of the Study

There are several limitations of this study that must be recognized. First, although most CBCL respondents were sufficiently familiar with the child to make adequate ratings (having known the child for at least 5 to 6 months), familiarity with the children varied. In some cases, the length of the placement with the foster family or relative was short, and, in other cases, a caseworker completed the form. Second, there was the possibility that CBCL and TRF scores were skewed if the caregiver or teacher who completed the form did not report accurately the children's competency areas or the frequency of the children's problem behaviors. If, for example, the child's current foster parent has not been reassured that Casey Family Programs serve children who have serious behavior problems, the parent may minimize the child's poor behavior in one or more areas to promote the child's opportunity for program admission.

Additional limitations of the study are related to characteristics of the CBCL and TRF instruments. Despite the diversity of the CBCL development sample and the number of

Table 9-8. Percentage of Casey Children with Problem Behavior Scores in the Borderline or Clinical Range[a] (*N*=362)

Scale	Child Behavior Checklist		Teacher's Report Form	
	Percentage of children in borderline range	Percentage of children in clinical range (Total %[b])	Percentage of children in borderline range	Percentage of children in clinical range (Total %[b])
Internalizing				
Withdrawn	8%	6% (14%)[a]	4%	4%(9%)[a]
Somatic Complaints	5	3 (8)	2	1(3)
Anxious/Depressed	6	9(14)	10	5(15)
Other[c]				
Social Problems	10	9 (19)	10	3(13)
Thought Problems	12	5 (17)	7	2(10)[b]
Attention Problems	11	10 (22)	6	3(9)
Externalizing				
Delinquent Behavior	10	15 (25)	7	2(9)
Aggressive Behavior	9	11 (20)	5	6(10)
Summary Data				
Internalizing	11	20 (31)	9	20 (29)
Externalizing	10	28 (38)	17	19 (36)
Total Problems	10	30 (40)	14	20 (34)

[a]Borderline clinical range includes scores between 67-70 for individual scale scores and 60-63 for summary scale scores. Clinical range includes scores 71 and above for individual scale scores and 64 and above for summary scale scores.

[b]Total percentage of children in combined clinical range may be different from the sum of Borderline and Clinical percents due to rounding. Normative rates are 5% for scales and 17% for summary scale scores.

[c]These scales do not statistically cluster with each other or in the other groups.

international studies that have been conducted using the CBCL and TRF, relatively few reports have been published that describe how various American ethnic groups differ with respect to scores on these measures. In addition, as with most behavioral assessment measures, the CBCL and TRF tend to highlight problem behavior. Thus, it is important to note that the lack of behavior problems in an area may indicate adaptive functioning and may be an area of strength. Finally, many statistical tests were performed in this study, and some of the significant findings may have occurred by chance. Additional studies are needed to ascertain whether the findings are reliable.

Other Research and Clinical Issues

This study raised a number of research and clinical issues. First, it became clear that the validity of checklist ratings depends on rater familiarity with the child. Practical methods for addressing this problem (such as employing multiple raters when appropriate or using rater familiarity with the child as a covariate in statistical analyses) are needed.

Second, issues arose as to how researchers should integrate CBCL and TRF reports. When using the two types of assessment forms, researchers and practitioners must determine how to weigh the reports and deal with the differences that appear in them. Based on validation and other studies of the CBCL and TRF, it is clear that the scores, while generally in agreement, do not correlate highly, and modest agreement was noted in this study as well. Although this result was not surprising given the different roles played by various types of raters, it raises the possibility that different environments elicit different kinds of behavior problems or strengths from children. A child in school, for example, may behave poorly if the school setting does not allow some gross motor experiences, whereas the home environment may provide more opportunities for the child to show more nurturing behavior. Differences in ratings may provide valuable information from a clinical perspective, however, as to where greater emphasis is needed. Differences in ratings from an outcomes research perspective may indicate that an intervention is having more success in one setting as opposed to another.

The third issue relates to the fact that adequate comparison data for children served by the child welfare system remain scarce. Specifically, despite the diversity of the CBCL norming sample and the number of international studies that have been conducted using the CBCL and TRF, there have been relatively few reports published in which variation in scores between American ethnic groups is addressed. Pooling research data from comparable studies would allow meta-analyses that would help address this issue (K. Wetherbee, personal communication, September 7, 1997).

Fourth, issues were identified regarding the use and analysis of CBCL and TRF measures to maximize their clinical sensitivity. Two studies using these instruments have found significant improvements in both internalizing and externalizing behaviors. In one study, improvements were found after 18 months (Clark et al. 1994) and in another study, after 16 months (Shennum, this volume). A number of researchers, however, have not found significant CBCL- or TRF-indicated behavioral changes in children in foster care or other programs after one year of service. In a recent, as yet unpublished study, for example, the researchers primarily found only insignificant changes after one year in a special foster care program, and as a result, the program instituted a two-year reassessment period (see Armsden et. al 1997). It is unclear whether there are factors that account for the failure to find significant improvements, other than the obvious explanations that the intervention was not effective or the gains made were not sufficiently large to be detected at the point in time they were measured.

Fifth was the issue of how best to use the measures in a strength-oriented agency. As with most behavioral assessment instruments, the CBCL and TRF highlight problem areas. It is important to note, however, that a lack of behavior problems in one area may indicate adaptive functioning and strength.

Sixth was the need to handle differences in raters between times 1 and 2 (and, in some cases, at time 3) in a time-series design approach. Results from at least one study (Berrick et al. 1994) suggest that differences in respondents on behavior rating scales may make a substantial difference in the reporting of problems. Methodological and statistical strategies are needed to account for or control changes in raters over time.

Seventh, the utility in using short forms of the CBCL and/or TRF was identified as an issue. Although staff and some parents would welcome shorter checklists, it may be that the validity of either instrument would be compromised in some cases if it were shortened. Smaller sets of items have been used in Tennessee and other states (see Glisson 1994). The advantages and limitations to the use of shortened forms need to be better understood.

Finally, individual item analysis versus scale analysis was seen as an issue. In general, scale scores are used most extensively when reporting CBCL, TRF, and YSR findings. Some of the individual problem behavior items, however, represent critical "sentinel" markers of service outcomes, such as physical fights or suicide attempts. Although there may be reliability and validity issues when item analyses are relied upon too heavily (see Anastasi 1982), the individual items may reveal important behavioral changes not easily detected by examining scale scores. The field could benefit from further discussions of the advantages and limitations of using individual checklist items versus scale scores.

Conclusion

The findings of the Casey Family Programs study indicate that children accepted into the program were functioning below the normative sample for the CBCL and TRF, but better than a large reference sample of children referred for clinical evaluation. Significant numbers of Casey children, however, scored in the clinical or borderline clinical range at intake, particularly as rated by caregivers. In addition, one-third of the children were functioning in the clinical range on academic performance upon entry into the program. Caregivers most frequently reported problems of an externalizing nature (delinquent or aggressive behavior) and attention problems. Teachers most frequently noted problems in school with aggressive behavior, anxiety/depression, and social problems.

If age or sex differences in CBCL and TRF scores are replicated in future studies, steps should be taken to focus on groups of children at the time of intake into foster care who are especially vulnerable to certain problems. Skilled, relevant intervention may ensure that further behavioral deterioration does not occur during this potentially difficult transition. At the time of a fresh start with a new family, some troubled children may be more open to focused intervention.

The diversity and complexity of these data underscore the importance of careful multi-axial assessment; individualized outcome-oriented case planning; and interventions that involve multiple systems, including the child, foster parent, birth family, peers, the school, and the broader community.

Acknowledgments

Collection of these assessment data was made possible through the efforts of the Casey foster parents, social workers, case assistants, and Division aides, who together with teachers ensured that the CBCL and TRF forms were completed. Thanks to Dr. Thomas Achenbach and David Jacobowitz for consultation regarding the scoring of the CBCL and TRF. We appreciate the review of early drafts of the technical report by Thomas Achenbach, Edith Fein, David Fine, and Glen Paddock.

References

Achenbach, T. M. (1991a). *Integrative guide for the 1991 CBCL/4-18, YSR, and TRF Profiles.* Burlington: University of Vermont Department of Psychiatry.

Achenbach, T. M. (1991b). *Manual for the Child Behavior Checklist/4-18 and 1991 Profile.* Burlington: University of Vermont Department of Psychiatry.

Achenbach, T. M. (1991c). *Manual for the Teacher's Report Form and 1991 Profile.* Burlington: University of Vermont Department of Psychiatry.

Achenbach, T.M. & Edelbrock, C. (1983). *Manual for the Child Behavior and Revised Child Behavior Profile.* Burlington: University of Vermont, Department of Psychiatry.

Anastasi, A. (1982). *Psychological Testing* (5th ed.). New York: MacMillan Publishing Co., Inc.

Armsden, G., Pecora, P.J. & Payne, V. (1997). *A profile of youth placed with The Casey Family Program using the Child Behavior Checklist/4-18 and the Teacher's Report Form.* Seattle, Washington: The Casey Family Program.

Berrick, J.D., Barth, R.P. & Needell, B. (1994). A comparison of kinship foster homes and foster family homes: Implications for kinship foster care as family preservation. *Children and Youth Services Review, 16*(1/2), 33–63.

Clark, H. B., Prange, M. E., Lee, B., Boyd, L. A., McDonald, B. A., & Stewart, E. S. (1994). Improving adjustment outcomes for foster children with emotional and behavioral disorders: Early findings from a controlled study on individualized services. *Journal of Emotional and Behavioral Disorders, 2*(4), 207–218.

Committee on Ways and Means, U.S. House of Representatives. (1996). *1996 Green Book.* Washington, DC: U.S. Government Printing Office.

Courtney, M. (1995).The foster care crisis and welfare reform. *Public Welfare, 53*(3), 27–33, 40–41.

Dubowitz, H., Feigelman, S., Harrington, D., Starr, Jr., R., Zuravin, S., & Sawyer, R. (1994). Children in kinship care: How do they fare? *Children and Youth Services Review, 16,* 85–106.

Dubowitz, H., Zuravin, S., Starr, Jr., R., Feigelman, S., & Harrington, D. (1993). Behavior problems of children in kinship care. *Developmental and Behavioral Pediatrics, 14,* 386–395.

Evans, M. E., Armstrong, M. I., Dollard, N., Kuppinger, A. D., Huz, S., & Wood, V.M. (1994). Development and evaluation of treatment foster care and family-centered intensive case management in New York. *Journal of Emotional and Behavioral Disorders, 2*(4), 228–239.

Fanshel, D. R. & Shinn, E. (1978). *Children in foster care: A longitudinal investigation.* New York: Columbia University Press.

Friman, P., Evans, J., Larzelere, R., Williams, G., & Daly, D. (1993). Correspondence between child dysfunction and program intrusion: Evidence of a continuum of care across five child mental health programs. *Journal of Community Psychology, 21,* 227–233.

Glisson, C. (1994). The effect of services coordination teams on outcomes for children in state custody. *Administration in Social Work, 18*(4), 1–23.

Henggler, S. W., Schoenwald, S. K., Borduin, C. M., Rowland, M., & Cunningham, P. B. (1998). *Multi-systemic treatment of antisocial behavior in children and adolescents.* New York: Guilford.

Hoffart, I. & Grinnell, R.M. (1994). Behavioral differences of children in institutional and group home care. *International Journal of Family Care, 6*(1), 33–47.

Hornick, J., Phillips, D., & Kerr, N. (1989). Gender differences in behavioral problems of foster children: implications for special foster care. *Community Alternatives, 1,* 35–52.

Hulsey, T. C. & White, R. (1989). Family characteristics and measures of behavior in foster and nonfoster children. *American Journal of Orthopsychiatry, 59*(4), 502–509.

Kluger, M., Alexander, G. & Curtis, P. (Eds.) (2000). *What Works in Child Welfare.* Washington, DC Child Welfare League of America.

Landsverk, J., Clausen, J., M., Ganger, W., Chadwick, D., & Litrownik, A. (In press). Mental health problems of foster children in three California counties. *Child Abuse and Neglect.*

Lipner, R. & Goertz, B. (1996). Child welfare priorities and expenditures. *W-Memo of the American Public Welfare Association, 2*(8), 3.

McIntyre, A. & Keesler, T. (1986). Psychological disorders among foster children. *Journal of Clinical Psychology, 14,* 297–303.

Paul, G.L. (1967). Outcome research in psychotherapy. *Journal of Consulting Psychology, 31,* 101–119.

Pecora, P.J., Massinga, R., & Mauserall, H. (1997). Measuring outcomes in the changing environment of child welfare services. *Behavioral Healthcare Tomorrow, 6*(2), 2–6.

Swire, M. R. & Kavaler, F. (1978). The health status of foster children. In S. Chess & A. Thomas (Eds.), *Annual progress in child psychiatry and child development* (pp. 626–642). New York: Brunner/Mazel.

Tatara, T. (1997). U.S. child substitute care flow data and the race/ethnicity of children in care for FY 1995, along with recent trends in the U.S. child substitute care populations. *VCIS Research Notes, 113* (March). Washington, DC: American Public Welfare Association.

10

Using the Child Behavior Checklist in Child Welfare Practice: Lessons Learned from One Agency's Experience

Kathleen Lenerz

The Child Behavior Checklist (CBCL) is used in child welfare settings for research, administrative, and clinical purposes. Researchers and program administrators use the instrument to evaluate programs, most often to examine the program's effectiveness in changing children's problem behavior. The CBCL also may be used as an aid in understanding the characteristics of the children served by a program and in assessing children's needs to ensure that appropriate treatment and services are provided. The multiple applications of the CBCL can be mutually reinforcing and provide useful feedback. When researchers, for example, describe aggregate characteristics of children or aggregate changes in their behavior, administrators and clinicians are able to place individual child behavior and their clinical work in a broader context. Similarly, when practitioners discuss individual case profiles, researchers develop a greater understanding of the clinical issues the program addresses.

At the same time, researchers, administrators, and social work practitioners may have different interests and orientations with respect to the CBCL. In most child welfare settings, researchers and administrators rely on social workers or other line staff to administer the CBCL and obtain reliable data. Practitioners, however, may not have training or experience in the use of standardized measures or may have a professional orientation to assessment that is incompatible with the use of standardized instruments. In such cases, social workers may not have a strong commitment to administering the CBCL in ways that would provide the most reliable data for researchers and program administrators.

There is little in the literature about the processes of administrating the CBCL in applied settings. A review of a 10-year bibliography of published articles using the CBCL (Vignoe & Achenbach 1997) shows only 12 references dealing with child welfare populations. The research on which those articles are based assumes that the administration of the CBCL followed appropriate research protocols. Discussions with colleagues in a variety of child welfare settings, however, suggest that compliance with protocols is often not the case.

To address the lack of literature in this area, this chapter identifies some of the key issues in the use of the CBCL in child welfare settings and discusses how these issues may ultimately affect the utility of the CBCL for research and administrative purposes. It also makes recommendations regarding the factors that should be taken into consideration when using the CBCL in child welfare settings. It further advances recommendations for implementation strategies to enhance the research, administrative, and clinical utility of the CBCL. This chapter is based on the experiences of one private child welfare agency, but the lessons learned may be relevant in other child welfare settings that offer similar programs and services. These experiences should be instructive for program evaluators, child welfare administrators, and children's services managers who wish to use the CBCL.

The Decision to Use the CBCL

Casey Family Services (CFS) is the direct services arm of the Annie E. Casey Foundation. The agency provides foster care and family-based services in 8 sites in the 6 New England states and Baltimore, and it serves approximately 550 children in foster care and approximately 450 families each year. The foster care programs include both long-term foster care, in which there is no expectation that children will return to their birth families and adoption is not feasible, and treatment foster care, in which emotionally disturbed children live in a family setting. Administrators and practitioners within the agency were interested in having a better understanding of the children served in the agency's long-term and treatment foster care programs and in supporting social workers' assessment of children's needs with information provided by a standardized measure. Agency researchers proposed a study of change in children's functioning during their stay in foster care and the use of the CBCL to meet the administrative and clinical needs that administrators and practitioners had defined. The CBCL was selected as the instrument for the study, marking the agency's first systematic data collection effort for program evaluation purposes and one of the first uses of a standardized instrument by social workers in the agency's foster care program.

Because CFS consciously strives to integrate program evaluation activities with clinical practice, a schedule for administering the CBCL was selected to meet research needs for regular data collection and to maximize opportunities for clinical use of the instrument. To integrate the measure with current practice, the agency decided to administer the CBCL to foster parents at intake and at subsequent six-month intervals, to take place just prior to the regular six-month case review.

The use of the CBCL was designed as an adjunct to existing clinical assessment that served as the basis for defining case goals and objectives and monitoring progress during the course of placement. As part of existing clinical practice at CFS, social workers conduct comprehensive assessments at intake to the program and obtain extensive information from referral sources and previous service providers. Such information typically includes placement history and reports of any psychological, psychiatric, and educational evaluations. During placement, children may receive a wide range of ancillary services intended to meet their individual needs. CFS social workers develop close working relationships with these service providers, maintaining ongoing contact and involving these service providers in case reviews. CFS social workers are able to obtain from these service providers substantial information on children's functioning and progress during the course of care. The CBCL complements these sources of information.

Implementation: Initial Training

As a first step in implementing the CBCL, CFS conducted a comprehensive one-day training in each site for all social workers and support staff who would use the CBCL scoring software. The agency consulted with clinical staff familiar with the instrument regarding methods for training staff who, for the most part, were unfamiliar with the CBCL or the administration of standardized instruments. Because the CBCL was to be used to complement rather than supplant existing case practice, the emphasis was on the instrument's clinical uses. The training included information on the administration of the CBCL and its scoring and interpretation; how to present the form to foster parents in an inclusive way that promoted their contributions to case planning; the use of the CBCL in assessing competencies and deficits; and the integration of the CBCL into extensive already-existing qualitative assessment procedures. The training included examples of how CBCL results could be used in team meetings and case reviews and as an aid in goal setting with individual youth.

To assist in ongoing implementation following the training, each site selected a "coach" or facilitator to aid social workers in integrating the use of the CBCL into their practice and to provide immediate, hands-on help with interpreting the results. Guidelines for administration were revised in response to social workers' experiences in using the instrument. Clinical supervisors in each site oversaw site administration and implementation of the CBCL, and research staff provided ongoing consultation and assistance throughout the initial implementation.

Initial Review of Implementation

The first systematic review of the clinical use and implementation of the CBCL took place approximately nine months after its introduction. Because the administration and use of the CBCL were new, it was expected that problems would arise in implementation. In fact, the first informal feedback suggested that CBCL administration was not a smooth process. In some instances, the instrument was not administered in a timely fashion or at all, and it appeared that the CBCL results were not necessarily being used in case reviews. These reports led to an assessment to determine the extent of CBCL implementation and staff perceptions regarding administration, interpretation, and integration of the CBCL into case practice. The focus was on whether the CBCL was being administered and whether it was being used for clinical purposes.

Based on a sample of data from the treatment foster care program only,[1] 57% of the 82 children had one or more CBCLs completed. Of those children who had an opportunity to have a second CBCL administration (children for whom more than 6 months had elapsed since their first CBCL, N = 16), 25% had a second CBCL. This data demonstrated that the CBCL had been administered twice for only 5% (N = 4) of all children in treatment foster care. Although it was not possible to determine from the CBCL data whether the measure was being used clinically, administration and scoring dates were used to indirectly determine the extent to which the data were used in case reviews. Because the CBCL forms must be computer-scored before their results could be used, a lag between completion of a form and its entry into the scoring program meant that the results were not available in time to be integrated into case reviews. To determine the length of this time lag, the date the form was administered was compared to the date of the computer file. On average, the time span between the dates was 42 days, or 6 weeks, although there was considerable variability across sites in the average time span. A number of factors were seen as possibly contributing to the time lag: foster parents not returning the form promptly, social workers losing the form, and support staff not entering the data when the forms were received. The fairly extensive time gap between the completion and the scoring of CBCL forms implied a lack of use of the results in case reviews.

These data suggested room for improvement in the administration of the CBCL and its full integration into practice. Feedback was provided to each site on completion rates and data entry time lags. Research and clinical management staff initiated discussions with team leaders, coaches, and staff to better understand implementation issues, and they found variability in the efforts that were being made across the sites to implement and use the CBCL. In only a few of the sites, for example, was the CBCL included as part of in-service training for foster parents, who then became actively involved in the interpretation of the results and their use for case reviews and planning. Method of administration varied. Although the initial staff training focused on the advantages of individual administration of the CBCL, some sites instead mailed the instrument to foster parents and teachers. When the instrument was mailed, there was a lower response rate and there were more errors in completion, including inappropriate responses, failure to follow instructions, multiple responses to a single item, and missing data. Variability also was found in the extent to which social workers incorporated the CBCL into treatment planning and case reviews. Social workers who described the use of the CBLC as difficult identified a number of barriers to the integration of the instrument into their case practice: practical considerations, lack of familiarity with standardized measures, and philosophical orientation to treatment.

Some social workers perceived the CBCL as a time-consuming requirement that negatively impacted the time available for direct service provision. Social workers reported that the CBCL required considerable extra time as they had to explain and administer the instrument to foster parents, discuss the results with them, and study the results for presentation at case reviews. They also reported that some foster parents felt that the CBCL was too time-consuming to complete or did not see the benefit of the instrument despite efforts to explain it to them. A frequent comment from social workers was that the profile did not tell them anything they did not already know after completing a thorough initial assessment of a child's needs and strengths and carefully monitoring ongoing needs and responses to treatment. In addition, despite training that emphasized that no single measure could capture everything of interest in an assessment, there continued to be a tendency among staff to see the CBCL as an all-purpose measure with a limited potential impact on case planning. Staff stated that the instrument provided information on only some areas of importance for children in foster care and that other critical areas—such as the ability to develop a family relationship, use good judgment, problem-solve, and demonstrate self-care and independent living skills—were not addressed by the instrument. Finally, social workers consistently expressed a lack of confidence in their ability to interpret and use the results of the instrument.

From a philosophical perspective, some social workers saw the CBCL and other standardized instruments as conflicting with their treatment orientation, which emphasizes the uniqueness and complexity of individuals and their strengths rather than their weaknesses (Pray 1991; Saleeby 1997; Weick et al. 1989). Pointing to the fact that the CBCL portrays children's behavior as scores relative to a normative sample, social workers saw the instrument as less valuable at capturing the richness and complexity that they felt were reflected in the more qualitative, narrative approaches they employed. They also expressed concern about the degree to which the CBCL "pathologizes" children through examining deviant or problem behavior as opposed to a focus on "normalizing" experiences and expectations for children in foster care. Specifically, some social workers reported difficulty in reconciling the use of the instrument in normalizing, strengths-based programs such as regular foster care, where behavioral difficulty is not the reason for children's placements.

The most common request from staff was for more training, particularly with regard to incorporating the CBCL into their already extensive assessments and using it in case planning and reviews and in monitoring change. Training was also requested in better incorporating foster parents into the process and in understanding how to interpret conflicting reports from foster parents, teachers, and youth. They asked for concrete demonstrations of the use of the CBCL in actual cases.

Implementation: Refresher Training

Following discussions with staff, the agency developed refresher training for supervisory staff, which focused on the clinical utilization of the CBCL. Actual case examples using the CBCL were provided by staff from a site that had been using the instrument for a number of years and that had developed methods for integrating it into their practice and six-month reviews. These staff members also shared ways to involve foster parents, use results to track a child's progress and refine case goals, and combine conflicting reports of multiple raters. As a result of this training, the use of the CBCL increased. In the largest program site, the CBCL completion rate tripled. Some social workers, however, continued to report difficulty in integrating the instrument into their practice and continued to raise issues related to treatment philosophy.

The agency also held discussions with foster parents to complement the discussions between research and clinical staff about the use of the CBCL and the refresher training for supervisory staff. In one session at an agency-wide foster parent conference, research staff, social work staff, and foster parents led a discussion of the overall goals for using the CBCL, its uses in treatment planning, and ways to include foster parents more fully in use and interpretation of the instrument. The exchange of ideas among participants reflected a diversity of views that mirrored the views of social worker staff. Participants, however, developed a greater understanding of the multiple philosophical and practice issues associated with the use of the CBCL.

Lessons Learned

Sladen's (1998) exploration of the issues that front-line staff face in implementing outcome measurement suggests that the experiences of CFS are not uncommon. Sladen identified a number of issues consistent with the experiences at CFS: social workers' sense of time pressures when asked to add tasks to their already heavy workloads; their concerns about the intrusiveness of standardized measures and the impact of such tools on the development of relationships with their clients; and their perceptions that such measures are not relevant in direct practice. She found that social workers need ongoing training that emphasizes the meaningfulness of standardized measurement results for their practice.

The description of the multidimensional process of change within organizations developed by Fullan (1982) provides a useful framework for examining and learning from the experiences at CFS. According to Fullan (1982), change occurs at three levels when innovations are introduced: materials, strategies, and beliefs. Complete change is possible, however, only when there is a change in underlying beliefs (Fullan 1982). When Fullan's framework is applied to CFS's implementation of the CBCL in its foster care programs, it is clear that change occurred to a greater extent at some levels than at others. At the level of materials, change was complete. Each site gained familiarity with the computer scoring program and had an adequate supply of forms, manuals, and training materials. At the level of strategies, there was not complete change. The administration of the CBCL improved over time but was not perfect, and there continues to be some difficulty in incorporating the instrument into practice.

At the level of beliefs, there also was incomplete change. Social workers did not hold strong beliefs in the clinical utility of the CBCL, nor did they view the instrument as providing a great deal of added value when compared to their existing practices. Their lack of faith in the instrument was a critical factor, as belief in a measurement's clinical utility is the foundation for change in practice. Because some social workers did not see the value of the instrument, they lacked commitment to administering and incorporating it into their clinical work.

Fullan's work on organizational change (1982) and the experiences of CFS in using the CBCL are consistent with studies conducted by Rosen and colleagues (cited in Lyons et al. 1997) on the introduction of new computer technology. These writers found three types of responses to new technology: eager adoption, hesitation or waiting until the technology had been proven, and resistance. In their review of a variety of studies on responses to computer technology, they found that about 30% to 40% of all individuals will actively resist; 50% to 60% will be hesitant; and only 10% to 15% are eager to adopt new techniques.

The experiences of CFS in implementing the CBCL provide a useful illustration of the principles described by Fullan (1982) and Rosen and colleagues (cited in Lyons et al. 1997) and reveal much about the implementation of such a measure in a diverse multisite agency. Equally important, these experiences illustrate the issues related to the reliability and utility of CBCL data when implementation does not follow a strict research protocol. These issues are particularly critical for researchers and administrators in child welfare settings and highlight the need for training practitioners in the administration of standardized instruments. The work of Fullan (1982) is helpful in suggesting ways to improve the research and administrative utility of CBCL data by focusing on the clinical utility of the measure.

Implementing the CBCL in a Child Welfare Setting

The CFS experience suggests a number of strategies and procedures for initiating the use of the CBCL in child welfare settings: monitoring implementation; refresher training; use of case examples; and collaboration among research, administrative, and clinical staff in implementation. The importance of monitoring the administration of the CBCL cannot be overemphasized (Lyons et al. 1997). The CFS experience suggests that monitoring should begin when implementation is initiated; should occur at several levels; should include assessment of the frequency and timeliness of instrument administration and the methods of administration; and most importantly, should examine the extent to which the instrument is integrated into practice. Integrating the CBCL into practice is the true indicator of the degree to which there is a commitment to using the instrument.

Refresher training is another useful technique for ensuring ongoing use of the CBCL. Learning principles (Mednick 1964) state that individuals do not maintain learning when practice occurs in short, intensive sessions, but, instead, they retain learning when there are spaced tutorials with time for practice. These principles were demonstrated in the CFS experience when the rate of CBCL administration improved dramatically after refresher training. Although a single training session may appear easier and less time consuming when introducing the CBCL, training that is incremental and multisession is likely to be more effective.

Social workers also reported that training that modeled the use of the CBCL with concrete, real-life examples was preferable to more didactic approaches. In child welfare settings, such modeling may involve demonstrating how the CBCL can be used to establish case goals and objectives; how it can be administered to foster parents or teachers in an interactive way that includes them in the assessment and interpretation process; and how to use the CBCL to monitor client progress. Consistent with the recommendation of Lyons and colleagues (1997) that standardized assessments be incorporated into the natural flow of work, such modeling may enhance social workers' understanding of how to incorporate the CBCL into their practice in a nonintrusive and meaningful way and, as a result, use it more effectively.

It also is important to involve a broad range of clinical staff in developing the training and planning the implementation. Involving staff from the inception is likely to result in greater feelings of inclusion, more relevant training, and a better fit between implementation guidelines and social workers' practice. Cognitive dissonance theory (Aronson, 1997; Girandola, 1997) suggests that the higher the level of social workers' participation in such training, the stronger their beliefs will be in the utility of the instrument. The efforts of CFS to seek staff input in the development of CBCL training, adjust the guidelines for CBCL administration based on social workers' feedback, and engage line staff as primary participants in developing and providing refresher training are examples of ways to promote staff involvement.

Close collaboration between research and clinical staff in the implementation of the CBCL is essential. When child welfare organizations create an environment that encourages research-practitioner collaboration and promote an atmosphere of mutual trust and respect, an investment in research and a commitment to struggle through difficulties in implementation are more likely (Epstein 1995; Hess & Mullen 1995a). The experiences of CFS demonstrate such positive outcomes. The decision to use the CBCL was reached by mutual agreement of research, administrative, and clinical managers; researchers and practitioners actively sought suggestions and information from each other throughout implementation; and researchers, administrators, and practitioners jointly designed the implementation procedures and training. All staff were committed to working collaboratively to improve the administration and use of the CBCL.

The Importance of Practitioner Values

Although monitoring implementation, refresher training, use of case examples, and collaboration provide means of ensuring cooperation with a new procedure, they alone are insufficient. Typically, researchers and administrators attribute implementation difficulties to practitioner' "lack of commitment" or "resistance" to the new procedure. Discussions with CFS social workers and Fullan's conceptualization of organizational change (1982), however, suggest an alternative perspective: that staff orientation to social work practice must be taken into account. The philosophical-epistemological perspectives of practitioners may be inconsistent with the use of the CBCL, either for clinical purposes or for research.

A guiding theoretical framework in social work today is that of the "person-in-environment" (Hess & Mullen 1995a). Social work training emphasizes understanding the complex, dynamic nature of people and their relationships in naturalistic settings (Burnette & Weiner 1995). Some social workers may find this phenomenology of practice to be inconsistent with the use of an instrument such as the CBCL that extracts information about individual behaviors without taking into account the larger context in which they occur. Moreover, some social workers may perceive the CBCL as labeling and categorizing children in a way that simplifies complex interpersonal and social dynamics (see Sladen 1998).

Although researchers and practitioners seek information when they use the CBCL (Epstein 1995), their orientations are different. Social workers are trained to use idiographic approaches to develop an understanding of individuals, whereas researchers typically employ nomothetic approaches to derive a more general understanding of principles of behavior and development.[2] Although Lyons and associates (1997) suggest that introduction of a new assessment tool to practitioners is essentially a marketing issue, the differences in worldview between social workers and researchers would suggest otherwise. Greater awareness of the multiple perspectives, disciplinary orientations, and environments of researchers and social work staff may be needed when employing the usual methods of introducing new procedures in an organization.

The Research and Administrative Utility of CBCL Data

When social workers lack faith in the clinical utility of an instrument, they may not complete it in a proper and timely manner. Response rates may be low; data may be collected at widely varying times; and the data may provide unreliable indicators of children's behavior. When data is of questionable utility, the power of any statistical test will be low, and it will be unlikely that any significant improvement in children's problem behavior will be found.

There is a strong relationship between clinical utility and research utility. When the clinical utility of the CBCL is perceived to be high, it will be administered appropriately and in a timely manner. Utilization of the measure by CFS staff increased, for example, after refresher training that emphasized the uses of the instrument in case planning. Social workers are likely to see the clinical utility of standardized instruments when researchers and administrators understand and address practitioners' perspectives and incorporate this information into collaborative efforts regarding its use. When such efforts are not made, researchers and administrators must be cautious in interpreting the meaning of the data obtained.

Conclusions

Whether and how to use the CBCL and other instruments in child welfare settings are not decisions to be made lightly. Although the addition of such a measure to line staff practice may seem a relatively straightforward task, it is, in fact, a multifaceted, multidimensional endeavor. Implementation of standardized measures involves initial and ongoing training that models use of the instrument in practice; ongoing monitoring and consultation; a close collaboration among research, administrative, and social work staff in the planning, training, and implementation of the measure; and most importantly, an understanding of social workers' beliefs and values. Absent such efforts, the instrument may be administered in a perfunctory manner, yielding data of questionable utility.

Given the increasing emphasis on accountability in social services and the reliance on line staff to collect data (Hess & Mullen 1995b), these considerations are likely to assume greater importance in the future. Although it is clear that social workers must be prepared to assume a role in research efforts, some schools of social work offer separate preparation for practice and for research or deemphasize the importance of research for future practitioners. It is increasingly important that professional education promotes the integration of research and practice to enhance both areas. Additionally, agencies can foster the integration of practice and research. As a result of such efforts, there can be greater confidence in the way in which outcome measures, such as the CBCL, are obtained and in their reliability for research and administrative purposes.

Endnotes

1.   At the time the implementation review was conducted, the agency's management information system was being developed and it was not possible to generate a list of all children in care from which to check CBCL completion rates. A secondary data base containing information on only the children in the treatment foster care program was available to use for the review.

2.   According to Babbie (1983, p. 56), the idiographic model of explanation "aims at explanation through the enumeration of the very many, perhaps unique, considerations that lie behind a given action." In contrast, the nomothetic model "does not involve an exhaustive enumeration of all the considerations that result in a particular action or event. Rather, it consciously seeks to discover those considerations that are most important in explaining general classes of actions or events" (Babbie 1983, p. 56).

References

Aronson, E. (1997). Back to the future: Retrospective review of Leon Festinger's—A Theory of Cognitive Dissonance. *American Journal of Psychology*, 110, 127–137.

Babbie, E. (1983). *The practice of social research* (3rd ed.). Belmont, CA: Wadsworth.

Burnette, D. & Weiner, A. S. (1995). Intersecting the parallel worlds of practice and research: An agency practitioner-academic researcher team. In P.M. Hess & E.J. Mullen (Eds.), *Practitioner-researcher partnerships: Building knowledge from, in, and for practice* (p. 138–150). Washington, DC: National Association of Social Workers.

Epstein, I. (1995). Promoting reflective social work practice: Research strategies and consulting principles. In P.M. Hess & E.J. Mullen (Eds.), *Practitioner-researcher partnerships: Building knowledge from, in, and for practice* (p. 83–102). Washington, DC: National Association of Social Workers.

Festinger, L. (1957). *A theory of cognitive dissonance.* Stanford, CA: Stanford University Press.

Fullan, M. (1982). *The meaning of educational change.* New York: Columbia University Press.

Girandola, F. (1997). Double forced compliance and cognitive dissonance theory. *Journal of Social Psychology, 137*, 594-605.

Hess, P. M. & Mullen, E. J. (1995a). Bridging the gap: Collaborative considerations in practitioner-researcher knowledge-building partnerships. In P. M. Hess & E. J. Mullen (Eds.), *Practitioner-researcher partnerships: Building knowledge from, in, and for practice* (pp. 1–30). Washington, DC: National Association of Social Workers.

Hess, P. M. & Mullen, E. J. (1995b). *Practitioner-researcher partnerships: Building knowledge from, in, and for practice.* Washington, DC: National Association of Social Workers.

Lyons, J.S., Howard, K.I., Mahoney, M.T., & Lish, J.D. (1997). *The measurement and management of clinical outcomes in mental health.* New York: Wiley.

Mednick, S.A. (1964). *Learning.* Englewood Cliffs, NJ: Prentice-Hall.

Pray, J.E. (1991). Respecting the uniqueness of the individual: Social work practice within a reflective model. *Social Work, 36,* 80–85.

Saleeby, D. (1997). *The strengths perspective in social work practice* (2nd ed.). New York: Longman.

Sladen, S. (1998). The impact of outcome measurement on frontline staff. *Fifth national roundtable on outcome measures in child welfare services: Summary of proceedings.* Englewood, CO: American Humane Association.

Vignoe, D., & Achenbach, T. M. (1997). *1997 Bibliography of published studies using the Child Behavior Checklist and related materials published through April 1, 1997.* [Computer program]. Burlington, VT: University of Vermont Department of Psychiatry.

Weick, A., Rapp, C., Sullivan, W. P., & Kisthardt, W. (1989). A strengths perspective for social work practice. *Social Work, 34,* 350–354.

Wicklund, R.A., & Brehm, J. W. (1976). *Perspectives on cognitive dissonance.* Hillsdale, NJ: Erlbaum.

11

Research with the CBCL: Methodological and Statistical Issues

Kathleen M. Wetherbee and Thomas M. Achenbach

The CBCL is widely utilized as an assessment instrument in research investigations. One need only glance at the over 3,000 studies using the CBCL and related forms to get a sense of how widely this instrument is used around the world (Vignoe, Berube, & Achenbach 1999). Much of the appeal of the CBCL is that, unlike many other instruments that measure only a single construct (such as depression), it measures multiple constructs. The CBCL yields diverse information on both competencies and problems through its numerous scales, both broadband and narrowband. The CBCL has demonstrated high reliability and validity and is generally accepted as the psychometrically strongest instrument for child assessment (Doll et al. 1998; Freeman 1985; Kelley 1985).

A vital aspect of research design when employing the CBCL is how best to use the information gleaned from the instrument while maintaining a powerful analytic strategy. The purpose of this chapter is to delineate analytic strategies and issues and thereby facilitate more useful research. The chapter is organized into two main sections. The first section deals with the scores that should be used when analyzing the CBCL. In this section, T scores, raw scores, and Z scores are reviewed, and recommendations are made regarding when to use which scores. The second section deals with issues of statistical conclusion validity (Cook & Campbell 1979), which often arise when planning research. Of the numerous threats to statistical conclusion validity, three seem to be particularly relevant to research when utilizing the CBCL and will be discussed in this chapter: fishing and error rate problem; low statistical power; and violated assumptions of statistical tests.

Selecting Which Score to Use: *T Scores, Raw Scores, and Z Scores*

T Scores

T scores are standardized scores that typically have a mean of 50 and a standard deviation of 10 and can be derived from the raw scores on a particular instrument. They facilitate comparisons between scores on different tests, as well as scores on different scales within a single test such as the CBCL. T scores on the CBCL, for instance, can be used to compare ratings of delinquent behavior to ratings of aggressive behavior using the same metric. When used for different scales on a single test such as the CBCL, T scores can help users compare a child's standing on each competence and problem scale. This information can then be used to target deviant areas for treatment and subsequent evaluation of outcomes.

T scores also respond to the fact that the raw score distributions for the normative samples on both the syndrome scales and competence scales of the CBCL are skewed. That is, raw scores in the nonclinical normative sample tended to cluster around the normal or nondeviant end of each distribution. The transformations to T scores reduce skewness to some extent. The T scores also maximize the differentiation of scores at the deviant ends while not exaggerating differences at the nondeviant ends of the distributions.

How CBCL T scores were assigned during test development may have implications for their utilization in research, depending on the focus of the research. One way that these procedures may affect research is through the truncation of the T scores. For the syndrome scales, the T scores are truncated at 50, which means that scores at or below the 50th percentile of the normative sample are all assigned a T score of 50. The purpose of this truncation is to give all syndrome scales the same starting point of 50 on the scale of T scores. On some syndrome scales, 50% of the normative sample obtained a raw score of 0 (i.e., no problems were reported). On these scales, truncation at 50 does not reduce variance among scores that are in the low normal range. On syndrome scales where less than 50% of the normative sample obtained a score of 0, however, two or more raw scores were assigned a T score of 50. Consequently, some of the variance among low problem scores is condensed into one T score.

If differences in the low end of the normal range are of interest, raw scores may be used in place of T scores. For statistical analysis, it is recommended that raw scores be used for syndrome scales and competence scales (Achenbach 1991) because they reflect all of the differences between individuals without truncation or other transformations. T scores for the Total Problem, Total Competence, Internalizing, and Externalizing scales, however, are not truncated and will typically produce the same statistical results as the raw scores (Achenbach 1991).

Raw Scores

The raw scale scores for the syndrome scales and competence scales are calculated by summing the scores for each item within each scale. The Delinquent Behavior scale, for example, has 13 items. If each item is scored 2, the maximum score would be 26. Missing data must be addressed when calculating the raw scale score for the competence scales. If data for any items of the School scale are missing, that scale is not scored. If an item is missing from the Activities or Social scales, the mean of that scale is substituted for the missing item. If more than one item is missing from the Activities or Social scales or any item from the School scale is missing, the Total Competence score is not calculated.

Raw scores are best utilized for research purposes because they provide a fully representative and unaltered range of variance. Therefore, when conducting statistical analyses on data, raw scores are preferred (Achenbach 1991). Raw scale scores can also be compared to the normative sample's raw scale scores as provided in Table 3-4 of the CBCL/4-18 manual (Achenbach, 1991). Raw scale scores for clinical samples are provided in Appendix B of that manual.

If a researcher wishes to combine data across both genders and/or across age groups, either T scores or other scores that are standardized by age and gender should be used. This approach is necessary because a raw score on a scale does not necessarily indicate the same degree of deviance for children of both genders at all ages. Aggressive Behavior raw scale scores, for example, are higher for boys aged 4–11 (M = 8.2, SD = 5.8) than for boys aged 12 to 18 (M = 6.8, SD = 5.7); for girls aged 4 to 11 (M = 7.0, SD = 5.2); and girls aged 12–18 (M = 5.7, SD = 5.2).

In sum, raw scores are the preferred scores for statistical analyses because there is no truncation when data across genders and age groups is *not* combined. When data are to be combined across genders and age groups, however, Z scores or other scores that are standardized by age and gender are preferred (Achenbach 1991).

Z Scores and Other Standard Scores

When combining data across genders and/or age groups for statistical analyses, the raw scale scores obtained for the research sample can be transformed to Z scores, T scores, or other standard scores having a mean and standard deviation chosen by the researcher (e.g., mean = 100, SD = 15). The raw scores should be standardized separately for each gender within ages 4–11 and 12–18 in the research sample. Z scores are standard scores with a mean of zero and standard deviation of one. As a standard score, Z scores enable comparisons between scores on different instruments and scores on different scales within an instrument such as the CBCL. Z scores and other standard scores can be obtained by converting raw scores via standard statistical software packages such as SPSS (Norusis 1993). Alternatively, raw scores can be converted to Z scores by using the following equation: $Z = X - M / SD$ with X representing an observation from a given sample, M representing the mean of the sample, and SD representing the standard deviation of the sample (Marascuilo & Serlin 1988).

When gender and/or age groups are combined for statistical analysis, the use of scores that are standardized separately for each gender within each age range is recommended. This approach is particularly important for research on the full range of behavioral functioning (normal and deviant functioning).

A summary of recommendations regarding which score to use under which circumstances is listed in Table 11-1.

Issues to Consider When Planning Analytic Strategies

Researchers should be aware of common methodological and statistical issues that arise during the design and planning of analytic strategies for multiple variables. A number of prominent journals have devoted entire issues to reviewing and delineating such problems (see *Journal of Clinical Child Psychology* 1995; *Journal of Counseling Psychology* 1987). Three issues seem particularly relevant when conducting research with the CBCL, all of which are threats to the statistical conclusion validity delineated by Cook and Campbell (1979). These three interrelated issues are the fishing and error rate problem, low statistical power, and violations of statistical assumptions. Because of the necessary brevity of this discussion, readers are referred to texts that treat each issue in greater depth (see, for example, Ryan 1959; Cohen 1970; Lindquist 1953).

The Fishing and Error Rate Problem

In studies utilizing the CBCL, the vast majority of researchers analyze multiple scales during their investigations, either as independent or dependent variables. An important methodological issue revolves around how to analyze multiple scales while keeping the overall Type I error (alpha error) rate in check. One strategy is to use each scale of the CBCL as a dependent variable with a subsequent univariate analysis of each. A problem that can arise with such an approach is sometimes called probability pyramiding (Haase & Ellis 1987). It involves Type I errors, which consist of inferring a significant relationship when, in fact, there is none (Rosenthal & Rosnow 1984).

The probability of a Type I error is measured by alpha, which is usually set at .05 or .01 in the social sciences. When a statistical test is conducted with alpha set at .05, there is a 5% chance that a statistically significant result may be spurious or simply due to chance. In other words, the obtained result does not reflect the true relation between the variables in the population.

When a second statistical test is conducted during the same study, the Type I error rate for a single dependent variable must be distinguished from the experimentwise Type I error rate, which is defined as "the probability of making one or more Type I errors in a series of analyses of dependent variables" (Haase & Ellis 1987, p.405). Although it is beyond the scope of this chapter to illustrate the calculations for determining the experimentwise error rate, numerous texts provide this information (see Kirk 1982; Marascuilo & Serlin 1988; Leary & Altmaier 1980).

One contributor to the experimentwise error rate is the number of dependent variables. As the number of dependent variables increases, the experimentwise error rate increases (Haase & Ellis 1987; Wampold & Poulin 1992; see also Dar et al. 1994). Leary and Altmaier (1980), for example, demonstrated that when two dependent variables are analyzed and alpha is set at .05, the experimentwise error rate is .0975. With nine dependent variables analyzed separately, the experimentwise Type I error rate increases to .37. In other words, almost 4 out of 10 significant findings would be expected to occur by chance alone. Consequently, when each variable or scale of the CBCL is analyzed utilizing univariate analyses and each statistical test's alpha set at .05, the experimentwise Type I error rate can quickly get out of hand and violate the statistical conclusion validity of the entire study (Cook & Campbell 1979; Heppner et al. 1992). The statistical conclusion validity of the study also is violated when many statistical tests are conducted on a data set without specific hypotheses, referred to as "fishing" (Heppner et al. 1992).

Table 11-1. Recommendations for Selecting which CBCL Score to Use for Research

Research focus	Recommended score for statistical analyses
Deviant behavior only	**T Scores**
Full behavior range (i.e., normal and deviant) and one age group or one gender	Raw Scores
Full behavior range (i.e., normal and deviant) and combining age groups and/or genders	Z Scores

Reviews of research journals have shown that the fishing and error rate problem is a common occurrence. One review estimated that approximately 4 out of 10 significant results reported would have been expected to occur by chance alone and hence, are not true effects but rather artifacts (Ryan, 1959). Because it is not known which results are true effects and which are not, one is left wondering about the validity of the knowledge base (Haase & Ellis 1987; Leary & Altmaier 1980).

A variety of methods, however, can be utilized to control the experimentwise Type I error rate. One suggested method is the use of multivariate statistical tests (Haase & Ellis 1987; Wampold & Freund 1987). Other techniques are suggested by Hays (1988), Huitema (1980), Sakoda et al. (1954), and Strahan (1982). In addition, there is the Bonferroni correction procedure of "divid[ing] the alpha rate selected by the number of tests performed explicitly or implicitly" (Rosenthal & Rosnow 1984, p. 255). Inherent in the Bonferroni method, however, is the assumption that the intercorrelations between dependent variables is zero. Accounting for the intercorrelations may considerably reduce the power of a study (Serlin 1982).

It also should be noted that multivariate techniques have inherent problems in omnibus testing. Should the omnibus F test in a MANOVA [Multiple Analysis of Variance)] prove to be significant, for example, further post hoc testing of variables accounts for the significant differences. This type of testing is often done through multiple linear combinations of the variables (Dar et al. 1994). The combination of variables found to account for the significant differences, however, can potentially lead to inferential ambiguity and a "set of most[ly] uninterpretable contrasts performed on mostly uninterpretable linear combinations of the dependent variables" (Serlin 1987, p. 370). Nonetheless, recommendations have been made regarding how to overcome some of the potential problems in omnibus tests, including the work of Bray and Maxwell (1982) in the use of discriminant analysis to follow up a significant MANOVA. The discriminate analysis can provide a variety of information, including the number of dimensions underlying group differences on the dependent variables; how each variable relates to those underlying dimensions; and which of the dependent variables most strongly differentiate between the groups (Bray et al. 1995).

A particularly simple approach to correcting experimentwise alpha is to determine the number (n) of tests expected to be significant by chance in a set of N tests. Tables provided by Sakoda and associates (1954), for example, show that in a study that has $N = 100$ statistical tests, the n expected to reach alpha = .01 by chance is 5 tests (using a p = .01 protection level for chance expectations). Researchers, therefore, can mark the 5 tests whose test statistics (such as t and F) exceed the .01 alpha level by the smallest amount. These are the 5 tests that can be considered most likely to reflect chance findings. Because any of the 95 remaining tests whose test statistics exceed p = .01 can be viewed as nonchance findings, there is little loss of statistical power.

Low Statistical Power

Another important consideration is the concept of statistical power, defined as the probability of accurately rejecting the null hypothesis when it is false or the probability of accurately detecting a relation that really exists (Rosenthal & Rosnow 1984). Power increases as the probability of making a Type II error (beta error) decreases. Alternatively, as power decreases, the probability of a Type II error increases. Power analysis can and should be used when designing research to determine the sample size that is needed to have a reasonable chance of detecting relations that exist in the population (Heppner et al. 1992; Wampold & Freund 1987). Further, low power threatens statistical conclusion validity (Cook & Campbell 1979; Heppner et al. 1992). A review of research journals has noted that a "disturbing proportion" of studies had such low power that they were very unlikely to detect a relation even if one existed (Orme 1990, p.518). Calculating power should and can be done utilizing a method developed by Cohen (1988), which can be done with the assistance of computer programs (see Borenstein & Cohen 1988).

Violated Assumptions of Statistical Tests

The third issue is the violation of the assumptions of statistical tests. Each statistical test has mathematical and distributional assumptions that need to be met for its proper usage (Betz 1987; Hays 1988). Parametric statistical tests, for example, require that scores be approximately normally distributed. Violations of assumptions may increase the probability of Type I and Type II errors, which can decrease the validity of a study. Such violations also may cause unnoticed errors during the calculation of statistics by computer programs (Wampold & Freund 1987). Testing the extent to which statistical assumptions are met is highly recommended and considered sound methodological practice.

The procedures involved for testing assumptions, however, become more complicated when utilizing multivariate techniques, which are often used to analyze the CBCL. The assumption of a multivariate normal distribution required for linear discriminant analysis, for example, may be difficult to test (Klecka 1980; Marascuilo & Levin 1983). One test for a multivariate normal distribution is to check for a normal distribution of each of the variables. Should any variables lack a normal distribution individually, they collectively will not yield a multivariate normal distribution. If, as separate variables, they are normally distributed, there may be a multivariate normal distribution, but not necessarily (Norusis 1993).

Another statistical assumption that seems particularly relevant when analyzing the CBCL concerns the correlations among the variables or scales, a concept known as multicollinearity. Intercorrelations can be problematic for some multivariate analyses such as multiple regression (Berry 1993). High correlations among the CBCL scales can prevent the scales from making substantial and unique contributions to the dependent variable. It is important to determine the nature and extent of the intercorrelations in their samples in order to understand the effect they might have on results.

Violations of statistical assumptions increase the risk that results may produce artifacts rather than reflect the true relations among variables. By examining whether particular data meet the assumptions of statistical tests, researchers will be better equipped to fully understand their results and determine whether alternative analyses may be appropriate (see Matkoski-Wetherbee 1997).

These and other issues have led the Task Force on Statistical Inference of the American Psychological Association (1996) to make recommendations for improving current practice. The Task Force's recommendations include approaches to improving the quality of data usage and protecting against potential misrepresentations of quantitative results. To ensure that the strengths and weaknesses of studies are understood and areas for additional work are identified, the Task Force recommended that researchers:

1. Provide more extensive descriptions of data (such as descriptions related to missing data, sample sizes, means and standard deviations, and graphical descriptive information);

2. Provide more extensive characterization of results (such as direction and size of effect, mean difference, regression and correlation coefficients, more complex effect size indicators, and confidence intervals); and

3. Use techniques to assure that reported results are not produced by anomalies or artifacts in the data (such as outliers, points of high influence, nonrandom missing data, selection, and attrition problems).

The Task Force also identified common misuses of computerized data analysis, including "reporting statistics without understanding how they are computed or what they mean" and reporting results to greater precision than is supported by the data (1996, p. 4). The Task Force emphasized that computerized analyses have placed far greater responsibility on researchers to understand and control their designs and analyses. These issues are especially relevant to the analysis of instruments with multiple scales such as the CBCL because the selection of research designs and analyses is more complex. When attention is paid to these issues throughout the investigation, much stronger designs and more powerful analyses will result.

Conclusion

This chapter has focused on a number of common methodological and statistical issues that arise when conducting research using multiple variables such as the scales offered in the CBCL. Researchers are encouraged to take these issues into consideration when planning investigations in order to strengthen designs and produce rigorous research that will contribute substantively to the knowledge base. Relevant as well as rigorous scientific investigations (Gelso 1979) are needed to push forward the boundaries of knowledge and solve the problems faced by the field of child welfare.

References

Achenbach, T. M. (1991). *Manual for the Child Behavior Checklist/4-18 and 1991 profile.* Burlington, VT: University of Vermont.

American Psychological Association Task Force on Statistical Inference (1996). *Initial report.* Washington, DC: Board of Scientific Affairs, American Psychological Association.

Berry, W. D. (1993). *Understanding regression assumptions* (Sage University Paper series on Quantitative Applications in the Social Sciences, series no. 07-092). Newbury Park, CA: Sage.

Betz, N. E. (1987). Use of discriminant analysis in counseling psychology research. *Journal of Counseling Psychology, 34,* 393–403.

Borenstein, M. & Cohen, J. (1988). *Statistical power analysis: A computer program.* Hilldale, NJ: Lawrence Erlbaum Associates.

Bray, J. H. & Maxwell, S. E. (1982). Analyzing and interpreting significant MANOVAS. *Review of Educational Research, 52,* 340–367.

Bray, J. H., Maxwell, S. E., & Cole, D. (1995). Multivariate statistics for family psychology research. *Journal of Family Psychology, 9,* 144–160.

Cohen, J. (1988). *Statistical power analysis for the behavioral sciences* (2nd ed.). Hilldale, NJ: Lawrence Erlbaum Associates.

Cook, T. D. & Campbell, D. T. (1979). *Quasi-experimentation: Design and analysis issues for field settings.* Chicago: Rand McNally.

Dar, R., Serlin, R. C., & Omer, H. (1994). Misuse of statistical tests in three decades of psychotherapy. *Journal of Consulting and Clinical Psychology, 62,* 75–82.

Doll, B., Furlong, J. J., & Wood, M. (1998). Reviews of the Child Behavior Checklist. In O.K. Buros, L.L. Murphy, Ed., *Thirteenth mental measurements yearbook,* 217–224. Lincoln, NE: Buros Institute.

Freeman, B. J. (1985). Review of Child Behavior Checklist. In J. V. Mitchell, Jr. (Ed.), *Mental Measurements Yearbook* (pp. 300–301). Lincoln, NE: Buros Institute of Mental Measurements of the University of Nebraska, Lincoln.

Gelso, C. J. (1979). Research in counseling: Methodological and professional issues. *The Counseling Psychologist, 8,* 7–35.

Haase, R. F. & Ellis, M. V. (1987). Multivariate analysis of variance. *Journal of Counseling Psychology, 34,* 404–413.

Hays, W. L. (1988). *Statistics* (4th ed.). New York: Holt, Rinehart, & Winston.

Heppner, P. P., Kivlighan, D. M., Jr., & Wampold, B. E. (1992). *Research design in counseling*. Pacific Grove, CA: Brooks/Cole.

Huitema, B. J. (1980). *The analysis of covariance and its alternatives*. New York: Wiley.

Kelley, M. L. (1985). Review of Child Behavior Checklist. In J. V. Mitchell, Jr. (Ed.), *Mental Measurements Yearbook* (pp. 301–303). Lincoln, NE: Buros Institute of Mental Measurements of the University of Nebraska, Lincoln.

Kirk, R. E. (1982). *Experimental design*. Monterey, CA: Brooks/Cole.

Klecka, W. R. (1980). *Discriminant analysis* (Sage University Paper series on Quantitative Applications in the Social Sciences, series no. 07-019). Newbury Park, CA: Sage.

Leary, M. R. & Altmaier, E. M. (1980). Type I error in counseling research: A plea for multivariate analyses. *Journal of Counseling Psychology, 27,* 611–615.

Marascuilo, L. A. & Levin, J. R. (1983). *Multivariate statistics in the social sciences: A researcher's guide*. Monterey, CA: Brooks/Cole.

Marascuilo, L. A. & Serlin, R. C. (1988). *Statistical Methods for the social and behavioral sciences*. New York: W. H. Freeman and Co.

Matkoski-Wetherbee, K. (1997). The relationship between family characteristics and the diagnosis of conduct disorder. *Dissertation Abstracts International.* (University Microfilms No. 9711002) University of Wisconsin-Madison.

Norusis, M. J. (1993). *SPSS for windows base system user's guide: Release 6.0*. Chicago: SPSS Inc.

Orme, J. G. (1990). Software review: Statistical power analysis: A computer program. *Social Service Review, 64*(3), 518–520.

Rosenthal, R. & Rosnow, R. L. (1984). *Essentials of behavioral research: Methods and data analysis*. New York: McGraw-Hill.

Ryan, T.A. (1959). Multiple comparisons in psychological research. *Psychological Bulletin,* 56 26-47.

Sakoda, J. M., Cohen, B. H., & Beall, G. (1954). Test of significance for a series of statistical tests. *Psychological Bulletin, 51,* 172–175.

Serlin, R. C. (1982). A multivariate measure of association based on the Pillai-Bartlett procedure. *Psychological Bulletin, 91,* 413–417.

Serlin, R. C. (1987). Hypothesis testing, theory building, and the philosophy of science. *Journal of Counseling Psychology, 34,* 365–371.

Strahan, R. F. (1982). Multivariate analysis and the problem of Type I error. *Journal of Counseling Psychology, 29,* 175–179.

Vignoe, D., Berube, R. & Achenbach, T. M. (1999). *Bibliography of published studies using the Child Behavior Checklist & related materials: 1998 edition*. Burlington, VT: University of Vermont.

Wampold, B. E. & Freund, R. D. (1987). Use of multiple regression in counseling psychology research: A flexible data analytic strategy. *Journal of Counseling Psychology, 34,* 372–382.

Wampold, B. E. & Poulin, K. L. (1992). Counseling research methods: Art and artifact. In S. D. Brown and R. W. Lent (Eds.). *Handbook of Counseling Psychology* (2nd ed.), 71–109. New York: Wiley.

12

Conclusions and Recommendations for Future Research

Peter J. Pecora, Gay Armsden, Nicole S. Le Prohn, and Thomas M. Achenbach

Situational Analysis Revisited

As Chapter 1 demonstrates, there is a great deal of interest and experimentation in increasing accountability in child welfare and mental health services in the United States. Some of the service delivery innovations involve outcomes measurement, managed care principles, and the delegation of planning and service delivery responsibilities to private entities. In some parts of the country, private agencies are rapidly taking over functions that historically have been governmental responsibilities. In place of detailed regulations describing how private entities are to carry out their new responsibilities, public agencies are attempting to judge the performance of private agencies according to the results that they achieve for children and families.

If public and private agencies are to be accountable for their results (as opposed to their compliance with government-prescribed procedures or requirements related to the provision of a certain level service), it is clear that a great deal of thought must be devoted to describing and defining the desired results. Clear descriptions and definitions are essential to the measurement and evaluation of staff performance. At the same time, the best performance measurement systems are based on a clearly articulated set of values or philosophical principles (American Humane Association et al. 1998) and utilize standardized measurement instruments and "functional" outcomes (Sechrest 1996). The CBCL, TRF, and YSR are among the standardized measures that may help address the major questions posed in Chapter 1:

- What are the needs and strengths of the children and families served?

- Which agency services are provided to whom?

- What short-term, intermediate, and long-term outcomes are achieved?

- Which services are most beneficial to whom?

- What does it cost to provide these services and achieve these outcomes?

CBCL Data Highlights

This book has summarized some of the research studies that have been completed using the CBCL, TRF, and YSR. Across these studies, what can be said about the CBCL and TRF? Some common findings are listed below and supplemented by other studies reviewed by Armsden and colleagues (2000).

A number of reports have been published that document the CBCL scores from samples of children in foster care. Table 12.1 summarizes data from 16 samples (13 studies) for which CBCL summary-score data are available, including the Casey Family Programs study (Armsden et al., this volume). All but two of these studies focused exclusively on behavior problems and did not report competence scores. The studies are listed approximately in order of the general age of the samples (mean age was not always reported). Although most studies included a wide age range, they typically did not report results by age. The majority of children were assessed pending placement or at entry into a program, although many children had previous placements. Foster parents served as respondents for children in regular foster care, and staff typically completed the form for children in residential treatment. Because of the small number of studies in the summary, caution should be used in interpreting the patterns of results.

Summary T Score Data

Ten studies have reported CBCL summary T score data. The samples consisted of 32% to 90% boys, with a median of about 55%. Among studies of children in regular or specialized foster care, those samples in which most children were under 12 years of age scored in the normal or borderline-clinical range. The single adolescent sample scored in the clinical range on all summary scales. Average scores for samples of children and youth in treatment or residential care were mostly in the clinical range, with some Internalizing scores in the borderline range. Courtney and Zinn (1997), in their study of a treatment foster care sample of adolescents, found overall better adjustment than did other samples with a similar age range. Children who left the program in their first 3 months (and, thus, possibly were functioning less well), however, were not part of the sample.

In order to summarize more precisely the CBCL studies reporting T scores, the samples listed in 12.1 were grouped into four categories and average T scores for each group were computed. Because the samples were so diverse, their scores were given equal weight in the calculation of mean scores. The study samples were divided into two groups: children in treatment care (residential treatment, group home, and specialized/treatment foster care) and children in regular care (including kinship care). Glisson's study (1994) was excluded because the type of care could not be categorized. All samples were further categorized according to whether they were predominantly preadolescent (mean or median age of less than 12 years) or predominantly adolescent (mean or median age of 12 years or older). Although not shown in table 12.1, data for the Casey sample were partitioned by age group because some age effects were present. The categorization of samples was not precise and some groups were small, but the data were considered adequate for some broad, cautious interpretations.

Figure 12-1. CBCL Mean *T* Scores by Type of Sample

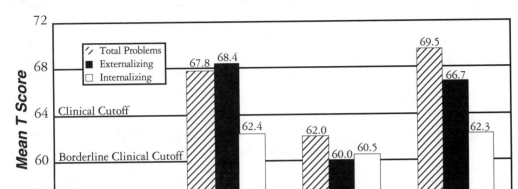

Type of Sample

Note: Preadolescent = mean or median ages of samples were under 12 years. Adolescent = mean or median ages of samples were at least 12 years. Tx = treatment. Ns varied by type of sample and score from 118 to 469. SD ranges by sample type: preadolescents in regular care, 1.4 - 3.5, and treatment care, 4.2 - 5.0; adolescents in regular care, 5.7 - 7.1, and treatment care, 2.1 - 4.5.

Source: Adapted from Armsden, G., Pecora, P., Payne, V., & Szatkiewicz, J. (2000). An intake profile of youth placed in long-term foster using the Child Behavior Checklist/ 4-18. *Journal of Emotional and Behavioral Disorders* 8(1), 60. Adapted with permission.

Figure 12.1 presents mean CBCL summary problem scores from 9 studies (13 samples) of children in care. On average, samples consisting primarily or entirely of preadolescents who were in regular care scored in the normal range (< 60) on all summary problem scales. Average summary scores for two samples of adolescents in regular care were in the borderline-clinical range (60-63), but this average belies the samples' disparate scores (Armsden et al., this volume; Hornick, Phillips & Kerr 1989). Both preadolescent and adolescent samples in treatment care scored in the borderline range on Internalizing scales and in the clinical range (> 64) on Externalizing scales and Total Problems.

Rates of Scoring in the Clinical Range

Table 12.1 also summarizes clinical-range data from 5 studies of children in care. Most commonly, these reports presented the percentage of children scoring in the clinical range on the problem summary scales. Not included were several studies that did not present separate data for the borderline and clinical ranges. The samples consisted of 32% to 60% boys, with a median of about 50%.

Table 12-1. *T* Score and Clinical Range Data from CBCL Studies of Children in Foster Care[1]

Study	Type of care	Rater	N	Age[a]	Internalizing	Externalizing	Total Problems
Hulsey & White (1989)	Foster care	Foster parent	65	M=6 (4–8)	NA[b]	NA	62
Comments: Assessed within 3 months of placement. First time in care. 88% African American.							
Dubowitz et al. (1993)	Kinship	Relative	223	(4–11)	18%	27%	39%
Comments: Data for 2–3 yr. olds were excluded (CBCL 4–18 not intended for use with those ages). Adolescent and full data are listed below. 90% African American.							
Evans et al. (1994)	Treatment foster care	Foster parent or parent	39	M=9 (5–14)	67	73	72
Comments: Referred for treatment foster care, but some randomly assigned to intensive home care. Assessed on enrollment. 90% male.							
Phillips (1997)	Foster care	Foster parent	39 (4–18)	57% < 12 yr. (for all samples)	56	57	58
	Specialized foster care		229		56	61	61
	Intensive treatment foster care		24		61	72	71
Comments: Assessed at 3 months post-intake.							
Shennum et al. (1998)	Residential treatment	Care workers	68	M=10 (6–12)	65 54%	68 74%	67 71%
Comments: Assessed at 4 months post-intake. 47% had previous placement in residential treatment or psychiatric setting. Average of 3.8 placements. 49% African American; 27% other ethnic minority.							
Armsden et al. (1999)	Long-term foster care	Foster parent	362	M=10 (5–18)	56 20%	54 28%	56 30%
Comments: Assessed at placement into long-term care.							
Clark et al. (1994)	Treatment foster care (primarily)	Parent or surrogate	109	Mdn=11.5 67% < 13 yr. (7–15)	63	68	NA
Comments: Assessed at entry. Children selected who had psychosocial disturbances. M years in care = 2.6. Averaged annualized rate of 3.8 placement changes.							

Study	Placement	Reporter	N	Age			
Heflinger & Simpkins (1997)	Foster care (42%); Family care (22%); Group residential (36%)	Caregiver	685	60% > 12 years (2-18)	20%	30%	30%
Comments: Sample is 64% of a random and representative sample of children in state custody.							
McIntyre & Keesler (1986)[b]	Foster care	Foster parent; administered by caseworker	158	M=12 (4-18)	NA	NA	37%
Comments: M of 4 years in care. Clinical-range % was computed from reported relative risk statistic.							
Friman et al. (1993)	Residential treatment	Parent or surrogate	84	M=14 (8-17)	62	69	68
Comments: Assessment at intake. % males/females not reported.							
Dubowitz et al. (1993)	Kinship	Relative	58	(12-16)	28% (Males: 50%; Females: 10%)	31% (Males: 46%; Females: 19%)	48% (Males: 65%; Females: 34%)
			281	All: (4-16)	20%	28%	41%
Comments: {See study entry above for children 4–11} Males 12–16 yrs.: n = 26. Females 12-16 yrs. : n = 32. Total Problems: all males = 46%; all females = 35%.							
Hornick et al. (1989)	Foster care	Foster parent	41	(12-16)	65	64	67
	Residential treatment	Care workers	34	(12-16)	67	69	71
Comments: Short-term foster care placement. Clinical-range data did not include summary scales. Short-term residential care pending placement. Clinical-range data did not include summary scales.							
Courtney & Zinn (1997)	Treatment foster care	Foster parent	259	(11-17)	58	62	NA
Comments: At least 3 months in care. Average of 3 prior placements. 75% Caucasian.							

Scores in italics are T scores. Percentages denote percentage of children in the clinical range (T score > 63). Unpublished data listed in this table are summarized with the authors' permission. Various versions of the CBCL were used in these studies.

[a] Age in years. M = mean; Mdn = median; range in parentheses.

[b] NA = data not available.

[1] Source: Adopted from Armsden, G., Pecora, P. J., Payne, V. & Sykawiecz, J. (2000). An intake profile of youth placed in long-term foster using the Child Behavior Checklist/4-18. *Journal of Emotional and Behavioral Disorders* 8(1), 50–51. Reprinted with permission.

The small number of reports that include CBCL clinical-range data permit estimated rates of severe problems for children ages 4–18 years who were in regular (nontreatment) foster care. These studies indicate that the disturbance rate among such children is on average 35% (range = 30% to 40%) based on CBCL summary data. These rates indicate a prevalence of clinically significant problem behaviors among children in regular care that is 3 to 4 times higher than the rate of 10% expected in the general population of children (Achenbach 1991a). Rates may be lower for preschool children and girls in kinship care (Dubowitz et al. 1993). There is some evidence that adolescents in regular care show higher rates of disturbance than do preadolescents, more on the order of 50% or higher, given the findings of Dubowitz and associates (1993) and Hornick and colleagues (1989) on T scores. The T-score results of the Casey study (Armsden et al., this volume) partially support the indication of greater problems among adolescents, at least for some Internalizing Problems.

Very limited clinical-range data indicate that children in residential treatment (Shennum et al. 1998) or state custody in general (Glisson 1994) may show as much as twice the rates of disturbance (i.e., more than two-thirds of children) shown in other samples. In addition, a number of studies of children in treatment care on average report T scores ranging well into the clinical range on Total Problems, providing further documentation of the extensive behavior problems among these children.

Most Prevalent Behavior Problems

Patterns of scores on the CBCL profiles show that across studies of children in care, behavior problems are most commonly of an externalizing nature (i.e., Delinquent and Aggressive Behaviors) rather than of an internalizing nature, with Attention and Social Problems the most prevalent of non-Externalizing problems (Armsden et al., this volume; Clark et al. 1994; Dubowitz et al. 1994; Friman et al. 1993; Glisson 1994; Hoffart & Grinnell 1994; Hornick et al. 1989; McIntyre & Keesler 1986). Low academic achievement as measured by the CBCL has also been documented for children placed with kinship care families (Dubowitz, et al. 1994) and in long-term foster care (Armsden et al., this volume), which is consistent with studies of children in foster care using other assessment methods (Fanshel & Shinn 1978; Runyan & Gould 1985). Of 11 CBCL studies that included preadolescents in the sample, only 3 have reported data for the Sex Problems subscale. The proportion of preadolescents in long-term foster care scoring in the clinical range on Sex Problems (11%) (Armsden et al., this volume) was similar to the 9% rate estimated from relative risk statistics reported by McIntyre and Keesler (1986), but less than the 18% rate found in study of children in residential treatment by Shennum and colleagues (1998).

Patterns of Competence Scores

Very little data have been published on the behavioral competence of children in care as assessed by the CBCL. One study of children in long-term foster care (Armsden et al., this volume) and one study of children in residential treatment (Shennum et al. 1998) have both reported that 27% of the samples scored in the clinical range on Total Competence. In the same studies, 19% of children in long-term foster care and 46% of the children in residential treatment were in the clinical range on the School scale. This finding is consistent with studies using other assessment methods that showed high rates of academic performance difficulties among children in foster or kinship care (Fanshel & Shinn 1978; Runyan & Gould 1985). Dubowitz and colleagues (1994) reported that 49% to 58% of school-age children in kinship care were performing below average in academic achievement.

Patterns of Age and Sex Differences

There is no consistent pattern of findings among CBCL studies of children in foster care regarding age and sex differences in psychosocial functioning (see Armsden, et al. 2000). Results from various studies suggest that age differences may be found when a wide age range is studied; age and sex interaction effects are considered; and individual subscales, rather than summary indices, are examined. Differential screening criteria may result in discrepant demographic findings among samples in various types of care.

TRF Data Highlights

Although few studies report TRF findings, some notable results can be highlighted. Hans et al. (this volume), for example, followed groups of drug-using and non-drug-using (comparison) women and their children over time (birth to age 10) and found few differences between groups of children at age 10. On the TRF, however, teachers rated the children born to drug-using women as behaving significantly less appropriately than children born to non-drug using mothers (T scores 41.6 vs. 46.6). Teachers rated children born to drug-using mothers as more withdrawn (raw scores 4.43 vs. 2.42) than comparison children. There were no significant differences between the two groups on the Internalizing scale (T scores for children born of drug-using mothers 52.89 versus 57.85 for children of non-users); the Externalizing scale (59.33 versus 54.98); and the Total Problems scale (58.08 versus 57.90).

Armsden and colleagues (this volume) found that children placed in long-term family foster care had higher mean problem T scores than the TRF normative sample. None of the mean TRF behavior problem scores were in the borderline clinical or clinical range, although many individual youth had elevated scores. Teachers rated Casey youth the highest for Anxious/Depressed (mean T score 55.8), Social Problems (mean T score 56.8), and Aggressive Behavior (mean T score 57.4). Overall, 34% of the Casey youths scored in the borderline clinical (14% of youths) or clinical (20% of youths) ranges on the Total Problems scale. These findings indicate that a substantial number of youth are experiencing difficulty in the school setting.

Challenges and Issues

Although the CBCL and the TRF have been cited among the most comprehensive assessment measures available, research and agency staff members have identified certain challenges and limitations associated with these measures.

Clinical Sensitivity

Because there is some evidence that the CBCL and TRF are sensitive to changes in youths' behavior over time (Mott 1997; Clark et al. 1994; Lenerz et al. 1995; Toprac 1997; MacCabe 1998), these measures qualify for use in evaluating social service programs and specific treatment interventions. Practitioners may use these measures to track the progress of individual youth after specific interventions such as treatment foster care, wilderness work experience, residential treatment, and psychotropic medication.

Some researchers, however, are concerned about the clinical sensitivity of the CBCL (see Phillips 1998; Heflinger & Simpkins 1998) and seek to maximize the instrument's utility by refining the analysis and reporting of CBCL data. Researchers note that averaging CBCL scores on a single behavior problem scale across ages and genders is methodologically incorrect and may distort true differences (Wetherbee & Achenbach, this volume). Mean scores often do not provide a complete or accurate picture. The unique needs of sub-groups of children should be examined. Second, clinical sensitivity issues arise because the disentangling of treatment-based changes in child behavioral functioning from developmentally-based changes is a complex endeavor. In response to this issue, some agencies have begun to analyze individual items on the CBCL to better understand why certain scores are elevated and determine whether changes are occurring in certain "sentinel" types of behavior problems, such as suicide attempts, physically attacking others, cruelty to animals, and fire-setting.

The Completion of Forms by Uninformed Raters

The CBCL form (and, to a lesser extent, the TRF form) does not indicate whether the person completing the form has sufficient familiarity with the child to accurately complete the items. Care must be exercised when selecting individuals to complete the CBCL, a particularly challenging undertaking when a child has been placed only recently in a new foster home or group care facility.

Inconsistency of Respondents and Changes in Setting

Armsden and colleagues (this volume) and Shennum and Moreno (this volume), among others, have noted the inconsistencies in ratings that may be introduced when, over time, different individuals complete the CBCL or TRF for a child. These effects may be compounded when child functioning is tracked through successive administrations in different settings, such as in the home, in foster care, and in residential treatment.

Importance of the YSR

Courtney and Zinn (this volume) found in their study that the YSR Internalizing scales identified youths in emotional distress but, caregiver and staff ratings on the CBCLs did not indicate the same level of distress. From both a clinical and research assessment perspective, this finding is important and suggests that those relying exclusively on the CBCL or TRF should use caution.

Using the CBCL, TRF, and YSR to Refine Practice and Program

Although CBCL resource books contain a wealth of information, there has been relatively little written in child welfare about how these data can be used to refine clinical case plans, improve services, and provide feedback to foster parents (Lenerz , this volume; Phillips, this volume). Research is needed on assessment procedures so that researchers and child welfare practitioners can more effectively share findings; guidelines can be developed; and networks of practioners/users and researchers can be established.

Foster Parents as Unique Raters

Phillips (this volume) notes that "foster parents are unique as raters of children's behavior." In reflecting upon his data, Phillips (this volume) further observes:

> They have fairly extensive experience with many challenging children and, as a result, their ratings may be based on generous internal baselines despite the CBCL's clear instructions. [However,] their subsequent ratings of the same children may then be resistant to change.
>
> ...The CBCL's potency, however, seems undeniable in describing important, clinically related characteristics of children. It effectively discriminated children who entered different foster programs, with children who entered ITFC evidencing more clinical-level behavioral difficulties, especially externalizing difficulties, than did children in RFC or SFC. Initial CBCL scores captured important information about these foster children that also was related meaningfully to their discharge status. Children who were discharged to less restrictive environments or who achieved most or all of their ISP goals had lower initial CBCL scores than did children discharged to more restrictive environments or who achieved none or some of their ISP goals.

What Phillips and other users of the CBCL have found is that foster parent completers of the CBCL often have unique and useful observations of the child's functioning.

Quality Control

The issues and challenges associated with the CBCL and TRF highlight the importance of properly training individuals who distribute the instrument to parents, foster parents, teachers, and others. When agency staff are unfamiliar with the CBCL and TRF, they may not give correct instructions. Quality control issues also may arise regarding the timely and consistent administration of the instruments (see Lenerz, this volume).

Respondent Bias

CBCL and TRF scores can be affected if the caregiver who completes the form does not report accurately the child's competencies or problem behaviors. As pointed out by Armsden et al. (this volume), a foster parent may minimize a child's poor behavior in one or more areas if the parent has not been reassured that the program serves children with serious behavior problems.

Limited Data for Various Ethnic Groups

Although some of the CBCL problem syndromes analyses were conducted on a sample of 4,455 children who were referred for mental health services (Achenbach 1993), the norms are based on a nationally representative sample of 2,368 youth between the ages of 4 and 18 years old, 27% of whom were children of color (Achenbach 1991a). The manuals report analyses of ethnic differences for each item and scale score, with socioeconomic status, gender, age, and clinical status controlled. These analyses included not only the nonreferred normative samples but clinically referred samples as well.

After controlling for clinical status and other demographic variables, ethnic differences the CBCL problem syndrome scales have generally been negligible. In addition, numerous cross-cultural comparisons have shown a rather narrow range of variation in CBCL problem scores for children from different countries (Crijnen, Achenbach, & Verhulst 1997; Crijnen, Achenbach, & Verhulst 1999). Child welfare agencies, nonetheless, may wish to develop specific profiles for the major ethnic groups that they serve and, through such profiles, alert worker to possible ethnic similarities and differences in problems and competencies.

Agency Misuse of the Forms for ADHD Classification

Some child welfare agencies have used the CBCL Behavior Problem scales to diagnose children as having Attention Deficit and Hyperactivity Disordered (ADHD). The relationship between the CBCL scale scores and the behaviors of youth with ADHD, however, is questionable. Although the CBCL is helpful in indicating whether further testing for ADHD should be done (Edelbrock 1984), a single measure should not serve as the sole basis for diagnostic conclusions.

Under-Reporting of Child Strengths on Parent-Reported Competence Scales

An examination of various youth profiles by Casey Family Service staff found two patterns that revealed underreporting of child strengths. First, the scales for the parent-reported competence section (addressing Activities, Social, and School functioning) allowed a child to score up to only the 69th percentile. Second, the parent-reported competence scales tended to show youth in a more negative light than their activities, participation in social events, and school achievement would normally indicate. These findings highlight the need to review carefully the open-ended questions of the first section of the competence section of the CBCL and to use other sources of assessment data as outlined in the Achenbach (1991a) Multi-Axial approach to assessment.

Supports for Future Research

In order to determine which interventions work best for which children, additional studies clearly are needed that combine the use of the CBCL and other outcome measures with complete descriptions of the population and interventions being studied. The chapters in this volume provide a foundation upon which such future research can build. The challenges and issues identified in this chapter also can guide studies that use the CBCL, TRF, YSR, and related measures.

Agency access to and use of the CBCL and other measures can be enhanced by Web-based versions that offer instantaneous scoring, as has been the case with the SF36 Health Survey (Ware et al. 1993, 1999) and the Ansell-Casey Life Skills Assessment (Nollan et al. 2000).

Alternative reporting formats also may promote use by practitioners, including the availability of less-technical scored report formats that use bar-graphs and other more intuitive presentations of the instrument scores. Many agencies, given the emphasis on strengths-based practice in wraparound and other service areas, may find graphing approaches that accentuate children's strengths more desirable.

New computer software, including, for example, the new Windows®-based software (released in 1999), can greatly facilitate interaction of data from the CBCL family of instruments with other kinds of data. Such software has other advantages. The Windows® software is available in network versions that allow accessibility by large numbers of users at multiple sites; provide for the presentation of results in simpler bar-graph formats; and permit the integration of textual summaries of information into users' reports. Web-based CBCL, TRF, and YSR applications will be available in Fall, 2001.

Conclusion

Outcomes-based decisionmaking draws on the values and principles that guide child welfare policy and practice and organizes the delivery of child welfare services into a results-driven system. In the current environment, however, many of the attempts to move the child welfare system toward outcomes-based services attach costs to outcomes and rely on the private sector to pilot outcomes-driven contracts. The decisions that prompt these efforts are, more often than not, driven by pressures on the state foster care and Medicaid budgets; by a lack of confidence in the public sector to "get the job done"; and by the many concerns of private providers regarding the need for more stable funding and more flexible service delivery models. Because child welfare agencies generally are not using the tools needed to monitor the desired outcomes in the new "models" of service delivery, they cannot be assured that the "new" way of doing things is any better than the old. The information needed to document "what works for whom" can be developed through practical and rigorous measurement systems that focus on a few key functional outcomes, describe those outcomes, and regularly collect data. The CBCL, TRF, and YSR are helpful tools for achieving a new level of accountability.

Acknowledgments

The first section of this chapter, Situation Analysis Revisited, was adapted from Pecora, Massinga, and Mauzerall (1997). The authors thank Vincent Payne and Charles Joyce for contributing to the section of this chapter that addresses challenges and issues.

References

Achenbach, T. M. (1991a). *Integrative Guide for the 1991 CBCL/4-18, YSR, and TRF Profiles.* Burlington: University of Vermont Department of Psychiatry.

Achenbach, T. M. (1991b). *Manual for the Child Behavior Checklist/4-18 and 1991 Profile.* Burlington: University of Vermont Department of Psychiatry not cited in text.

Achenbach, T. M. (1993). *Empirically-based taxonomy: How to use syndromes and profile types derived from the CBCL 4-18, TRF, and YSR.* Burlington: University of Vermont Department of Psychiatry.

American Humane Association, Children's Division, American Bar Association, Center on Children and the Law, Annie E. Casey Foundation, Casey Family Services, the Institute for Human Services Management and The Casey Family Program. (1998). *Assessing outcomes in child welfare services: Principles, concepts, and a framework of core indicators.* Englewood, CO: American Humane Association

Armsden, G., Pecora, P. J., Payne, V., & Sykawiecz, J. (2000). An intake profile of youth placed in long-term foster care using the Child Behavior Checklist/4-18. *Journal of Emotional and Behavioral Disorders, 8*(1). 49-64.

Clark, H. B., Prange, M. E., Lee, B., Boyd, L. A., McDonald, B. A., & Stewart, E. S. (1994). Improving emotional adjustment outcomes for foster children with emotional and behavioral disorders: Early findings from a controlled study on individualized services. *Journal of Emotional and Behavioral Disorders, 2*, 207–218.

Courtney, M., & Zinn, A. (1997). *Use of the Child Behavior Checklist in a longitudinal study of treatment foster care outcomes.* Paper presented at The Child Behavior Checklist 1997 Roundtable, Seattle WA, September, 1997. Madison: University of Wisconsin at Madison.

Crijnen, A.A.M., Achenbach, T.M., & Verhulst, F.C. (1997). Comparisons of problems reported by parents of children in twelve cultures: Total Problems, Externalizing, and Internalizing. *Journal of the American Academy of Child and Adolescent Psychiatry, 36*, 1269-1277.

Crijnen, A. A. M., Achenbach, T. M., & Verhulst, F. C. (1999). Comparisons of problems reported by parents of children in twelve cultures: The CBCL/4-18 syndrome constructs. *American Journal of Psychiatry, 156*, 569–574.

Dubowitz, H., Feigelman, S., Harrington, D., Starr, Jr., R., Zuravin, S., & Sayer, R. (1994). Children in kinship care: How do they fare? *Children and Youth Services Review, 16*, 85–106.

Dubowitz, H., Zuravin, S., Starr, Jr., R., Feigelman, S. & Harrington, D. (1993). Behavior problems of children in kinship care. *Developmental and Behavioral Pediatrics, 14*, 386–395.

Edelbrock, C., Costello, J., & Kessler, M. D. (1984). Empirical corroboration of attention deficit disorder. *Journal of the American Academy of Child Psychiatry, 23*, 285–290.

Evans, M. E., Armstrong, M. I., Dollard, N., Kuppinger, A. D., Huz, S., & Wood, V. M. (1994). Development and evaluation of treatment foster care and family-centered intensive case management in New York. *Journal of Emotional and Behavioral Disorders, 2*, 228–239.

Fanshel, D., & Shinn, E. (1978). *Children in foster care: A longitudinal investigation.* New York: Columbia University Press.

Friman, P., Evans, J., Larzelere, R., Williams, G., & Daly, D. (1993). Correspondence between child dysfunction and program intrusion: Evidence of a continuum of care across five child mental health programs. *Journal of Community Psychology, 21,* 227–233.

Glisson, C. (1994). The effect of services coordination teams on outcomes for children in state custody. *Administration in Social Work, 18,* 1–23.

Heflinger, C. A., & Simpkins, C. G. (1997). *The clinical status of children in state custody.* Paper presented at The Child Behavior Checklist 1997 Roundtable, Seattle WA, September , 1997. Nashville, TN: Vanderbilt Center for Mental Health Policy.

Hoffart, I., & Grinnell, R. M. (1994). Behavioral differences of children in institutional and group home care. *International Journal of Family Care, 6,* 33–47.

Hornick, J., Phillips, D., & Kerr, N. (1989). Gender differences in behavioral problems of foster children: Implications for special foster care. *Community Alternatives, 1,* 35–52.

Hulsey, T. C., & White, R. (1989). Family characteristics and measures of behavior in foster and nonfoster children. *American Journal of Orthopsychiatry, 59,* 502–509.

Lenerz, K., Cannon, B., Johnson-Meester, N., & Peterson, J. (1995). *Intensive family preservation services: An examination of program-specific outcomes.* (Mimeogaph). Boys Town, NE: Father Flanagan's Boys' Home.

MacCabe, N. A. (1998). *Average pre and post CBCL T-scores and difference scores for post CBCLs administered at different stages of treatment for clients served in regular and treatment foster care.* (Mimeograph). Austin: Texas Department of Mental Health and Mental Retardation, Research and Evaluation.

McIntyre, A., & Keesler, T. (1986). Psychological disorders among foster children. *Journal of Clinical Psychology, 14,* 297–303.

Mott, M. (1997). *Clinical change scores of children placed in residential treatment* (Mimeograph of unpublished data). Boystown, NE: Father Flanagan's Boys' Home.

Nollan, K. A., Horn, M., Downs, A. C., & Pecora, P. J. (2000). *Ansell-Casey Life Skills Assessment (ACLSA) and Life Skills Guidebook Manual.* Seattle, WA: Casey Family Programs.

Pecora, P. J., Massinga, R., & Mauserall, H. (1997). Measuring outcomes in the changing environment of child welfare services. *Behavioral Healthcare Tomorrow, 6*(2), 2–6.

Phillips, R. (1997). *Professor Achenbach meets Mick Jagger: Using the Child Behavior Checklist in foster care.* Paper presented at the Child Behavior Checklist 1997 Roundtable, Seattle Washington, September, 1997. Whitehall, PA: Pinebrook Services for Children and Youth.

Runyan, D., & Gould, C. (1985). Foster care for child maltreatment. II. Impact on school performance. *Pediatrics, 76,* 841–847.

Sechrest, L., McKnight, P., & McKnight, K. (1996). Calibration of measures for psychotherapy outcome studies. *American Psychologist, 51,* 1065–1071.

Shennum, W. A., Moreno, D. C., & Caywood, J. C. (1998). *Demographic differences in children's residential treatment progress.* Revision of a paper presented at the Child Behavior Checklist 1997 Roundtable, Seattle ,Washington, September. Los Angeles: Five Acres—The Boys and Girls Aid Society of Los Angeles County.

Toprac, M. G. (1997). *Comparing the outcomes of public sector children's mental health providers: The Texas experience.* Workshop presented at the Children's Services Outcome Management Program, Pittsburg, PA.

Ware J. E., Snow, K. K., Kosinski, M., and Gandek, B. (1993, 1999). SF-36 Health Survey Manual and Interpretation Guide. Boston, MA: New England Medical Center, The Health Institute.

About the Editors and Authors

Thomas M. Achenbach, PhD, Professor of Psychiatry and Psychology, is Director of the Center for Children, Youth, and Families at the University of Vermont Department of Psychiatry. A graduate of Yale University, he received his PhD from the University of Minnesota and was a postdoctoral fellow at the Yale Child Study Center. Before moving to Vermont, he taught at Yale and was a Research Psychologist at the National Institute of Mental Health. Dr. Achenbach has been a DAAD Fellow at the University of Heidelberg, Germany; an SSRC Senior Faculty Fellow at Jean Piaget's Centre d'Epistémologie Génétique in Geneva; Chair of the American Psychological Association's Task Force on Classification of Children's Behavior; and a member of the American Psychiatric Association's Advisory Committee on DSM-III-R. He is the author of *Developmental Psychopathology, Research in Developmental Psychology; Empirically Based Taxonomy*; and manuals for the Child Behavior Checklist, Teacher's Report Form, and Youth Self-Report Form.

Gay Armsden, PhD, is a developmental psychologist and research consultant in Seattle, Washington. She received her PhD from the University of Washington. She has published in the areas of adolescent attachment, chronic illness in the family, assessment of children in foster care, and long-term effects of early intervention on maltreated children. She has collaborated on a number of studies with Casey Family Programs.

Victor J. Bernstein, PhD, is a research associate professor at the University of Chicago. He received his PhD in developmental psychology from Loyola University in 1975 and is a licensed clinical psychologist. Since 1979 he has worked at the University of Chicago on a variety of research studies focusing on parent-child interaction with families living in troubled communities. He is particularly interested in how the early parent-child relationship can function as a source of resilience for high-risk children. He spends much of his time training intervention program staff to improve developmental outcomes of children born at risk by strengthening relationships in parallel—the trainer-trainee, supervisor-staff, staff-parent, and parent-child relationships. Dr. Bernstein is currently working on a project funded by the Substance Abuse and Mental Health Services Administration to implement and evaluate the effectiveness of substance abuse and mental health services offered to parents through Head Start centers.

JoAnna Caywood, BA, is a graduate from the School of Social Welfare at the University of California, Berkeley, and is currently employed in a human services agency in the San Francisco area. She previously served as Research Associate at Five Acres, Los Angeles, California, where she was responsible for management of program evaluations. She also has worked as a counselor of autistic children and in a range of nonprofit charitable organizations.

Mark Courtney, PhD, is an associate Professor at the School of Social Service Administration and an Affiliate of the Chapin Gall Center for Children at the University of Chicago. Dr. Courtney's research has focused on the correlates of children's pathways through the child welfare services system, including family reunification, adoption, and reentry to out-of-home care. He is currently involved in longitudinal studies of the post discharge functioning of former foster youth, and the impact of welfare reform on child welfare. He co-authored *Unfaithful Angels: How Social Work Abandoned its Mission* (with the late Harry Specht) and *From Child Abuse to Permanency Planning: Child Welfare Services, Pathways and Placements* (with Richard Barth, Jill Duerr, and Vicki Albert).

Sydney L. Hans, PhD, is a research associate professor and director of the Unit for Research in Child Psychiatry and Development at the University of Chicago. Since receiving her PhD in developmental psychology at Harvard University in 1978, she has conducted research in Chicago on the development of high-risk infants and children. Her research explores how biological and social factors interact to contribute to developmental risk and resilience over time and how parental mental illness and substance abuse impact child development. Dr. Hans currently serves as principal investigator for two studies funded by the National Institute on Drug Abuse exploring how parent-child relationships are affected by maternal opioid dependence, comorbid psychopathology, and history of traumatic experiences affect parent-child relationships.

Craig Anne Heflinger, PhD, is a child clinical psychologist, Associate Professor of Human and Organizational Development, Peabody College of Vanderbilt University, and Fellow at the Center for Mental Health Policy, Vanderbilt Institute for Public Policy Studies, Nashville, Tennessee. Her professional and research efforts for the past 20 years have been directed at improving clinical and community services and policies for children with serious emotional disturbance and their families. She was the initial project manager and implementation study coordinator of the Ft. Bragg Evaluation Project, a large-scale evaluation of an innovative continuum of care for delivering mental health services to children and adolescents of military personnel. Dr. Heflinger has examined the use of psychiatric hospitals for children in state care, and improving the measurement of family-related issues in mental health services research. She continues to study the impact of managed care on children with serious emotional disorders and adolescents with substance abuse problems through research funded by the Substance Abuse and Mental Health Services Administration and the National Institute on Drug Abuse. She serves on the Tennessee Statewide Mental Health Planning Council, the Tennessee Voices for Children Board of Directors, the TennCare Partners Monitoring Group, and the Steering Council for the Tennessee Alliance for the Mentally Ill Evaluation of TennCare Implementation.

Linda G. Henson, MA, began her work as a research project professional in the Department of Psychiatry while a graduate student in the Division of Social Sciences at the University of Chicago. For over 20 years, she has been involved in studies of maternal substance abuse, children at risk for schizophrenia, and adolescent parents. She has been responsible for recruiting and maintaining a sample of families affected by substance abuse in which parents and children have been followed longitudinally from pregnancy through the children's fourteenth birthdays.

David B. Hickel, PhD, is a clinical psychologist who currently serves as the director of research, assessment, and performance improvement at The Sycamores in Pasadena, California. He also maintains a private practice with children and adults in Pasadena, California. Dr. Hickel received his PhD in clinical psychology from Fuller Theological Seminary in 1991. He has been working with children in out-of-home care for nearly 20 years. In addition to outcomes research, Dr. Hickel specializes in the assessment of Attention Deficit Hyperactivity Disorder as well as learning disorders in children and adults.

Charles Joyce, MSW, is the social work supervisor with the Bismarck Division of Casey Family Programs, Bismarck, N.D. He received his BA in social work from Moorhead State University, Moorhead, Minnesota, and his Masters of Social Work degree from the University of Iowa, Iowa City, Iowa. He has approximately 25 years of professional experience, primarily in the areas of mental health and child welfare.

Elena Lamont, BA, is a research administrative assistant with Casey Family Programs. Ms. Lamont organized the 1997 Child Behavior Checklist Roundtable. She has a background in publishing and coordinated the production of this book. Ms. Lamont holds a BA in cultural anthropology from The University of Washington.

Kathleen Lenerz, PhD, is a research associate at Casey Family Services in Shelton, CT. She received her PhD in Human Development and Family Studies from Pennsylvania State University, then spent two years as a National Institute of Mental Health postdoctoral fellow in applied human development at the University of California–Los Angeles. For the past seven years, she has worked in child welfare settings, where she has conducted program evaluations in the areas of treatment foster care, family preservation, family reunification, and permanency planning for HIV-affected families. Her particular areas of interest include the development of agency self-evaluation capacity, research from a multi-disciplinary perspective, and the social and emotional development of children and adolescents.

Nicole S. Le Prohn, MSW, PhD, is the Director of Practice Research for Casey Family Programs in Seattle, Washington. Before joining Casey, Dr. Le Prohn was an Assistant Professor at the University of Southern California School of Social Work, where she taught courses in research, social work practice, and human behavior. As director of practice research, Dr. Le Prohn oversees a variety of agency-based program evaluations. She trains staff in the use of the CBCL and oversees the reporting and analyses of the data.

Debra Moreno, MA, is a research associate at Five Acres, Los Angeles, California. She is responsible for data collection and reporting in support of agency program evaluation and quality improvement. Ms. Moreno also is an instructor in the Psychology Department at Pasadena City College. She previously held the positions of child care worker and activity therapist at Five Acres. Her research interests include cognitive/educational assessment and child development. She holds a MA in psychology from California State University, Los Angeles.

Vincent H. Payne, BA, is a Research Specialist for Casey Family Programs in Seattle, Washington. He received a baccalaureate degree from Clark Atlanta University. Mr. Payne's work focuses on the design, coordination, and planning of research studies. He has published articles and research reports on mentoring African American youth, use of the CBCL and TRF in foster care, and intensive aftercare services for juvenile delinquents. Other projects with The Casey Family Program include the Specialized Family Care Project and the Boise Technical Assistance Project.

Peter J. Pecora, MSW, PhD, has a joint appointment as the Senior Director of Research Services for Casey Family Programs, and a professor in the School of Social Work, University of Washington, Seattle, Washington. He was a program coordinator in a number of child welfare service agencies in Wisconsin before serving on the faculty at the Graduate School of Social Work at the University of Utah from 1982-1990. Dr. Pecora has provided training in evaluation of family-based services programs, risk assessment, and other areas to child welfare staff in a number of states. He is co-author of a number of articles and books on child welfare practice, administration, and evaluation, including *Quality Improvement and Program Evaluation in Child Welfare Agencies: Managing into the Next Century); Evaluating Family-Based Services; The Child Welfare Challenge; Families in Crisis: The Impact of Family Preservation Services;* and *Managing Human Services Personnel.* Dr. Pecora has provided consultation regarding evaluation of child and family services to the U.S. Department of Health and Human Services, and a number of foundations including the Annie E. Casey Foundation, Colorado Trust, Edna McConnell Clark Foundation, McKnight Foundation and the Stuart Foundation.

Roger D. Phillips, PhD, currently is Director of early intervention and preschool services at The Arc/Warren County in Washington, New Jersey. When the present research was conducted, he was director of research at Pinebrook Services for Children and Youth, Pinebrook, Allentown, Pennsylvania, and instructor in psychology at Cedar Crest College in Pennsylvania. He received his PhD from the University of Rochester and was a postdoctoral research fellow at the Human Emotions Laboratory, University of Delaware. Dr. Phillips currently provides mental health/child development consultation to Head Start/Early Head Start programs in U.S. Department of Health and Human Services Regions 2 and 3; program development/evaluation consultation to Binney & Smith, Inc. for the Art as a Way of Learning Project; and consultation to early intervention programs. He has served on the editorial board of Children's Health Care and reviews manuscripts for a number of professional journals. He is principal investigator for Preventing Intergenerational Transmission of Abuse and Neglect, Pinebrook Parenting with Purpose Program, and Systemic Reform for Children. He is active in the leadership of regional policy groups concerned with child and family issues.

William A. Shennum, PhD, is the director of research and evaluation at Five Acres, Los Angeles, California. He is responsible for program evaluation and quality improvement in a range of child and family services, including family preservation, home-based services, treatment foster care, community-based group care, and residential treatment. His specific interests include outcome measurement, analysis of individual differences in outcomes, and applied research and evaluation. He has participated in a number of interagency collaborative efforts concerned with program evaluation and child/family outcome measurement. He received a PhD in psychology in 1981 from the University of California, Santa Barbara.

Celeste G. Simpkins, AA, has been a research associate with Vanderbilt University since 1968. Her expertise lies in linking data from diverse sources (state wide fiscal, services, and census data) and analysis of complex design data. She has been with the Center for Mental Health Policy, Vanderbilt Institute for Public Policy Studies since 1993 as the primary staff person for a project that examines the use of psychiatric hospital and residential facilities by children in state custody. She also is presently involved in projects that examine the impact of managed care on services provided for children with severe emotional disturbances and alcohol or drug disorders.

Kathleen M. Wetherbee, PhD, formerly with Casey Family Programs, is a psychologist in private practice in Lynnwood, Washington. She received her PhD from the University of Wisconsin–Madison in Counseling Psychology with a specialization in children and families and in research design and analysis. She subsequently completed a year of clinical residency at the Illinois Masonic Medical Center in Chicago. For the past 14 years, Dr. Wetherbee has been active in both clinical treatment and research across a range of child and family issues. She has worked on a number of National Institute of Mental Health grants through the University of Rochester and New York State Psychiatric Institute. Her research work has included examining risk factors in juvenile fire setting, improving the validity and reliability of the diagnosis of Conduct Disorder, and investigating the interaction and emotional climate in families with schizophrenic family members. Dr. Wetherbee has been involved in evaluating the effect of a capitation payment system on deinstitutionalization and the development of critical pathway protocols for healthcare utilization and cost-effectiveness.

Andrew Zinn, MSSW, was the independent living coordinator for the Rock County Human Services Department in Jansville, Wisconsin. He has also worked as a Child Protective Services case manager for the same agency. His professional experience extends to community development, youth recreation, and child and family advocacy. Mr. Zinn is currently working toward his PhD in social welfare at the University of Wisconsin–Madison.